THE
CHALLENGES
OF THE
U.S.-JAPAN
MILITARY
ARRANGEMENT

THE
CHALLENGES
OF THE
U.S.-JAPAN
MILITARY
ARRANGEMENT

COMPETING SECURITY TRANSITIONS
IN A CHANGING
INTERNATIONAL ENVIRONMENT

Anthony DiFilippo

AN EAST GATE BOOK

M.E. Sharpe
Armonk, New York
London, England

An East Gate Book

Library of Congress Cataloging-in-Publication Data

DiFilippo, Anthony, 1950–
    The challenges of the U.S.-Japan military arrangement : competing security transitions
in a changing international environment / Anthony DiFilippo.
    p. cm.
"An East Gate Book."
Includes bibliographical references and index.
ISBN 0-7656-1018-3 (alk. paper)
    1. United States—Military relations—Japan. 2. Japan—Military relations—United States.
3. United States—Foreign relations—Japan. 4. Japan—Foreign relations—United States. 5.
United States—Military policy. 6. Japan—Military policy. 7. National security—United
States. 8. National security—Japan. I. Title.

E183.8.J3 D54 2002   2002019093
355′.031′09730952—dc21

Printed in the United States of America

BM (c)   10   9   8   7   6   5   4   3   2   1

To My Family

Contents

List of Tables and Figures

Tables

Figures

Acknowledgments

Since fall 1998, when I began working on this book, I have received much support. First I must acknowledge the support of the members of my family who in different ways encouraged me to write this book. My conversations with many individuals were also important, as they often helped me to see some things in different ways or focus more on issues that I had largely ignored or given too little attention to in this work. Several Japanese friends were especially important in this respect, including Teiichiro Tonoue of the Tokyo Physicians for Elimination of Nuclear Weapons, Hiroshi Katsumori, chairperson of the Article Nine Society in Japan; and Kenji Urata of Waseda University. Subsequent to a meeting on the abolition of nuclear weapons arranged by Kenji Urata in early August of 2001, Hiro Umebayashi of the Peace Depot and I had a useful conversation that helped me rethink the importance of making Japan's three nonnuclear principles national law rather than policy.

Lincoln University supported my research by providing me with some research stipends that helped to offset some of the financial cost of conducting the research for this book. The university also twice provided me with funds that helped to defray much of the cost of two visits to Japan. These trips were important, as they helped to add definition and clarity to the book. For example, when I was in Tokyo in July of 2000, Axel Berkofsky, then affiliated with the German Institute for Japanese Studies, kindly notified me of an important discussion on Japanese security issues being held at the Japan Institute of International Studies, a policy arm of the Japanese Foreign Ministry. It was during this discussion that I became convinced that to acquire a credible role in international security, many in Tokyo were too easily sacrificing public opinion for a stronger alliance with Washington.

THE
CHALLENGES
OF THE
U.S.-JAPAN
MILITARY
ARRANGEMENT

1

Introduction: Challenges of the Twenty-first Century

The U.S.–Japan security relationship has existed for five decades. Begun during the Korean War, the alliance early on had two interrelated objectives. First, by bringing Tokyo into Washington's foreign policy camp, the expectation was that the Soviet Union would not develop any political designs relating to Japan. Second, it became clear to proponents of the treaty in Washington and Tokyo that because of the position of neutrality advocated by some divisions of the Japanese political left during the early postwar years, these forces could be kept at arm's length. This attempt by Washington and many in Tokyo to marginalize the left nearly collapsed in 1960, when massive opposition to the renewal of the bilateral security treaty led to large protests in Tokyo.

Stability versus Instability

While these objectives have historical value, they are not especially germane today. What is important today is that the U.S.–Japan security alliance survived the Cold War and, since the mid-1990s, has been strengthened. Justified for a while by the argument that even though the Cold War had ended in the early 1990s, this was not the case in East Asia; more recently, Washington and Tokyo have shed the bipolar rationalization and now rely on the more generalized contention that the bilateral alliance brings stability to the region.[1] An ad hominum nuance of this justification is that the existence of the alliance has prevented war and loss of lives in the region. During the G-8 summit held in Okinawa in July 2000, President William Clinton took time to visit U.S. marines there and told them two things: to act like "good neighbors" (a euphemistic way of instructing them to behave responsibly so that in the future the United States can avoid any more embarrassments connected with the poor conduct of some of its servicemen in the prefecture) and to keep in mind that, because of the bilateral security alliance and the U.S. presence, no wars have occurred in the region.[2] Clinton, however, failed to remind U.S. troops of even recent security catastrophes that had occurred despite the existence of the bilateral alliance, such as the nuclear tests conducted by India and Pakistan in 1998, and that continued to destabilize the Asia-Pacific region.

Having long jettisoned the Cold War rhetoric associated with presumed superpower aggression, today the need to maintain stability in East Asia is justified by an amalgamation of political possibilities. Or, put differently, regional instability can come from different sources. As the new 1997 "Guidelines for U.S.–Japan Defense Cooperation" indicate, both Washington and Tokyo are very much concerned about "situational" problems in the East Asia–Pacific region that can occasion instability.[3] Within East Asia, these problems could conceivably arise from several sources, such as North Korea invading South Korea, China forcefully taking over Taiwan, or, less likely but nonetheless part of the consideration, Russia deciding to extend its sphere of military influence.

In the eyes of many policy makers in Washington and Tokyo, regional instability in East Asia could also emerge from rogue activities. Foremost on the list of possible threats is North Korea, which, in the wake of its hurling a missile over Japanese territory in August 1998, caused Tokyo to decide to become involved with Washington in TMD (theater missile defense) research. Although unlikely, rogue activities in East Asia could also come from beyond the region, as a result of possible misconduct by Iraq or Iran. Instability also relates to the problems associated with potential terrorist activities (North Korea remains on the U.S. terrorist list), which may or may not be sanctioned by a government. In brief, to contend with virtually all conceivable security threats to East Asia and beyond, now including nonstate terrorist activities, the U.S.–Japan security relationship has been evolving into an alliance that is becoming the regional equivalent of NATO.

Critics charge that the U.S.–Japan security alliance is an anachronism, since its Cold War justification is no longer relevant today. However, this is far too simplistic. To show its irrelevance to the current period, it is necessary to identify specific sources of instability occasioned by it. Moreover, the provision of anecdotal information would also demonstrate the current tenuousness and uncertainty associated with the bilateral security alliance, as would a thorough analysis of Japanese public opinion data.

This book is about the sources of instability that connect to the continuation of the U.S.–Japan security alliance—an arrangement that presupposes enemies and therefore definitively answers the question of which side is right and which is wrong. It is about the regional tension, distrust, and suspicions that the alliance precipitates. It is about the manifest contradictions that emanate today from Japanese security policy, which typically reflects Washington's military objectives, as well as Tokyo's persistent desire to be aligned with a military superpower so that Japan can acquire international credibility in the twenty-first century. It is about Tokyo disregarding Japanese public sentiment on security matters to satisfy the interests of policy makers, both at home and in Washington. This problem manifests itself every so often when a U.S. military incident exasperates the Japanese people to such a point that parts or all of the bilateral security alliance are called into question. It is about Japan's failure to develop a security policy consistent with national sentiments and about the abolition of nuclear weapons and a strong United Nations. Ending on a sanguine note, this book is about how Tokyo can build on these national sentiments by playing a leading role both in designing an international nuclear disarmament agenda and in strengthening UN global security mechanisms, which need to be linked to capable regional institutions.

Seeing Better Times

Since the end of the Cold War, the U.S.–Japan security alliance has outlived its usefulness. It is now associated with visible domestic dissatisfaction. Even when dissatisfaction cannot be discerned, there is some amount of public uncertainty about the alliance. Another problem is that the bilateral security alliance must also contend with growing external suspicion and distrust in some countries outside the alliance.

In early February 2001, when the U.S. submarine *Greeneville* carelessly surfaced and sank the Japanese fishing ship *Ehime Maru*, a training vessel that, as the Japanese strongly emphasized, had many young people on board, the tenuousness of the bilateral security alliance immediately became apparent. Although an inexcusable and reckless tragedy, it was not intentional. Nonetheless, popular perception in Japan was that Washington displayed arrogant insensitivity to the seriousness of the incident, leading to visible dissatisfaction among many Japanese with the bilateral security arrangement. Many Japanese quickly connected the submarine tragedy to the serious and continuing problems stemming from the presence of American troops in Okinawa—one of which was a string of arson attacks by a U.S marine in January 2001—and reasoned that the security alliance was not serving their interests the way it should.[4] While some in the United States felt that the Japanese public overreacted to the submarine incident and that American apologies were sufficient, what is incontrovertible is that the tragedy was an accident, albeit one that should have not occurred, that instantly provoked popular indignation and demonstrated the fragility of the bilateral security alliance.

In Okinawa, local disgruntlement with the disproportionate presence of American troops in the prefecture has been intensified by the U.S.–Japanese failure to reach an agreement about the relocation of the U.S. Marine Futenma Air Base. Although tension has remained permanently high in Okinawa for the past several years, at different times it has waxed, because of the irresponsible activities of U.S. servicemen in the prefecture, and eventually waned somewhat. Okinawans were especially outraged when three U.S. servicemen raped a young Japanese schoolgirl in 1995, a tragedy that forced thousands into the streets in protest. In the wake of yet two other tragedies involving U.S. servicemen in July 2000, Okinawan protest became vocal again, prompting the politically savvy president Clinton to abandon the White House plan to have a public discussion with local citizens on the presence of American troops in the prefecture when he was there attending the G-8 Summit. In a speech to Okinawans, Clinton reaffirmed the need to maintain the U.S.–Japan security alliance and offered what many locals saw as incomplete and unsatisfactory answers to the bases' problems.[5] Dissatisfaction with the size of U.S. forces in Japan, however, is not restricted to Okinawa. In Japan, there is discernible resentment among a large part of the public about the presence of U.S. troops and bases there and continued problems associated with them.

Beyond these domestic concerns, not China or Russia or North Korea is going to sit back indefinitely and watch the United States and Japan continue to strengthen their security relationship. In the twenty-first century, attempting to maintain security by relying on an alliance structure and undiluted military power supported by sophisticated technologies is not a particularly safe course to follow. Developments in science and technology have driven societies to change and adapt for centuries. Why Russia, China, and North Korea will not consider or even implement changes that will permit them to resist the perceived hegemony associated with the maturing military U.S.–Japan security arrangement is left completely unexplained by advocates of the alliance. Although winning the Cold War resulted at least in part because the United States outspent the Soviet Union, this strategy is unlikely to work in the East Asia–Pacific region during the twenty-first century. Already there is evidence that China, North Korea, and Russia are considering cooperative ways to offset the perceived challenge represented by the U.S.–Japan security alliance. Moreover, in contrast to the situation in the Cold War, individual or cooperative strategies to thwart the bilateral alliance do not necessarily have to rely on spending to the point of depletion. Rather, these countries can find more cost-effective ways to undermine and circumvent the bilateral security alliance by developing niche strategies, if the need arises.

While Washington and Tokyo publicly endorse regional security efforts, specifically the ASEAN Regional Forum (ARF), their first line of security is the bilateral arrangement. This is problematic. Compared with their enthusiasm for the bilateral security alliance, Washington and Tokyo's commitment to ARF appears tepid at best. Both Washington and Tokyo have been willing to bolster the bilateral security alliance, for example, with new guidelines for defense cooperation; however, they demonstrate much more reserved behavior when it comes to taking steps to strengthen ARF. So, as Washington and Tokyo publicly acknowledge the importance of ARF for the future of security in the Asia–Pacific region, their immediate concerns and energies focus on the biliteral security alliance. Multilateral security in the Asia–Pacific region is something to support publicly; it is not something that either Washington or Tokyo has gone out of their way to promote and develop.

Washington and Tokyo have developed an analogous posture toward the United Nations—analogous but not identical—because U.S. arrogance toward the United Nations has been evident since the mid-1990s. Because of the U.S. influence on the United Nations, it has been very difficult for this multilateral institution to evolve to the point where its security mechanisms serve the needs of all countries. Coupled with a deliberate U.S. policy of alienation from the United Nations, this arrogance and Tokyo's typical compliance with the security decisions of Washington have left Japan still waiting to experience the expectation of its 1957 Basic Policy for National Defense: that the United Nations will provide Japan with security. This expectation is the political linchpin that, if ever realized, will become the reason, according to Article X of the U.S.–Japan Security Treaty, for ending the accord.

Because policy makers in Washington and Tokyo have been working to shore up the security alliance, the United States and Japan have not been enthusiastically embracing multilateral options. The upshot is that in East Asia, Tokyo and Washington have security preferences that are inconsistent with those of some other countries in the region. Post–Cold War politics pushed to prominence the prospect of realizing a multipolar world and multilateral security. This is the global environment and security response favored by Russia and China. Even North Korea, a very recent member of ARF, has recognized the significance of multilateral security as an alternative to alliance politics.

Advocates of the U.S.–Japan security alliance, which some countries in the East Asia–Pacific region perceive as a threat, must constantly attempt to identify malleable and easily shifting justifications for its continued existence. China's alleged work on modernizing its nuclear weapons "soon" is a strategic public relations move intended to promote the imminent need for defensive shields. In its 2000 report the Japanese Defense Agency, moreover, recently identified China as a potential security threat to Japan. While increasingly today stability means preventing nuclear proliferation, alliance politics and the threat of military force offer no guarantee that nuclear nonproliferation will prevail. Thus, labeling North Korea a "rogue state," as many Washington and Tokyo policy makers routinely do, contributes to regional instability, since it obstructs the formation of genuine diplomatic and cooperative efforts,[6] and creates a political wall where threats of force are made on both sides.

Korean unification and the desire of North Korea to establish normal relations with the United States and Japan present an especially big challenge to those who continue to seek justifications for the bilateral alliance. Unifying the Korean Peninsula and improving relations among the United States, Japan, and North Korea will make it difficult to maintain American troops in South Korea. Even though it once suggested that it would accept the presence of U.S. troops in South Korea, Pyongyang continues to press very hard for their removal[7]; indeed, justifying their presence there will become increasingly more difficult for any American administration. Working especially hard during the past two years to cast off the nefarious labels of both a rogue and a reclusive state, North Korea has recently been making it clear that it wants to be integrated into the regional and world communities and that it is willing to put on a cooperative suit to do this. However, the Bush administration's early 2001 hard-line approach toward North Korea has made reconciliation between Seoul and Pyongyang much more difficult, since it neutralizes the South's "sunshine policy" and creates considerable angst in the North. Even worse, the Bush administration's hard-line position, wittingly or not, maintains the North Korean threat scenario, the core of which is that the Democratic People's Republic of Korea (DPRK) is a rogue state. This helps to justify plans to develop TMD and NMD (national missile defense)[8], now conjoined and simply called missile defense.

In the aftermath of the U.S. bombing of the Chinese embassy in Yugoslavia in May 1999, Sino-American relations took an obvious and precipitous turn for the worse. But time managed to heal some of the acrimony that the Chinese expressed toward the United States for months following the bombing. By the middle of 2000, Beijing and Washington had become more inclined to work with each other, affording some improvement in both security and economic relations. However, the U.S. bombing of the Chinese embassy made clear—as did the 2001 spy-plane incident and the American argument that China has plans to modernize its nuclear arsenal—that major problems between Washington and Beijing can emerge at anytime and lead to the quick deterioration of bilateral relations. So, despite some maturation in the Sino-American relationship, a significant amount of distrust and tension still exists between Washington and Beijing. These problems could easily be exacerbated, since Beijing perceives the Bush administration's emerging China policy as more abrasive and more focused on containment than was its predecessor.[9]

China makes no bones about its position that the United States is determined to exercise hegemonic control over the East Asia–Pacific region and at least suggests that Japan has been enlisted to cooperate in this effort, all of which, Beijing stresses, undermines the responsibilities of the United Nations.[10] Beijing is emphatic about its belief that the recent strengthening of the U.S.–Japan security arrangement has introduced instability and imbalance into the Sino-American-Japanese relationship.[11] This perceived heightening of regional instability is exactly the opposite of what Washington and Tokyo maintain. With the unification of the Korean Peninsula, China may very well become the primary justification for the security alliance between Washington and Tokyo and for maintaining American troops in Japan. Even now, some in Beijing believe that North Korea provides a convenient pretext for the strengthened U.S.–Japan security alliance; the accord's real reason for existence today, they contend, is China.[12] Thus, the unification of the Korean Peninsula would likely mean that the U.S.–Japan security alliance would be the only remaining policing structure in East Asia, leaving little doubt in the minds of Beijing policy makers that it is hegemonic in design.

Meanwhile, the Pentagon has already taken a precautionary step to guard the U.S.–Japan security alliance, should unification occur on the Korean Peninsula. A recent Pentagon report to the U.S. Congress maintains that China is seeking to become the "preeminent power among regional states in East Asia." The report maintains that Beijing is determined to bring Taiwan under the control of China and that it opposes the recently strengthened security arrangement between Washington and Tokyo because of Japan's expanded regional military role and because of its concern about the resurgence of Japanese militarism.[13] Another recent Pentagon report stresses the modernization of Chinese weapons of mass destruction, including nuclear and ballistic missile programs, and indicates that, with North Korea, China "will present serious proliferation challenges to the United States and its Allies in the region," and is one of just a handful of countries that can pose a military threat to the American mainland.[14]

The crisis in Yugoslavia also took a toll on U.S.-Russian relations. Since Washington circumvented the United Nations during the crisis, Moscow saw U.S.-led NATO actions in Yugoslavia as politically unacceptable and got the distinct impression that America had hegemonic intention. Complicating the relationship between Washington and Moscow was the proposal by the Clinton administration to alter the 1972 Anti-Ballistic Missile (ABM) Treaty so that the United States could develop a NMD system. For some observers, both the Yugoslavian crisis and the American proposal to change the ABM Treaty has put the United States in the position of aggressor (the Soviet Union was cast in this role during the Cold War). Certainly, President Bush's decision to withdraw from the ABM Treaty has increased Moscow's concerns. In

East Asia, almost any conceivable military action that brings into play the U.S.–Japan security alliance will be seriously criticized by Russia and will critically damage Moscow's bilateral relationship with both Washington and Tokyo. But even without any activities that involve the actual deployment of American and Japanese military forces, Moscow has been very critical of statements by the United States that it plans to develop and deploy an NMD system, and given Japan's relationship to TMD,[15] Moscow has become skeptical of Tokyo's objectives in East Asia.[16]

Today, Washington and Tokyo must work harder than they did in the past to find reasons for maintaining their bilateral security alliance, an integral part of which is America's military presence in the East Asia–Pacific region. Justifying the U.S.–Japan security alliance has become metaphorically tantamount to locating a moving target. Is North Korea the reason? Perhaps China really should be feared, given its nuclear weapons and the U.S. allegation that Beijing will be modernizing them. Adding to China's likelihood of precipitating regional instability from the perspective of Washington and Tokyo is that Beijing refuses to dismiss the possibility of using force to bring Taiwan under Chinese control. Or, maybe Moscow will strategically endeavor to acquire control of East Asia, first by attempting to influence politics on the Korean Peninsula and then by refusing to settle with Tokyo the matter of the Northern Territories, the islands that the former Soviet Union occupied after Tokyo surrendered in World War II.

Tokyo is facing an even more difficult task than Washington in justifying the bilateral security alliance. Tokyo began working on normalizing relations with Pyongyang in 1999. As time has passed, small steps have been taken by Tokyo and Pyongyang in this direction. Continued movement on this path will eventually collide with Japan's current security policy, since it includes both the desire to normalize relations with North Korea and simultaneously to view it as the most serious threat to Japanese national security. The establishment of completely normal relations between Japan and North Korea is itself no small challenge, given historical and even recent problems between these two countries. But by constantly accusing North Korea of representing a missile threat to Japan and especially by joining the United States in performing research on TMD, Tokyo is making it very difficult to have a strong normal relationship with Pyongyang. In short, Tokyo is sending mixed signals to Pyongyang. On the one hand, it is saying that as neighbors Japan and North Korea should have a reasonably amicable relationship.

On the other hand, which is the dominant one, Tokyo is saying, we distrust you; we believe that you are capable of launching missiles at Japan that will cause many deaths and will inflict serious damage on our country. This manifestly ambivalent political posture, which is weighted in one direction because of enduring suspicions and mistrust and which Tokyo attempts to neutralize by retaining its alliance with the United States, is not the grounds on which it should be working to normalize relations with Pyongyang.

Because Japan has maintained normal diplomatic ties with China since 1975, because it may be moving in this direction with North Korea, and since the settlement of the Northern Territories disagreement is the only visible and serious bilateral problem remaining in Russo-Japanese relations, the rationalization for the Tokyo–Washington security alliance is wearing away. In conjunction with a relatively large defense budget, the maintenance of the security alliance with the United States leaves Japan wide open to the criticism that at least some Japanese policy makers are seeking remilitarization. Some critics also argue that current Japanese discussions on constitutional change, which began in both houses of the Diet in early 2000, are linked directly to emergent interests in remilitarization and are therefore largely aimed at revising Article 9, the war-renouncing clause of the Japanese constitution. While ultraconservative forces support a stronger and more independent (of the United States) military for Japan, today this is a minority position. However, when combined with domestic discussions on constitutional change, recent efforts to present the bilateral alliance as still necessary to stabilize East Asia create the foundation upon which remilitarization can actually take place in the future, especially since today what is demanded of Japan is more regional responsibility. Presently, a prominent, though not necessarily dominant, position in Tokyo is to continue to strengthen the security alliance with Washington, and after having exposed the public to an extended discussion of why Article 9 needs to be changed, to do so within five to ten years. Thus, political efforts to maintain a security alliance that is more difficult than ever to justify are being undertaken by Tokyo policy makers who are determined to make Japan a "credible" international power that is directly and strongly linked militarily to the United States. To accomplish this, however, they must ignore the serious contradictions in Japan's security policy and constantly promulgate an exaggerated version of the prospects of regional threats to the public.

The Opposite Perception: Promoting Instability and a New Arms Race

One thing that has not changed about the U.S.–Japan security alliance in the fifty years that it has existed is that it is supposed to have maintained regional stability. If stability is defined as a state where war or the high-level threat of war does not exist, then the alliance has not been terribly effective. Although the Soviet Union never attacked Japan during the Cold War, other serious destabilizing forces have appeared despite the continued existence of the bilateral alliance. The Korean War, which began in June 1950, did not end after the signing of the U.S.–Japan Security Treaty in 1951 nor after the accord went into effect in 1952. The alliance did not prevent China from developing nuclear weapons—hardly a stabilizing event in the region. The U.S.–Japan alliance did not prevent or end the Vietnam War. More recently, the U.S.–Japan security alliance did not stop the Democratic People's Republic of Korea (North Korea) from beginning a nuclear weapons program in the early 1990s, thwart Pyongyang's missile development efforts, or discourage it from launching a projectile over Japan without prior notice in August 1998. With the bilateral alliance in effect for decades, China went ahead with nuclear testing in 1995 to assure that its nuclear arsenal was capable of neutralizing the threats it perceives from the other nuclear powers.

It is increasingly difficult today to convince Beijing, Pyongyang, and, most recently, even Moscow that the U.S.–Japan security alliance does not represent a regional threat. Since the U.S.–Japan security alliance is a bipolar rather than a multipolar structure—which is now being advocated by China, Russia, and North Korea—it represents a real or at least a potential threat to them. Because the U.S.–Japan security relationship is an alliance between the two biggest economies in the world with a combined military power that would be difficult to challenge, it is increasingly being perceived by China, North Korea, and Russia as a destabilizing, or at least threatening, regional force. Moreover, there is growing regional concern about Tokyo's military intentions. For example, Beijing has recently expressed apprehension about Japan's five-year defense plan for the period 2001–2005. Tokyo proposes to raise Japanese defense spending by more than ¥930 billion ($8 billion) from the previous five-year period (1996 to 2000). Of particular concern to Beijing is the more "offensive" looking military that Japan wants to develop, with the introduction, for example, of in-flight refueling planes.

Perplexing to Beijing is the unanswered question of why Japan is plan-ning to increase its military spending in light of the fact that its economy has been lethargic for the past decade.[17] In brief, what officials in Beijing as well as in some other countries in East Asia now fear is that Japan is moving away from *senshu boei* (an exclusively defense-oriented policy).

The primary cause of the instability produced by the U.S.–Japan se-curity alliance is the suspicion and mistrust that it harbors. Perceptions *do* matter, particularly when focused on a strengthened security alliance between the world's two most advanced countries.[18] Although the United States has been working for a decade to shed the image of the global policeman, it has been unsuccessful. This label has been difficult to get rid of because in East Asia, Washington, with Tokyo's assistance, has taken steps that run counter to shedding this perceived role. The 1996 joint security agreement for the twenty-first century between the United States and Japan was meant to create the perception of unity, since Wash-ington and Tokyo had become concerned that the bilateral security ar-rangement had lost its meaning soon after the Cold War ended. The 1997 Completion of the Review of the Guidelines for U.S.–Japan De-fense Cooperation have put the bilateral arrangement on an entirely new path, one that unnecessarily raises regional suspicions and distrust. In addition to symbolically strengthening the bilateral security alliance, the new guidelines legitimate regional security responsibilities for Ja-pan. The enlargement of the bilateral security arrangement has been perceived as the incontrovertible preference of Washington and Tokyo for alliance solutions to regional security problems. Lurking not too far in the background is the suspicion that Japan is readying itself for remilitarization, something many countries in Asia do not really want to think about. To some extent, the expeditious passage of anti-terrorist legislation by the Japanese Diet in the fall of 2001 has added to this suspicion.

What some governments and millions of people must think about in East Asia—and indeed all over the globe—is that the world is at the threshold of a new arms race. That evidence for this new arms race should appear in East Asia should not be too surprising, since in this part of the world the Cold War never really ended. As the U.S. Department of De-fense has made clear, four of the five enduring communist countries in the world (North Korea, China, Laos, and Vietnam) are in East Asia.[19] The fact that all countries in East Asia do not share "common values" has been the fundamental political reason for sustaining the Cold War–

like milieu. The East Asian region serves as the incubator of the new arms race, since three of the world's five declared nuclear powers—the United States, Russia, and China—have significant interests in this area. While not technically in East Asia, India and Pakistan, the two countries most recently to have tested nuclear weapons, are part of the larger Asia–Pacific region. Directly connected to its rogue status, North Korea's military intentions have been perennially suspect, expecially its nuclear weapons and missile programs, despite a lack of current evidence of the former and the DPRK's declared moratorium on launchings associated with the latter until at least 2003.[20] China has been accused of espionage, was alleged to have stolen information on U.S. nuclear weapons,[21] and was severely rebuked by Washington for unjustifiably detaining an American surveillance crew and impounding its aircraft. According to some in the U.S. intelligence community, China will be modernizing its nuclear weapons. China has also been accused of helping Pakistan with missile technology development; recently, the Bush administration has charged that Beijing has provided Iraq with sensitive military technology. Washington has been warming up to New Delhi, which is one of the few governments to support NMD openly, and, perhaps most important, moved away from its strong criticisms of the Indian nuclear weapons program. This nascent Washington–New Delhi friendship can easily precipitate stronger ties between China and Pakistan. In an event reminiscent of the Cold War atmosphere, Russian concerns with the effects of the reaffirmed U.S.–Japan security alliance surfaced in September 2000 when one of its diplomats, who had been working in Japan for three years, was caught receiving sensitive military information from a researcher in Japan's National Institute for Defense Studies. And Russian and U.S. espionage agents have continued to be exposed long after the end of the Cold War.

Compounding all of this is the fact that increases in military spending by countries affecting the East Asian political environment are especially ominous indicators of an imminent arms race. In recent years, by all accounts, China's defense expenditures have been growing.[22] Even Russia, whose persistently lackluster economy has been a major concern for observers all over the world, has allowed its military spending to increase in 2000 as a part of gross domestic product. Apart from the massive and growing U.S. defense budget, China is very worried about the recent growth in India's military expenditures and has voiced particular concern about the 67 percent increase in Japanese defense spending that took place between 1998 and 2000.[23] Some Japanese observers are quick to point out that Japan's military budget is big relative to that of most other countries because of the high salaries of the Self Defense Forces. While high salaries are a factor (along with food costs they make up about 45 percent of the defense budget), they certainly do not account for all of the growth in Japanese military spending.

Although the continuation of U.S. security alliances with Australia, Thailand, South Korea, and the Philippines are indicative of America's regional influence, currently Washington's cornerstone relationship with Japan portends by far the most problems, as it has engendered early symptoms of a new arms race. Because of the 1997 guidelines for defense cooperation between Washington and Tokyo, military strategists must now factor into the equation Japan's increased security obligations, especially its new regional responsibilities. Directly tied to the perception of a strengthened U.S.–Japan security alliance is the decision by Tokyo to begin cooperative work on TMD with Washington. If developed and deployed, TMD and NMD (missile defense) will be the most likely catalysts of a new arms race. Rather than assuring protection, these missile defense systems will instead produce a proliferation of nuclear weapons or other military countermeasures. How else will China sustain its deterrence? Even cash-strapped Russia has already indicated that it will not sit idly and permit these defensive systems to be developed and deployed; it will attempt to circumvent them. Moreover, the missile defense system has rekindled interest in the relationship between Russia and China, as well as that between Russia and North Korea.[24] In brief, these proposed defensive systems have exacerbated the regional distrust and suspicion that some nations feel toward Japan.

Given Japan's exceptionally strong technological infrastructure, a few important questions emerge that create the impetus for a regional arms race. If it is to be developed, how much of its resources will Japan ultimately be willing to commit to missile defense? To what extent will a defensive system prod Tokyo to consider a more independent (of the United States) military posture? Exactly how will China, North Korea, and Russia respond to a decisive U.S.–Japan advantage in regional defensive technology? Reacting to TMD and NMD, China's director of arms control, Sha Zukang, stated that: "If a country seeks to develop advanced theater missile defense or even national missile defense in an attempt to maintain absolute security, other countries will be forced to develop more advanced offensive missiles."[25] Moreover, not only will nations have to develop offensive means to immediately circumvent a U.S.–Japan defensive shield, eventually they will also need to commit resources to building defensive systems that will engender a response by Tokyo and Washington.

The fundamental problem with the U.S.–Japan security relationship today is that it is extremely difficult for it to remain dormant. There are too many structural forces pushing for its expansion. Policy makers and military planners in Washington and Tokyo place far too much value on the bilateral security alliance for several reasons. First, the United States and Japan benefit economically from each other and from the East Asian region, and so the security alliance provides a mutual perspective on and reciprocal commitment to the overall bilateral relationship. Second, there are currently fewer immediately perceived military repercussions to Japan's commitment to the alliance than there were during the Cold War when rivalry prevailed between military superpowers. In short, today the U.S.–Japan security alliance is better able to "handle" North Korea (e.g., the Korean Economic Development Organization)—whose rogue state position provides a convenient and plausible justification for the bilateral security arrangement—than it could the Soviet Union. Third, while North Korea's putative unpredictability serves as the most accessible explanation for the bilateral security alliance, China and Russia remain visibly reachable reasons for its maintenance; they, therefore, can be quickly pulled to the political forefront if the need arises. Finally, there is the technological reason. An alliance between the world's two leading technological powers creates the momentum for finding technical remedies to security matters—even to the point of exaggerating problems—to ensure maintenance of the status quo. Taken together, these structural forces that propel the U.S.–Japan alliance, along with the desire to be technologically prepared for any security contingency, establish the impetus for a new arms race in the twenty-first century.

Presently, Japan's security dependence on the United States is eerily similar to a situation in the past. A previously classified American National Security document of June 1960 stated that: "Because Japan's dependence on the United States is almost total in the security area and also heavy in the economic field, America is in a position to be able to exert a decisive influence on that country's international policy."[26] By maintaining this security dependence today, Tokyo policy makers have ignored important Japanese concerns relating to the abolition of all nuclear weapons and a strong United Nations that is capable of providing effective leadership in international security.[27] Present in the Japanese political culture are patent contradictions that reflect the duality of national concerns: continued commitment to Article 9, but a very large defense budget; a security alliance with the world's only military superpower, but for more than four decades still maintaining that the United Nations is a major pillar of the country's defense policy; and an evident, globally public opposition to the existence of nuclear weapons, yet clear willingness to sustain the bilateral security alliance and remain under America's nuclear umbrella. On this last point, a Japanese government official recently wrote in a policy paper about the need to maintain the bilateral security alliance that "Japan relies upon [the] U.S. nuclear deterrence against the threat of nuclear weapons, yet it actively participates in international efforts for realistic and steady nuclear disarmament, aimed at establishing a world free from nuclear weapons."[28] Perhaps the biggest contradiction currently ascertainable in Japanese politics is that while it has been common for officials to speak about the need to abolish nuclear weapons, these words ring hollow, given that Japan maintains the bilateral security alliance, which is a major cause of the proliferation of regional tension and suspicion. It is difficult to deny that today the U.S.–Japan security arrangement, which now includes Japanese involvement in missile defense, is sowing the political seeds that will contribute to a new arms race, rather than bring about regional or global disarmament.

Reaching a Security Policy Decision

During the Persian Gulf War, it became especially clear to Tokyo that Japan needed to assume more responsibilities in the area of international security. While the 1992 Peacekeeping Operations Bill was designed to move Japan in this direction, Tokyo soon realized that this was not enough. Because Japan had attained the status of an economic superpower, the dominant view in Tokyo was that Japan had to establish "credibility" in international security in the eyes of the other major countries. Tokyo briefly entertained multilateral security options but deemed them inadequate and requiring U.S. leadership.[29] However, this did not mean that Tokyo wanted to abandon the idea of developing multilateral security. So, while publicly supporting the development of embryonic multilateral security systems, such as ARF, Tokyo acknowledged the continuing need to maintain the bilateral security alliance.[30] Following the lead of Washington, Tokyo soon concluded that the best route to take was to reaffirm the U.S.–Japan security alliance. Accordingly, in Tokyo on April 17, 1996, Prime Minister Hashimoto and President Clinton signed the "U.S.–Japan Joint Declaration on Security—Alliance for the Twenty-first Century"; on September 23, 1997, in New York City, Washington and Tokyo issued the "Completion of the Review of the Guidelines for U.S.–Japan Defense Cooperation," which was approved by the Diet in May 1999; and in December 1998, Tokyo gave the green light to TMD and within weeks authorized about $8 million for the project. In short, Tokyo got what it was seeking: a strengthened security arrangement with the world's only military superpower, which afforded international credibility to Japan and simultaneously allowed Japan to cast off the disparaging "free ride" label that it had been forced to wear during the Cold War.

The problem for too many in Tokyo, however, is that the strengthening of the bilateral security alliance in many ways has been more symbolic than substantive. Because Article 9 of the Japanese constitution prohibits Japan from assuming any semblance of an offensive military posture, some Tokyo policy makers and other observers have been pushing for constitutional change, notwithstanding the fact that recent survey data indicate that nearly three-fourths of the Japanese public want to maintain Article 9. The reasoning behind the proposed change is that altering Article 9 to permit Japan to participate freely in military operations outside of Japanese territory will gain additional international credibility for the country. Not only will Japan be able to take part in UN security operations like a "normal country," it will be free to join forces with the United States, without constitutional debate or restriction, in regional military engagements—the latter currently the more likely of the two possible events. According to this line of thinking, even without nuclear weapons, Japan is in the position of becoming a responsible and credible world power. Constitutional change, specifically of Article 9, is therefore the ultimate objective of Japanese nationalists and others who seek to enhance Japan's credibility internationally by expanding the parameters of its authorized security responsibilities.

However, for what is now a minority group, constitutional change is only the penultimate objective. Those making up this group want Tokyo to seriously reconsider possessing nuclear weapons, thus forcing it to abandon the nation's three nonnuclear principles, which, although not fashioned into law, remain fundamental to Japanese national policy (*kokuze*). Although this position is diametrically opposed to popular sen-

timent in Japan, where an overwhelming majority of citizens believe
that their country should never possess nuclear weapons, Tokyo policy
makers have certainly not felt compelled in the past or in more recent
times to yield to the public's will. For example, despite public support
for Japan's ceiling on defense expenditures at 1 percent of gross national product, Prime Minister Nakasone's cabinet broke through it in
January 1987.[31] Recent survey data similarly show that Tokyo tends to
overlook public sentiment in security matters.[32]

Especially since 1996, Tokyo has been attempting to acquire for Japan international recognition as a reliable U.S. ally by strengthening the
bilateral security alliance. Tokyo has been working hard to create an
understanding of Japan that can be interpreted only as its willingness to
assume more regional security responsibilities sanctioned by the bilateral security arrangement with the United States. A big problem for Japan is that efforts made to strengthen the alliance with the United States
are inconsistent with the UN multilateral security option endorsed by
the 1957 Basic Policy for National Defense, which is still recognized as
fundamental to the country's security posture. As alluded to above, even
the bilateral security treaty indicates the ephemerality of Japan's dependence on the United States for protection, as it projects a time when the
United Nations would assume this responsibility. So, Tokyo's push for
credibility has not only resulted in strengthening the security alliance
with Washington, it has also put into political abeyance genuine work to
implement effective multilateral security mechanisms.

For decades, Japan has had a special affinity to the United Nations. Since
the end of the Cold War, however, the security alliance with the United
States has prevented Japan from moving determinedly in the direction of
strengthening multilateral security mechanisms. While the renewed attention to UN security in the early 1990s and the recent appearance of
ARF in 1994 generally heightened interest in multilateral security, today
Washington and Tokyo are markedly more concerned with the strength
of the bilateral alliance. Especially since the middle of the 1990s, Tokyo,
like Washington, has viewed multilateral security as something for the
future, that is, not quite ready to handle today's regional and international problems. Ironically, the observed weaknesses of multilateral security serve to legitimate the attention Tokyo has given to strengthening
the security alliance with Washington. As a result, Tokyo has not contributed nearly enough leadership to help make multilateral security effective in dealing with the inevitability of regional and international problems.

Tokyo has not yet confronted the fact that international credibility does not have to mean remaining committed to a security arrangement with the United States. Credibility can be acquired in a different way: building legitimately effective multilateral security mechanisms and promoting nuclear disarmament. Since the vast majority of the Japanese people support the abolition of all nuclear weapons, promoting nuclear disarmament is an activity that directly corresponds to an international norm that they want to see established. A perfectly legitimate question that Tokyo cannot fully answer is why it is not doing much more to promote multilateral security and nuclear disarmament. Added to this is the strong public support for Japan to participate actively in the United Nations by promoting global security and world peace. Thus, it is fair to question the extent to which Tokyo is working to satisfy the interests of the Japanese public in matters pertaining to security. Rather than developing policies that are consistent with popular interests, Tokyo has been working hard to convince the public to accept extensions to the Cold War security regime.

All of this means that Tokyo needs to separate Japan's security policy from that of the United States. Tokyo will need to announce an end to the bilateral security treaty and come out from underneath America's nuclear umbrella if it intends to promote a viable international nuclear disarmament agenda that appears credible to other countries. Taking the lead in building effective multilateral security structures will contribute to Japan's protection. By authenticating its interest in instituting a global nuclear disarmament process and by disassociating itself from the suspicion harbored by some countries that it has been assisting the United States in establishing hegemony in East Asia, Japan can bolster its international credibility. Thus, this kind of international credibility requires that Japan establish a neutral security policy so that it can take meaningful steps forward in the areas of multilateral security and nuclear disarmament.

It is unlikely, however, that Tokyo will assume these responsibilities completely on its own initiative. Facing Washington has not been one of the hallmarks of policy making in Tokyo. But there are at least three major ways that significant change could take place in Japan's security policies.

First, because the bases issue in Okinawa is an ever-present political cauldron linked to the U.S.–Japan security alliance, it could very quickly become heated to the point where residents are unrelenting in their demands that American military installations and troops be removed from their prefecture. The removal of U.S. troops from Okinawa could persuade either Washington or Tokyo or both that major revisions are needed in the bilateral security alliance. Thus, it is conceivable that without bases in Okinawa, Washington would abandon the security alliance or Tokyo would decide that without the presence of American troops it might be better to rely completely on its own forces for defense.

The second potential source of change in Japan's security policies involves civic groups and nongovernmental organizations (NGOs) supporting peace and opposed to nuclear weapons.[33] Already, there is a significant amount of concern in Tokyo and Washington that should there come a time to activate the new guidelines for defense cooperation, local Japanese port communities—some of which have previously made known their objections to visits by U.S. warships suspected of carrying nuclear weapons—will resist or even fail to comply with implementation orders. Civil society can play an even bigger part than it does presently in increasing public awareness and in this way move the central government toward a different security trajectory. At the same time, NGOs would need to continue applying pressure on the United Nations for more substantive activity on nuclear disarmament.

Local government action, the third way that Japan's security policies can change, is also important. Local governments in Hiroshima and Nagasaki, as well as elsewhere in Japan, must raise the level of public consciousness relating to the immediate need to abolish nuclear weapons and come to the realization that the existing U.S.–Japan security alliance makes this an arduous task. Civic groups, NGOs, and local governments, finally, must all link their efforts to abolish nuclear weapons to the urgent necessity of shoring up the security mechanisms of the United Nations as well as those of regional institutions.

2

The Bilateral Security
Relationship: What It Is Today

Introduction

The Persian Gulf War produced the widespread expectation that the United Nations' security mechanisms could be fully activated in the not-too-distant future. The Persian Gulf War, therefore, was responsible for creating the impression that cooperative global security, though then in a nascent stage, could evolve into a potent and significant international system. When the Soviet Union collapsed bringing a proclaimed end to the Cold War, the idea previously spawned during the Persian Gulf crisis that America would no longer have to assume the role of world's policeman became, however superficially, an accepted mode of political and academic thinking in the United States as well as elsewhere. Although proving to be transitory, it seemed that cooperative international security would replace the hegemonic struggles that had dominated global politics for more than four decades. Why would the United States continue to embrace this costly role? With Cold War tensions gone and with the Persian Gulf crisis seemingly demonstrating that nations could respond cooperatively when international security emergencies appeared, the United States could reap the benefits of a "peace dividend." Even Japan appeared willing to rethink its complete ban on participation in international peacekeeping. Largely because of *gaiastu* (foreign pressure) politics by the United States, the Japanese government passed the Peacekeeping Operations Bill in 1992.

But almost as quickly as the idea of an America no longer playing the role of the world's policeman emerged, it was quickly jettisoned by a myopic political read of the post–Cold War security environment. Ethnic and regional conflicts quickly replaced the Soviet problem. In Asia, North Korea had to be carefully monitored; China had to be "engaged" or "contained," depending on one's interpretation of U.S. security policy, and Russia, while less of an immediate threat, still had to be reminded of the strong U.S. military presence in East Asia. Thus, almost as quickly as it appeared, the United States had literally abandoned the widespread optimism that centered on UN security that had surfaced only a few years earlier. Lacking restraint, Washington readily accepted the post–Cold War reality that it was the world's singular (military) superpower and openly declared its objective of continuing military superiority. Identifying itself as the "world's only superpower today," the United States pledged to remain "politically and militarily engaged in the world over the next fifteen to twenty years, and that it will maintain military superiority over current and potential rivals." Washington adopted the policy that the United States had to be prepared to fight and win "two major theater wars nearly simultaneously" and that it place "greater emphasis on the continuing need to maintain continuous overseas presence in order to shape the international environment and to be better able to respond to a variety of smaller-scale contingencies and asymmetric threats."[1]

Mainly because of the size and strength of the American economy, cultural hegemony had already become an accomplishment of the United States. Now with the Cold War over, another opportunity became clear to U.S. policy makers. Rather than relinquishing the role of world's policeman, the United States seized the opportunity to capitalize on the peace dividend, more in the way of establishing indisputable global hegemony than in reducing military spending.[2] Accordingly, it became quite easy for the United States to be very critical of the potential for a viable and potent UN security system. Many Washington policy makers, some of whom had never particularly inclined toward accepting international security under the auspices of the United Nations anyway, demonstrated a continuing commitment to security structures that had been utilized during the Cold War. As a result, during the first half of the 1990s, Washington had identified a key policy objective: to create a global understanding of the United States as a "benevolent hegemon."

With NATO serving as a strong security bulwark in the West, Asia remained the security challenge that the United States had to confront single-handedly. With the Cold War declared over, Washington was free to shift somewhat the interpretation of national security from largely military concerns to include a very healthy dose of economic interests. This made Asia, and particularly East Asia, more attractive to the United States. Japan, with one of the largest economies in the world,[3] has remained a strong ally, and, despite the opposite impression given by some Washington bureaucrats, U.S. exports there have grown sharply over the last decade.[4] U.S. economic concerns in Asia, however, extended well beyond Japan. China, Singapore, Hong Kong, Indonesia, and South Korea, as well as other Asian countries, have become fundamentally important to U.S. economic interests. Apart from Cuba, America's neighbor to the south, Asia is where several communist governments still exist. China and North Korea have been identified as the biggest threats to regional instability, with the latter the more immediate problem and the former, a declared nuclear power with a big and growing economy, seen as a potential source of trouble in the years ahead.[5] Thus, since East Asia had become vital to U.S. economic interests and because it was presumed that this part of the world promised to be an area of future growth, a strong American presence had to be maintained in the region.

In the immediate aftermath of the Cold War, the United States began to reaffirm the importance of its bilateral security alliances in the East Asia and Pacific region. Bilateral security relations with Japan, Australia, South Korea, Thailand, and the Philippines were said to account for America's "forward military presence" in the region.[6] Although the presence of American military personnel in the East Asia and Pacific region declined since the end of the Cold War, in 1999 the United States still had more than 98,000 troops in that region. Japan is home to over 41 percent of American troops in the East Asian and Pacific region; more than half of U.S. troops in Japan are in Okinawa.[7]

An Enduring Security Alliance

The U.S.–Japan security relationship began during the Occupation period with the signing of the Treaty of Mutual Cooperation and Security in 1951. While different Japanese political groups debated the advantages and disadvantages of the bilateral security alliance for Japan, the treaty survived the 1950s. From the onset, its purpose was clear: to align

Tokyo with Washington so that the Soviet Union would be deterred from making an aggressive move on Japan. The treaty did, however, come to have an underlying purpose, which was to serve as a countervailing force to the position of "unarmed neutrality" for Japan, a theme resounded by the Japan Socialist Party, particularly by members of its left wing. Despite initial beliefs pertaining to the ephemerality of the bilateral pact, since there existed the expectation that the United Nations would assume control of international security and hence the protection of Japan, and significant political resistance over the renewal of the treaty in 1960, which included opposition of others besides the socialists,[8] the U.S.–Japan bilateral security alliance survived the Cold War.

It was at the end of the Cold War that questions began to emerge in Japan concerning the need for the security alliance with the United States. For Japan, a cooperative international security system guided by the United Nations meant that the United States no longer had to play the role of world's policeman. In addition to this, according to Japan's Ministry of Foreign Affairs, by the early 1990s there was evident a growing expectation that the United Nations would assume the responsibility of implementing collective global security.[9] Understand that this was an expectation that Japan had allowed to lie dormant for several decades because of its "choice" to remain tied to a U.S.-dominated security structure.

Appearing in the summer of 1994, the Higuchi Report was an attempt by Japan to introduce a security policy that at least superficially carried a Japanese signature.[10] Though seeing the continued need for the U.S.–Japan Security Treaty, this report also emphasized that both regional and multilateral security structures would be emergent parts of the new international order. According to the Higuchi Report, multilateral security would be centered on the United Nations, but U.S. leadership was still necessary, at least for the foreseeable future. This report struck a very sensitive political nerve in Washington by conjecturing that "[t]he question is whether the United States, its preeminent military power notwithstanding, will be able to demonstrate leadership in multilateral cooperation, and the answer to the question will depend to a certain extent on actions by nations in a position to cooperate with the United States."

Since the publication of the Higuchi Report, America's capability to perform effectively as the leader of an international security system has been placed in serious doubt on two occasions. In the winter of 1998, the United States was unable to get consensus from the international community, including within the Security Council, to use military force against Iraq when it failed to comply fully with UN inspection demands.[11] This discernible weakness in U.S. security leadership, was a prelude to an even more disturbing international event: the wave of nuclear testing performed by India and Pakistan during the spring of 1998. In its leadership role, the United States was compelled to castigate India and Pakistan publicly for their nuclear testing. But it was quite easy to see through the political facade. U.S. criticism of India and Pakistan for nuclear testing—neither country had signed the Comprehensive Test Ban Treaty—could hardly be justified because of America's substantial nuclear arsenal and because of its repeated subcritical nuclear testing. Nonetheless, it was evident to American policy makers that leadership required sanctioning of India and Pakistan. Thus, the United States, as well as Japan,[12] responded by imposing economic sanctions on India and Pakistan. However, within weeks of India and Pakistan's nuclear testing, U.S. abhorrence of this activity nearly disappeared when, pressured by American agricultural groups, Washington lawmakers voted to eliminate much of the economic sanctions. The Asian financial crisis and making *gaiatsu* (foreign pressure) suggestions to Japan to repair its economic problems upstaged the nuclear-testing catastrophe, soon to be joined by Iraqi noncompliance with UN arms inspectors and the terrorist bombing of two U.S. embassies in east Africa. Relying on the guidelines set forth in its Official Development Assistance charter, Japan retained its economic sanctions of India and Pakistan.[13] Thus, unnoticed by the international community, the onus of security leadership regarding the important matter of nuclear testing by India and Pakistan rested squarely on the shoulders of Japan. However, Japan, while very much disturbed by India and Pakistan's nuclear testing and the potential to ignite a post–Cold War arms race, remained comfortably under the U.S. nuclear umbrella.

The contradiction of Japan remaining under America's nuclear umbrella while vehemently opposing the existence of nuclear weapons and nuclear testing is clearly not new. For some time, Tokyo's security alliance with Washington has not only afforded Japan the guarantee of American protection but also the U.S. nuclear shield. When the Cold War ended, the United States continued to stress to Japan that, while the world was perhaps a safer place, it was still very troubled. Cold War complaints of the Japanese "free ride," which amounted to a sustained effort by the United States to get Japan to increase its military spending, were transfigured into pronouncements of an "equal partnership."[14] For the United States this new alliance required the maintenance of the bilateral security alliance, and continued high levels of Japanese spending for foreign economic assistance. There is hardly any doubt that the new "equal partnership" was really not equal, since America's dominance of the security alliance and its role as the ultimate protector of Japan ramified the entire bilateral relationship, from trade and other economic matters to science and technology.[15]

Sustaining the Bilateral Security Alliance

It is commonly stated by officials in both Tokyo and Washington that the U.S.–Japan security alliance, the nucleus of which is the extant 1960 U.S.–Japan Treaty of Mutual Cooperation and Security, is the "cornerstone" of the bilateral relationship. While the United States values all of its bilateral security alliances in the East Asia–Pacific region, its most important security relationship in the area is with Japan. For Washington, there are two reasons why it especially values this alliance today: (1) it is considered according to Department of Defense reports on East Asia, "the linchpin of the United States security policy in Asia," where threats still exist, including the survival of communism; and (2) the economic significance of the East Asia–Pacific area, and particularly Japan, requires a strong U.S. security presence. Tokyo also has two important reasons for wanting to preserve the bilateral security alliance, albeit they are quite different from Washington's. First, Tokyo wants to establish credibility as a world power, and so by agreeing to strengthen the bilateral security alliance, Japan has a vicarious link to the military superpower status of the United States. Second, Tokyo very much wants to retain the nuclear shield provided by the United States in the security alliance.

Since the end of the Cold War, the United States has worked very hard to minimize the threats to the continued existence of the security alliance with Japan. Questions pertaining to the need for the continuation of the alliance in both the United States and Japan were answered by Washington and Tokyo policy makers in a string of official documents that have attempted to demonstrate the present and future significance of the bilateral security arrangement. The U.S. Department of Defense published its first post–Cold War document on the need to maintain the security status quo in the East Asia–Pacific region in 1992. This report states that the "U.S.–Japan relationship remains key to our Asian security strategy," and notes that the "continuing U.S. presence in Japan and the strength of the U.S.–Japan security relationship are reassuring to many nations in the region." This report made clear that the United States wanted to deter North Korean adventurism and that its "quest for nuclear weapons capability continues to be the most urgent threat to security in Northeast Asia."[16]

Problems on the Korean Peninsula date back to the Korean War (1950–1953). However, since 1990 an inordinate amount of attention has been focused on North Korea as a major source of instability in East Asia. The normalization of diplomatic relations between the Soviet Union and South Korea in September 1990 prompted the Democratic People's Republic of Korea (DPRK) to reconsider its national policy agenda. This included the DPRK's nuclear program, which Moscow had nurtured since 1956 when it signed a nuclear research agreement with Pyongyang. By 1990 Moscow was attempting to dissuade Pyongyang from developing nuclear weapons. The dissolution of the Soviet Union created additional concerns about Pyongyang's nuclear objectives. Although there was a cooling-off in the bilateral relationship between Pyongyang and Moscow during the first half of the 1990s and although Russia too remained concerned about DPRK's nuclear intentions, at least twice during this period—in 1992 and in 1994—the Russian government emphatically maintained that North Korea did not yet possess nuclear weapons.[17]

Because of mutual concerns about the development of nuclear weapons on the Korean Peninsula, Seoul and Pyongyang held discussions on denuclearization during 1990. On December 31, 1991, Pyongyang and Seoul signed the Declaration on the Denuclearization of the Korean Peninsula. Fulfilling a commitment it made when it assented to the Nuclear Nonproliferation Treaty (NPT) in 1985, North Korea signed an inspections agreement with the International Atomic Energy Agency (IAEA) in late January 1992. In January 1993, North Korea refused to give inspectors from the IAEA access to two sites suspected of being used for nuclear waste, increasing suspicion about Pyongyang's nuclear weapons program. Two months later, on March 12, 1993, Pyongyang announced its intention to withdraw from NPT because, it believed, insufficient progress on the denuclearization accord had created problems between North and South Korea. Bilateral talks between Washington and Pyongyang in June 1993 produced a

North Korean agreement to defer its withdrawal from NPT.[18]

In May 1993, North Korea launched a Rodong missile. This event got the attention of Washington and Tokyo, since it exacerbated the nuclear issue by indicating DPRK delivery capability. The Japanese Defense Agency eventually concluded that the missile did not fly over Japan, but that it landed in the Sea of Japan. Contrary to the Defense Agency's findings, the United States in early 1998—demonstrating its continuing suspicion of Pyongyang's military objectives and its desire to maintain a regional-threat environment—informed Tokyo that the missile might have crossed over Japanese territory.[19]

A major crisis emerged in the spring of 1994 when North Korea began drawing fuel from its nuclear reactor, further raising suspicions about Pyongyang's objectives. With approval from the Clinton administration, former president Carter went to North Korea in June 1994 to try to resolve the crisis. The formal resolution of the crisis occurred on October 21, 1994, when the United States and North Korea signed the Agreed Framework. As a result of this bilateral accord, Pyongyang re-committed North Korea to the NPT and agreed to end the development of its graphite-moderated nuclear reactors, essentially freezing DPRK's nuclear weapons program. For its part, the United States agreed to establish an international consortium, which later appeared as the Korean Peninsula Energy Development Organization (KEDO) in March 1995.[20] With the objective of keeping Pyongyang disengaged from nuclear weapons development by providing both financial assistance for the construction of two civilian light water reactors and heavy oil, KEDO was established less than six months after the United States and the DPRK finalized the Agreed Framework. The original members of KEDO were the United States, Japan, and South Korea.[21]

Meanwhile, Russian foreign minister Kozyrev's emphatic statement in June 1994 that North Korea did not possess nuclear weapons and that it would be unable to produce them for at least another three years[22] fell on deaf ears. By this time, a near consensus had developed in the United States and Japan that the DPRK had nuclear weapons. The growing concern that North Korea had nuclear weapons was indeed widespread in Japan. By the beginning of 1994, a survey sponsored by the United States Information Agency showed that 94 percent of the respondents thought that North Korea then possessed nuclear weapons.[23]

While Tokyo largely remained on the sideline and reasoned it worthwhile to hold talks on normalizing relations with North Korea, Washington maintained a cloud of suspicion over Pyongyang's military intentions. The U.S. State Department charged that Pyongyang was not cooperating with IAEA—which it was obligated to do under the Agreed Framework—making it hard to monitor the extent of North Korea's commitment to freezing its suspected nuclear weapons program. More problematic, said the State Department, was getting access to information relating to North Korea's past nuclear weapons activities.[24] Despite the existence of the Agreed Framework and KEDO, Washington continued to paint the picture of a nuclear weapons threat from North Korea. In mid-August 1998, U.S. intelligence made specific the impending nuclear threat coming from North Korea. Having located a large underground site approximately twenty-five miles from Yongbyon, which is where—until the 1994 Agreed Framework—the DPRK allegedly had been manufacturing plutonium for use in several nuclear weapons, U.S. intelligence sources concluded that the new location was being used to restart North Korea's frozen nuclear weapons program.[25] This conclusion by the U.S. intelligence community proved to be unfounded, as we will see below. However, this well-publicized statement from U.S. intelligence sources did accomplish three important things: it sustained the belief in the threat of an impending nuclear weapons problem coming from the DPRK, it reinforced the image of North Korean adventurism, and it served to justify the strengthening of the U.S.– Japan security alliance.

In February 1995, the Department of Defense published its second post–Cold War security report on the East Asia–Pacific region. This report stressed the need to keep 100,000 U.S. troops in the region "for the foreseeable future" and emphasized that Washington desired greater transparency of Beijing's military intentions. Even though the U.S.– DPRK Agreed Framework had been in place for more than three months by the time of the publication of this report, which explained the benefits of implementing this accord, it characterized North Korea as unpredictable and as a potentially destabilizing force in East Asia. Helping to keep the DPRK military threat, including the nuclear weapons, politically alive, this reports stated that

> North Korea's history of aggression, threats to peace, and exports of missile technology have created a context in which its development of nuclear weapons would be an extremely dangerous threat to security on the Peninsula, in Asia, and for global non-proliferation. At the same time, North Korea's conventional military threat to the Republic of Korea has not

abated, and requires continued vigilance and commitment of United States forces.[26]

More than the previous report, this one emphasized the "equal partnership" status of the bilateral relationship, that is, Japan would be an important partner in the East Asian security structure designed and led by the United States. In addition, this report emphasized that Japan is the leading provider of foreign aid to developing countries in the world, and it also stressed that "Japan's new global role involves greater Japanese contribution to regional and global stability."[27]

This new global role that Japan had to assume was critical. During the 1980s, as Japan was establishing itself as a major economic and science and technology superpower, Tokyo became aware that the nation had to make a major contribution to the international community— a growing foreign assistance budget was not enough. Because of the Persian Gulf War and the end of the Cold War, Tokyo became even more aware than it had been before of the need for Japan to play a major role in international affairs. Somehow Tokyo had to reconcile Japan's desire for an important international role, its pacifist constitution, its concerns about the existence of nuclear weapons, and its belief in a strong United Nations with the largely unchanged security position of the United States in the East Asia–Pacific region.

Despite questions arising in Japan concerning the need for the continuation of the security treaty with the United States, Japanese policy makers concurred with the American position that the security status quo had to be maintained in the East Asian region. This, however, did not occur without prodding from the United States. Just a little over two months after the publication of the Higuchi Report, Secretary of Defense William J. Perry visited Tokyo and met with Japanese defense minister Tokuichiro Tamazawa. In late September 1995, the U.S.–Japan Security Consultative Committee met in New York to discuss strategic issues dealing with the bilateral alliance. This was the twentieth meeting of the Security Consultative Committee. Setting this meeting apart from the nineteen preceding it was the fact that this was the first time that this forum involved cabinet-rank officials from both Japan and the United States. Representing Japan was Yohei Kono, deputy prime minister and minister of foreign affairs, and Seishiro Eto, minister of state and director general of the Defense Agency; Secretary of State Warren Christopher and Secretary of Defense William J. Perry represented the United States.[28]

One year later, in September 1996, the twenty-first meeting of the U.S.–Japan Security Consultative Committee convened in Washington, again involving cabinet-level representation from both countries. Now exposed to the crises that took place in Okinawa—first the brutal rape of a young Okinawan schoolgirl by U.S. servicemen and then the mounting Okinawan opposition to U.S. military presence on the island—former secretary of state Christopher felt that it was important to stress the following at the meeting: "Today's second cabinet-level meeting of the U.S.–Japan Security Consultative Committee reflects the fundamental importance of the security partnership between our two great nations." Christopher went on to say: "The renewal of our security partnership has been at the heart of the strengthening of our overall relationship." Former secretary of defense Perry meanwhile emphasized the continuing importance of U.S. military troops in the Asia–Pacific area, including maintaining the existing number in Japan, and stressed that both President William Clinton and Prime Minister Ryutaro Hashimoto recognized the significance of the Mutual Security Treaty as well as the need to begin work to build a stronger bilateral security relationship, of which the first step was to review the 1978 Guidelines for U.S.–Japan Defense Cooperation.[29]

The United States and Japan had already taken this first step a few months earlier. Directed by the Subcommittee for Defense Cooperation but under the general administration of the U.S.–Japan Security Consultative Committee, the review of the 1978 guidelines was underway in June 1996. The Interim Report on the Review of the Guidelines for U.S.–Japan Defense Cooperation appeared a year later, in June 1997.[30] Three months later, on September 23, 1997, Washington and Tokyo finalized the new Guidelines for U.S.–Japan Defense Cooperation at the twenty-second Security Consultative Committee meeting in New York City.

The realization that Japan and the United States were working to strengthen their security relationship has been especially disturbing to both North Korea and China. Exasperating Beijing was the phrase in the new guidelines, "areas surrounding Japan,"[31] which, according to the public statements issued by Tokyo and Washington, refers not to a geographical area, but rather "situations" that will affect Japanese security. Beijing feels that this apparent strengthening of the U.S.–Japan security arrangement, which broadens Japan's regional responsibilities, would effectively give America, with Japanese support, the discretionary power to intervene in China–Taiwan problems. Speaking to this issue, Chinese president Jiang Zemin said, "Taiwan should not be covered by the new guidelines." From China's vantage point, the U.S.–Japan security alliance has been evolving beyond just the protection of Japan and in the direction of establishing regional security. Because Beijing harbors the view that the United States is a hegemon,[32] which runs counter to China's stated foreign policy,[33] from the Chinese perspective the new bilateral guidelines reinforce this position.[34]

Although relying on political hyperbole to some extent, nonetheless, North Korea's initial response to the new guidelines—well before its improved relations with South Korea, Japan, and the United States—was that they are equivalent to an act of war. Just a few days subsequent to the appearance of the new guidelines, a spokesperson for North Korea's Foreign Ministry stated that the United States and Japan had "entered a phase of attaining their wild design on a full scale to gain supremacy over Asia by means of military solution."[35] Pyongyang has interpreted the new guidelines between the United States and Japan as a bilateral mandate that legitimates the use of military force on the Korean Peninsula, and that specifically targets the DPRK.

The new guidelines have been controversial. Not only have they troubled Beijing and Pyongyang, but also in South Korea there have been reverberations from the new guidelines, which, as they do for China and North Korea, create the prospect of Japanese remilitarization.[36] Even in Japan, serious concerns arose when Tokyo formally acceded to what appeared to be a stronger security relationship with the United States at a time when the implicit value of the security alliance itself was being questioned. A political consensus on the new guidelines had not been established, and Japanese public opinion was definitely not solidly behind their creation. In Tokyo, Osaka, and Okinawa, as well as elsewhere throughout Japan, many people saw the new guidelines as a form of political retrogression, in that they suggested some degree of Japanese remilitarization; moreover, a concern surfaced that the new guidelines would make Japan a target, should the United States become involved in a military dispute in the Asia–Pacific region.[37]

Then there were constitutional questions. Was it constitutionally permissible for Japan to enter into these new security guidelines with the United States? Does not Article 9, the war-renouncing clause of Japan's constitution, prohibit it from assuming a belligerent military position? These are the types of questions asked by those in

Japan who were in a position to know the answers. A survey of constitutional scholars in Japan conducted by one of the country's major daily newspapers, *Asahi Shimbun*, found that approximately 80 percent of them thought that the new guidelines are in violation of the constitution.[38]

Signed by Liberal Democratic Party prime minister Hashimoto and President Clinton during the latter's April 1996 visit to Tokyo, the Japan–U.S. Joint Declaration on Security Alliance for the Twenty-first Century became the catalyst symbolizing bilateral efforts to strengthen the security alliance. The Joint Declaration reaffirms U.S. and Japanese commitment to the bilateral security alliance, stresses that it is still necessary for the protection of Japan and for the stability of the Asia Pacific region, which requires the "positive regional engagement of the U.S."; and concludes by pointing out that security, political, and economic issues, which are the three "legs" of the relationship, depend on shared democratic values and ultimately rest on the 1960 Treaty of Mutual Cooperation and Security. The Joint Declaration also states that both Clinton and Hashimoto agreed to begin a review of 1978 guidelines.[39] Thus, it was the Joint Declaration that initiated the reorganization of the Subcommittee for Defense Cooperation, which directed a review of the 1978 guidelines and within months led to the new guidelines for defense cooperation.[40]

The Subcommittee for Defense Cooperation's review of the 1978 guidelines relied on the Joint Declaration and Japan's National Defense Program Outline. Approved by the Japanese government in late November 1995, the latter document, like the Joint Declaration, stressed the importance of the Japan–U.S. security alliance. Less than a month later, the Japanese government adopted the Mid-Term Defense Build-up Plan (1996–2000), which also underscored the importance of the bilateral security arrangements.

The new guidelines for bilateral defense cooperation were not created in a political vacuum. Rather, they emerged in an environment in which the United Sates had been fortifying its efforts to establish regional stability or, devoid of the euphemism, hegemony, with Japan working diligently in a supporting role. However, constitutional restrictions and the stream of pacifism that flows through Japan lend a symbolic character to Tokyo's commitment to a strengthened security alliance with Washington. For the time being, notwithstanding the new guidelines, it is unlikely that Japan—where collective security is unquestionably a sticky political and constitutional issue because of enduring national pacifism—will quickly rush to support the United States should a military problem emerge in the East Asian region. Nonetheless, the new guidelines for defense cooperation created the impression that Washington and Tokyo had taken a significant step in the direction of forming a NATO-like security structure in East Asia. The terrorist attacks on the United States in September 2001 gave Tokyo the opportunity to remove some of the lingering criticism experienced by Japan since the Gulf War when its role was largely limited to providing financial support. Because of the horrific human tragedies precipitated by these attacks, Tokyo was able to expedite through the Diet anti-terrorist legislation, which is different from the new guidelines, that authorized Japanese participation in the international war on terrorism in Afghanistan in a noncombat capacity. Still, many Japanese remain uneasy about Japan's involvement in the conflict.

If conservative forces in Japan succeed in changing Article 9 of the constitution, the Japanese willingness to get involved in regional security activities is likely to change as well. Should this occur, symbolism will be replaced by substantive military action. Constitutional change will legitimate Japan's involvement in military activities, other than those directly connected to the defense of its territory, and open the door to complete Japanese remilitarization. By pushing Japan down the path of remilitarization, constitutional change may ultimately be responsible for getting it involved in non–UN related military matters outside of East Asia, something that Tokyo has been reluctant even to offer to the public for consideration. Indeed, the Japanese government did not even demonstrate unequivocal verbal support of Washington, its staunchest ally, in August 1998 when it retaliated against the terrorist bombings of two American embassies in Africa by sending cruise missiles to Sudan and Afghanistan. Instead, Tokyo opted to indicate that while it "understands" Washington's position, it was not informed beforehand of U.S. intentions, suggesting that it did not have all the facts.[41] Days later, still without direct support from Tokyo, Secretary of State Madeleine Albright thanked Japan for its "understanding" the U.S. decision to respond to the terrorist attacks.[42]

Ongoing political resistance coming from Okinawa has been diverting some attention away from the strengthening of the bilateral security alliance. When three U.S. servicemen raped a young Okinawan schoolgirl in September 1995, massive protest quickly erupted, demonstrating not just a widespread revulsion at the crime, but also the fact that the many citizens of Okinawa had for some time been very dissatisfied with the continued presence of U.S. forces there—a much larger political issue. An especially strong pacifist sentiment exists in Okinawa. Alongside this is the enduring sentiment in favor of neutrality; thus, the continuing Okinawan commitment to "unarmed neutrality." Together these sentiments translate into some uncertainty about Tokyo's security alliance with the United States and the significance of the security treaty. This uncertainty about the mutual security treaty, however, is not restricted to Okinawa. A 1996 survey performed by *Nihon Yoron Chosakai* (Japan Public Opinion Survey Association) found that 51 percent of those polled thought that the bilateral security treaty should be brought to an end.[43]

Tokyo's treatment of the Okinawan crisis has mainly been to yield to Washington's objective of maintaining a strong military presence in Japan; many of the people of Okinawa feel that this comes at their expense. To deal with the crisis that had arisen in the prefecture, Washington and Tokyo created the Special Action Committee on Okinawa (SACO) in November 1995. The Security Consultative Committee approved the SACO Interim Report during its mid-April 1996 meeting. In early December 1996, SACO issued its final report. The report's main objective was to provide the Security Consultative Committee with recommendations that, "when implemented, will reduce the impact of the activities of U.S. forces on the communities in Okinawa." All actions resulting from the SACO report are to be compatible with the bilateral security treaty and other associated arrangements.[44]

A big part of the strategy laid out by Washington and Tokyo was to improve the relationship between the people of Okinawa and U.S. military forces and facilities. The bilateral Security Consultative Committee announced its endorsement of the SACO report on December 2, 1996, on the same day that SACO held its final meeting. At that time the committee also stressed the need for better relations between the U.S. military and local communities by calling for the creation of a U.S. Forces–Community Day.[45] Some major points outlined in the SACO Final Report are plans to return approximately 21 percent of the land used by American forces to Okinawans, relocation of troops, and efforts by the U.S. military to reduce noise and the number of night flights.[46]

One of several major issues in Okinawa's dispute with Washington and Tokyo is the future of the Futenma Air Station. The SACO Interim Report issued in April 1996 recommended that options be identified for the relocation of the Futenma Air Station. The mid-September 1996 Status Report established the Special Working Group on Futenma, which identified three options for the future of the air station: (1) to absorb the heliport in the operations of Kadena Air Base; (2) to build a heliport at Camp Schwab, a U.S. Marine base near Nago, Okinawa; and (3) to construct a sea-based facility. On December 2, 1996, the Security Consultative Committee accepted SACO's recommendation to construct a sea-based facility off of the east coast of the Okinawan mainland. The Security Consultative Committee charged the Futenma Implementation Group with the responsibility of coming up with a plan and a location for the heliport by December 1997.[47]

The selection of the sea-based facility off the shore of the city of Nago has been controversial. Well after the selection of Nago for the relocation of Futenma Air Station, serious problems have persisted between Okinawa and Tokyo. Even though Tokyo has tied financial benefits for Okinawa to the building of the sea-based facility near Nago, no settlement has been reached. In August 1998, Okinawans saw a renewal of the tensions that were evident months earlier between their prefecture and Tokyo.[48] Although Okinawan governor Masahide Ota continued to display a staunch resistance to the building of the heliport off the shore of Nago, in late August 1998 he reportedly said that he was willing to think about relocating Futenma Air Station somewhere else in the prefecture.[49] In 2000, Okinawan governor Keiichi Inamine was still struggling with the base issue. The governor supported a fifteen-year limit to the U.S. Futenma Air Station. Washington and Tokyo continue to oppose the time limitation proposed by Inamine.

The main problem with the way Tokyo has handled the Okinawan negotiations with Washington is that is has proceeded as if there is no alternative to a visibly strong U.S. military presence in Okinawa. The underlying justification from both Washington and Tokyo has continued to be based on the argument that the world is still a very dangerous place and that this most certainly applies to the East Asia–Pacific area, particularly since North Korea, China, or perhaps even Russia or some other country or terrorist group could strike and create regional havoc at any time. Because of these potential threats, U.S. troops are still needed in Okinawa, as well as in other places in Japan. However, policy makers do not address the question that if North Korea is the most immediate threat to Japan and to the region, why are there more U.S. troops in Japan (40,338) than in South Korea (35,913)?[50] Simply stressing that the existence of a quasi-alliance between Japan and South Korea (quasi because each country has a separate security arrangement with the United States) continues to ensure regional stability ignores the presumed significance of a North Korean adventurism and invasion into the southern half of the peninsula.[51]

It is important to understand that there is a cultural dimension to the continuation of the Cold War security alliance between Japan and the United States and, accordingly, the need to keep a disproportionately large share of American troops in Okinawa. Having accepted and lived with U.S. military protection for decades, the people of Okinawa have not so much become accustomed to this way of life, but have come to tolerate it. In other words, they feel a sense of hopelessness. This explains why a recent Japanese government poll found that for the first time since 1985, when Okinawans were initially asked about the presence of U.S. bases in their prefecture, more respondents, 45.7 percent, accepted them than opposed them, 44.4 percent.[52] Mitigating this serious matter somewhat is the fact that the majority of Japanese political leaders have accepted the bilateral security relationship as a way of life, particularly those affiliated with the U.S.-leaning Liberal Democratic Party. Periodic remarks by Japanese and U.S. political leaders rest squarely on an unproven syllogism: The existence of the bilateral security alliance has protected Japan and helped to maintain regional peace, so there is a continuing need to sustain it. Even the socialist leader Tomiichi Murayama, who served as prime minister from June 1994 to January 1996, succumbed to the cultural pressure to maintain the Cold War security relationship with the United States, moving from rejection of the alliance for many years prior to assuming office to acceptance of it while in office.

Since the dissolution of the Soviet Union, Japanese and American policy makers have relied on a shifting regional enemy (North Korea, China, maybe Russia, or some other threat) to help justify the bilateral security alliance. At the very least, this suggests an attempt by Tokyo policy makers to certify that Japan is a credible participant in power politics. Tokyo policy makers further rationalize that the Japanese people—but especially Okinawans, who have had to bear most of the burden connected with the bilateral alliance—must make the sacrifices associated with the presence of American forces for the protection of Japan and for regional stability. To help alleviate some of the burden of their sacrifices, conciliatory gestures by Tokyo have centered on the suggestion of financial assistance to Okinawa, a Japanese prefecture that continues to experience economic difficulties. Added to this is the intermittent reminder that the presence of American bases and troops in the prefecture has been economically beneficial to some Okinawans.

Tokyo has examined the bilateral security arrangement, not with a critical eye seeking alternatives, but by predisposing Japan to the position that the alliance is imperative for the country's protection and for the stability of all of East Asia. That the bilateral security alliance is a product of the Cold War and was designed specifically to deal with the problems of that period generally has had no effect on Washington and Tokyo policy makers. By developing a threat scenario that is adaptable to different regional situations, or more specifically, contingencies, Washington and Tokyo have concluded that the omnipresence of virtually any potential threat is sufficient reason to maintain the bilateral security alliance. Erstwhile assistant secretary of defense for international security affairs Joseph Nye went as far as to remark that the existence of "enduring and convergent interests . . . has not made the U.S.–Japan security alliance obsolete. On the contrary, if the alliance did not already exist, we would have to create it now."[53]

Understand that the revitalization of the bilateral security alliance in recent years has kept Japan integrally linked to America's strategic plan for the East Asia–Pacific region. In addition to its growing economic interests in the area, which Japan also shares, Washington has concluded that it must retain security presence and influence in the East Asia–Pacific region. A forfeiture of this presence and influence would reduce America's ability to apply *gaiatsu* (foreign pressure) on Japanese economic policies and simultaneously undermine its international identity as a good hegemon.

Concerns for Change

It has been argued that it is necessary to keep Tokyo committed to the bilateral security alliance, since in its absence, Japan would abandon its antimilitarist culture and remilitarization would be forthcoming.[54] In other words, the existence of the bilateral security alliance helps to pacify several of Japan's neighbors, who have not forgotten its militarist past. Therefore, in one important way this argument supports the United States acting as a good hegemon, because it is consistent with Tokyo's position, which is that for Japan there is no practical alternative to the bilateral security alliance. Conversely, to argue simply that the bilateral alliance and the new guidelines sustain Japanese security dependency on the United States and that Japan should abandon Article 9 and adopt an independent, activist position—that is, remilitarize—so that the economic burden of its defense can be lifted from America's shoulders ignores a fundamentally important matter.[55] The absence of U.S. hegemony in the East Asia–Pacific area would give Japan, for the first time in the postwar period, the chance to act independently to satisfy its interests in nuclear disarmament and to galvanize interests in regional security.

There have been calls on both sides of the Pacific Ocean for U.S. and Japanese policy makers to implement major changes in the bilateral security arrangement so that the alliance can accurately reflect current conditions and, in particular, to deal with the discontent in Okinawa. Some of these calls for change in the bilateral security alliance have specified moving U.S. forces out of Japan, and especially Okinawa.[56] Okinawa hosts most U.S. troops in Japan, but discontent there also stems from the fact that 75 percent of the land controlled by American military forces in the country is in this prefecture and also that 10 percent of the Okinawan land mass is occupied by American military facilities.[57]

However, the removal of U.S. forces from Japan would not end the bilateral security alliance, nor would this adjustment take Japan out from under America's nuclear umbrella. While removing or reducing U.S. forces in Japan and relocating them to other places in the Asia–Pacific region would perhaps noticeably decrease Okinawan discontent, China, North Korea and Russia would still be very uncomfortable with bilateral efforts to strengthen the security alliance. Beijing, Pyongyang, and Moscow strongly oppose the most recent bilateral security effort of the United States and Japan, that is, theater missile defense (TMD). Japan, moreover, would remain susceptible to American trade and economic demands, since the existence of the security alliance would leave in place the United States' decided advantage in attempts to resolve bilateral issues.

There have also been those who support the end of the bilateral security alliance. Most who support this position propound the notion of Japan still taking a "free ride." Bad enough that the United States spent billions of dollars during the Cold War to protect Japan, but it continues to do so today. Japan should be assuming the responsibility of providing for its defense; this may require a rescission of Article 9.[58]

But ending the existing bilateral security arrangement and effectively endorsing Japanese remilitarization would cause a precarious situation, to say the least, to emerge in the East Asia–Pacific region. Although China and North Korea already oppose the existing U.S.–Japan security alliance, its demise, if coincident with Japanese remilitarization, would invite additional rancor in the region. Both China and North Korea would become deeply concerned with what they would perceive as a potential military threat emerging in Japan. South Korea would also become quite uneasy with these changes, as would Russia. A strong and independent Japanese military posture would not be welcomed by Moscow today, especially since there is a discernible nationalist sentiment pushing its way to the surface in Japan. Even the reasonably strong expectation of reemergent Japanese militarism would be sure to aggravate Tokyo and Moscow's inability to work out the Northern Territories/southern Kurile Islands dispute, which had originally been expected to be resolved by the end of 2000. In short, given its historical record of military aggression directed at its neighbors, Japan would have a very difficult time convincing several countries in the region that its remilitarization is politically benign.

Recent Regional Fragilities

To deal effectively with the problems in East Asia, much more change is currently needed in the U.S.–Japan security alliance than the presentation of concessions to Okinawa. The threat of nuclear proliferation is a serious one in the world today and the East Asia–Pacific region is no exception to this. The United States, Japan, China, Russia, and North Korea must continuously grapple with this and related security issues. Beijing had to contend with the fact that India's five nuclear tests conducted in the spring of 1998 were not only a signal to Pakistan, but also to China. While choosing sides in the India–Pakistan conflict is easy for China, what is difficult is the problem of nuclear weapons proliferation and the understanding that New Delhi, now with nuclear capability, sees Beijing as a potential enemy. Placed in this context, improvements in Sino-Japanese relations face serious political hurdles not just because of historical problems, but recent attempts to strengthen the U.S.–Japan security alliance further expand China's band of external threats and cause it to be overly suspicious and defensive and thus add to regional tensions.

As we have seen, the impending nuclear threat from North Korea remained a serious regional concern even after the signing of the 1994 U.S.–DPRK Agreed Framework in which Pyongyang promised to end its nuclear weapons program in exchange for financial assistance to procure nuclear-powered facilities.[59] The belief that the reclusive North Korean government had maintained a subterranean nuclear weapons program had become so widespread by the end of the 1990s that it was tantamount to common knowledge in the United States and Japan. The United States insisted that it wanted to inspect a suspected DPRK underground facility at Kumchang-ni. North Korea initially balked at the proposal of inspection by the United States, but eventually, in March 1999, agreed to permit American access to the site. From May 18 to May 24, 1999, a U.S. Department of State team traveled to North Korea to inspect the activities at Kumchang-ni. The State Department's report indicated that North Korea cooperated with the U.S. team and pointed out that:

> The site at Kumchang-ni does not contain a plutonium reactor or reprocessing plant, either completed or under construction. Given the current size and configuration of the underground area, the site is unsuitable for the installation of a plutonium production reactor, especially a graphite-moderated reactor of the type North Korea has built at Yongbyon. Based on the data gather by the U.S. delegation and the subsequent technical review, the U.S. has concluded that, at present, the underground site at Kumchang-ni does not violate the U.S.–DPRK Agreed Framework.[60]

In November 1998, President Clinton appointed former secretary of defense William Perry to lead a policy review team to examine the U.S. policy on North Korea. Perry was part of the U.S. group that visited North Korea in May 1999. Regarding DPRK nuclear weapons program, Perry's report indicated the following:

> The Agreed Framework of 1994 succeeded in verifiably freezing North Korean plutonium production at Yongbyon—it stopped plutonium production at that facility so that North Korea currently has at most a small amount of fissile material it may have secreted away from operations prior to 1994. . . . Yet, despite the critical achievement of a verified freeze on plutonium production at Yongbyon under the Agreed Framework, the policy review team has serious concerns about possible continuing nuclear weapons–related work in the DPRK. Some of these concerns have been addressed through our access and visit to Kumchang-ni.[61]

Both U.S. government reports on Kumchang-ni published in 1999, at the very least, indicated that work on nuclear weapons was not taking place at this location. A subsequent U.S. inspection of the Kumchang-ni site in May 2000 also produced no evidence that Pyongyang had been attempting to develop nuclear weapons.[62] It is, however, important to emphasize that Perry's 1999 report on Kumchang-ni strongly implies that Pyongyang could still be supporting work on nuclear weapons, perhaps elsewhere in North Korea. Indeed, although it lacks any evidence, Washington has kept alive the suspicion that Pyongyang may have maintained its secret nuclear weapons program—and this has happened since the 1999 Perry report.

In addition to pointing to the chemical and biological weapons threat coming from North Korea, in September 2000 the Department of Defense, in a report to Congress on security issues dealing with the Korean Peninsula, stressed that the DPRK had "suspected nuclear weapons capable of missile delivery."[63] In late September 2000 Secretary of Defense William Cohen stated at a South Korean news conference that: "North Korea's chemical, biological, nuclear, and long-range missile programs continue to pose a threat to South Korea, the U.S. and other countries."[64] On the same trip to East Asia, Cohen remarked in discussions with Japanese prime minister Yoshihiro Mori and foreign minister Yohei Kono that even though North Korea has demonstrated some peaceful intentions, "there are still many dangers, including arsenals of biological, chemical, and possibly nuclear weapons."[65]

Tokyo also continued to point to a possible nuclear threat from North Korea after the U.S inspection of Kumchang-ni. Even the Tokyo Forum for Nuclear Nonproliferation and Disarmament, a project initiated by the Japanese government, draws attention to the continuing possibility of a nuclear threat coming from North Korea. The forum's July 1999 report states: "All nuclear weapon and missile-related activities in North Korea must cease." Referring to the American inspection of the North Korean location, the forum's report states: "The May 1999 visit by U.S. representatives to an underground site suspected of being intended for a nuclear weapon program produced no evidence to support such allegations. This was a positive development, but it is too early for considered judgment."[66]

Together, Washington and Tokyo recently cast suspicion on North Korea by pointing to threats posed by the apparent continuation of its ballistic missile and nuclear programs. During the press conference that followed the official discussion of the 2000 U.S.–Japan Security Consultative Committee, which is known as the "2 plus 2" meeting, Washington and Tokyo continued to create the impression of a North Korean threat to regional peace and stability. U.S. Secretary of State Albright commented that efforts are continuing to bring North Korea out of isolation, "while addressing the concerns of the international community about its nuclear and long-range missile programs." Showing complete insensitivity to the ramifications on normalization discussions taking place between Japan and the DPRK, Japanese defense minister Torashima emphasized that: "North Korea—it is most likely that it is [*sic*] deployed No-Dong, which covers virtually all Japanese territories, and we do not really see any change as of this moment in the military situation on the Korean Peninsula."[67] Pyongyang argued that since both Washington and Japan have regional military interests, their comments represent a continuing attempt to undermine efforts to bring about an improving security environment on the Korean Peninsula.[68]

On August 31, 1998, regional relations worsened when North Korea launched a projectile that flew over Japan. Gravely disturbed by the episode, Japan and the United States initially concluded that the North Korean launch had been a Taepo Dong 1 missile. North Korea remained almost totally silent on the specifics of the launch for several days, stating only through its deputy ambassador to the United Nations that his country was displeased with Japan's military alliance with the United States. However, Tokyo reacted the day after the DPRK launching, announcing that "technical study on the ballistic missile defense system will be further continued, and the bills related to the U.S.–Japan Defense Guidelines are expected to be approved and enacted soon." Tokyo also announced at this time that it was ending food aid and assistance to the DPRK, halting efforts to normalize bilateral relations with North Korea, and canceling financial assistance to KEDO.[69]

In its review of the incident, Japan's Defense Agency concluded at the end of October 1998 that the DPRK had launched a Taepo Dong ballistic missile; that if the rocket did have a satellite attached, it was a pretext for testing the ballistic missile.[70] At the same time, Tokyo announced that it was going to develop and deploy four surveillance satellites by 2002.[71] This further aggravated regional tension. Since Japan had relied on satellite information from the United States, Beijing and Pyongyang interpreted Tokyo's deployment plan as an important step in the direction of developing an independent Japanese military posture.

The real extent of Japanese mistrust of North Korea surfaced a few days after the launch. Japan announced that it would make final plans during the September meeting of the Security Consultative Committee in New York to develop a cooperative TMD system with the United States, with Japan developing the radar and satellites and the United States responsible for construction of the interceptor missiles. Initially, Japan had been reluctant to commit to TMD with the United States, fearing that China would interpret this as a threat.[72] Catching both Japan and the United States by surprise, North Korea subsequently announced that it had launched a civilian satellite and not a missile. Despite Pyongyang's claim that the satellite launch would "contribute to promoting scientific research for peaceful use of outer space," Tokyo felt it important to stick to the initial decisions it made concerning its relations with North Korea.[73] The United States acknowledged that the launch could have been a satellite or both a satellite and a missile. While neither Japan nor the United States could initially verify that a civilian satellite had been launched by North Korea, Russian officials announced that they had confirmation that the projectile was a satellite.[74]

Some officials in the White House, the Pentagon, and the State Department, along with several members of Congress, expressed deep concern about the North Korean launch. However, nearly two weeks after the incident took place, the Department of Defense informed Tokyo that North Korea had indeed attempted to put a satellite into orbit. The satellite evidence notwithstanding, the Department of Defense saw a need to reaffirm North Korea's label as a regional security risk. The Department of Defense stressed that, although the launch was a satellite, North Korea's action should still be seen as a threat since it showed that its technological achievements could present a security problem.[75]

Relations deteriorated even more when the U.S. intelligence community, reacting to data obtained from American satellite technology, claimed that North Korea was preparing another missile launch. Washington responded to this by telling Pyongyang that it should not proceed with another launching. An article appearing in the *New York Times* in late December 1998 reported a partial and jaundiced version of this issue.[76] With McCarthy-like hysteria, the article began by stating that Pyongyang "warned the United States that it was prepared to launch another medium-range missile." Quoting directly from the Korean Central News Agency, the official news agency of the DPRK, the *Times* article pointed out that Pyongyang said that it would be "foolish for the U.S. to expect any change in our attitude." What the *Times* article did not point out was that Pyongyang indicated in the Korean Central News Agency story that: "We are fully ready to launch an *artificial satellite* again when we think it is necessary."[77] By stressing that the DPRK was warning the United States that it was prepared to launch another medium-range missile, rather than an artificial satellite, the *Times* article was unambiguously reinforcing the rogue status of North Korea. The actual warning that the DPRK was sending to Washington was that: "The United States had better not try to test our faith and will." Also serving to reinforce the image of North Korea as a rogue state was the report in the *Times* article that Washington suspected that Pyongyang was continuing its nuclear weapons development.

Like the Rodong missile launch in 1993, Pyongyang's more recent decision to send a projectile over Japanese territory was a provocation. Whether or not this was the intention does not matter; this is the perception that it created. Pyongyang should have given Tokyo advance notice that a projectile would be launched and that it was going to fly over Japanese territory. However, relations between Japan and North Korea were not particularly good prior to the August 1998 projectile launching. The failure of the two countries to settle historical differences had been exacerbated by other problems, such as the continued allegations that North Korea was secretly developing nuclear weapons and that it posed a missile threat to Japan and by Tokyo's decision to strengthen the security alliance with the United States. When Tokyo decided to strengthen the security alliance with the United States, Pyongyang became very worried and, as we have already seen, reacted harshly to the new guidelines for defense cooperation between Japan and the United States. Thus, *any* North Korean launching, with or without prenotification, would have raised serious suspicions in Washington and Tokyo.

Although Washington had announced the DPRK launching was a satellite, this does not mean that it was trying to get Tokyo to react soberly to the emergent crisis. Washington continued to define North Korea as a rogue state, capable of almost anything that would undermine the stability of East Asia. About two weeks after the United States informed Japan that the North Korean launch in August was a satellite, a South Korean news agency, citing a document from an American military expert on ballistic missiles, reported that North Korea *might* have exported sensitive Rodong ballistic missile parts to Pakistan in the spring of 1996.[78]

Japan later recommitted its financial assistance to KEDO and Pyongyang has been making a sustained effort to demonstrate that it does not want North Korea to be viewed as an isolated rogue state. In 2000, Pyongyang established diplomatic ties with several countries and even improved its relationship with the United States. As a result of bilateral discussions that took place in late 1999, it appears that Pyongyang also genuinely supports normalizing relations with Japan.[79] Although his first trip to North Korea was cancelled, former prime minister Tomiichi Murayama's visit to North Korea in early December 1999 marked the beginning of another attempt to normalize Japan–DPRK relations.

It must be stressed that the U.S.–Japan security alliance, a remnant of the Cold War security paradigm, is built on mistrust and suspicion. This means that virtually any regional issue can be misunderstood and spun out of control as long the U.S.–Japan security arrangement still exits and some countries perceive that it targets them in any way. It also means that the existence of normal bilateral relations, while an optimal condition, is not a panacea for regional stability. Despite having established normal bilateral relations in 1978, mistrust and tension still exist between Japan and China. For example, some observers in Beijing believe that once relations on the Korean Peninsula started to improve, Tokyo began to shift its claims of a regional military threat away from the DPRK and toward China. Chinese concerns center on the Japanese Defense Agency 2000 white paper, which, unlike that of the previous year, specifically calls attention to China's missile threat to Japan—a claim that Beijing says further helps to justify Tokyo's involvement in TMD research.[80] In a situation reminiscent of the Cold War atmosphere, generally improving relations between Russia and Japan turned abruptly sour for a short time in September 2000 when Tokyo accused a Russian diplomat of illicitly gaining access to classified defense information. Moscow responded to the espionage allegation by maintaining that some in Japan want to undo the improvements in Russo-Japanese relations. Like Beijing and Pyongyang, Moscow had already expressed much anxiety over the U.S.–Japan decision to begin research on TMD. So, the alleged spying incident—to the extent that it is true—will only aggravate remaining tension and suspicion in the Russo-Japanese relationship and in this way add to regional instability.

Sacrifice and Contradiction: Japan, the United Nations, and the U.S. Nuclear Umbrella

When Japan became a member of the United Nations in 1956, and for some time thereafter, many Japanese, including policy makers, maintained the expectation that in time this multilateral organization would provide the country with security; thus, there would be no need for a security alliance with the United States. Article IV of the 1951 treaty states:

> This Treaty shall expire whenever in the opinions of the Governments of the United States of America and Japan there shall have come into force such United Nations arrangements or such alternative individual or collective security dispositions as will satisfactorily provide for the maintenance by the United Nations or otherwise of international peace and security in the Japan Area.[81]

Article X of the 1960 treaty similarly stresses that:

> This Treaty shall remain in force until in the opinion of the Governments of Japan and the United States of America there shall have come into force such United Nations arrangements as will satisfactorily provide for the maintenance of international peace and security in the Japan area.[82]

Reflecting the nonbelligerent sentiment of the Japanese constitution (Article 9), the government approved the Basic Policy for National Defense in 1957. This document, which today remains fundamentally important to Japan's defense policy, pledges

> [t]o deal effectively with external aggression on the basis of Japan–U.S. security arrangements, pending effective functioning of the United Nations in the future deterring and repelling such aggression.[83]

The Gulf War raised global expectations that the United Nations would become an effective force in international security. For Japan, in particular, this expectation did not emerge but rather resurfaced from the dormancy brought on by the Cold War. The demise of the Soviet Union and the end of the Cold War further raised Japan's interest in revitalizing the United Nations.[84] The "new world order" portended the end of America's role as the world's policeman; the international climate appeared to be right for the United Nations to assume the position of principal steward of global security. Would not a strengthened and effective

UN security system mean that Japan would no longer need the security arrangements it had with the United States? This question was certainly being asked in Japan; however, far too many policy makers in Tokyo and Washington had different thoughts on this matter. As a result, there was a concerted effort by policy makers in Washington and Tokyo to assure the continuation of the Cold War bilateral security alliance.

The United States eventually withdrew its support for the United Nations as the chief administrator of global security at the same time that it failed to meet its financial obligations to this organization.[85] However, Japan, perhaps because of its lingering historical sentiment, still sees a need to strengthen UN operations. But this is fundamentally different from working to revitalize the United Nations so that it can assume the responsibility of global security and therefore the protection of Japan. That the United States has issued a resounding no to comprehensive UN security has made it too easy for Japan to continue to live with the Cold War bilateral security alliance. That Japan endorses strengthening the United Nations, including its security mechanisms, but has not worked particularly hard to make this a reality is an abandonment of the principles set out in both security treaties and in the Basic Policy for National Defense. Moreover, Japan's involvement with ARF (Asian Regional Forum) is hobbled by its failure to demonstrate to its membership, which includes China and North Korea,[86] that it is pursuing a nonthreatening regional security system independent of U.S. security interests.

But because of its continuing security relationship with the United States, there is more at stake for Japan than just foregoing its interests in and concern for a comprehensive UN security system. As the only nation that has suffered the devastating and catastrophic consequences of the use of nuclear weapons, Japan has long advocated that they should be completely abolished from the planet. Japan endorsed the elimination of nuclear weapons when it became a member of the United Nations more than forty years ago, and it still does today. Subsequent to the nuclear testing by India and Pakistan in 1998, former prime minister Keizo Obuchi stated that: "Realizing a nuclear-free world is the strong desire of the Japanese people." Encouraged by the nation's peace constitution, the Japanese people believe that they should play an important role in helping to realize nuclear disarmament.

Because of the American and Soviet arms race that characterized the Cold War, Japan could ignore the fact that it supported deterrence and remained protected by America's nuclear shield. Thus, the contradiction between Japan's position under America's nuclear umbrella and its strong opposition to the continued existence of nuclear weapons was generally overlooked because of its commitment to pacifism and need for national security. Since Japan's hands were tied during the U.S.–Soviet nuclear arms race, it appeared reasonable to conclude that Japan had to choose sides during the Cold War and could do no serious work on the elimination of nuclear weapons.

The end of the Cold War ushered in major changes in the conditions surrounding international security. Japan's official post–Cold War policy on the United Nations is that: "The world has undergone structural changes with the end of the Cold War, and the international community is striving to create a new framework for peace and prosperity."[87] But because Japan has not made structural changes in its security policy, it not only still maintains the alliance with the United States, it also still depends on America's nuclear shield. The new guidelines for bilateral defense cooperation state specifically that "the United States will maintain its nuclear deterrent capability."[88] Accordingly, sustained, substantive work by Japan on the abolition of all nuclear weapons—work that clearly demonstrates that this problem has been targeted as an achievable goal with a specific timetable—has been sacrificed because of the security alliance with the United States and because of Tokyo's failure to act on widespread Japanese sentiment that endorses nuclear disarmament. It is true that Japan has taken some steps in recent years to emphasize the importance of disarmament. The most recent initiative by Japan has been its role in forming the Tokyo Forum for Nuclear Nonproliferation and Disarmament.[89] Another important step that has been taken is that since 1989 Japan has been the host country for the UN Conference on Disarmament.[90] Still another was former prime minister Obuchi's address to the fifty-third session of the UN General Assembly in 1998 in New York, where he stressed the need to develop a nuclear nonproliferation regime to end nuclear testing and "to see the sincere implementation of nuclear disarmament by nuclear weapons states."[91] But if there is a genuine conviction about addressing the global problem of the existence of nuclear weapons, Tokyo must first confront and then change its contradictory situation of desiring to abolish them completely and accepting America's nuclear deterrent. Announcing an end to the bilateral security alliance and moving out from under America's nuclear umbrella are structural changes that would put Japan in an unrestrained political position that would permit it to deal forthrightly and decisively with the problem of nuclear weapons.

Tokyo maintains that its position on nuclear weapons is not contradictory. Tokyo argues that Japan must continue to accept the U.S. nuclear deterrent because there is no other reasonable alternative; however, this does not mean that its desire to see the abolition of nuclear weapons is not genuine. Tokyo further justifies its position by arguing that the reduction of nuclear weapons should rely on a "realistic and incremental modus operandi."[92] Tokyo reasons that a gradual approach to the elimination of nuclear weapons without a specified timetable is best, since nuclear disarmament is a long-term process that, if abbreviated, would lead to serious security problems. Thus, Japan has exhibited some timidity on the question of the abolition of nuclear weapons. Although Japan's position on nuclear weapons is very different from that of the United States, it has refused to challenge the United States directly on this matter.

This can be seen in Japan's appearance before the International Court of Justice (World Court) at The Hague in the Netherlands in fall 1995. The UN General Assembly asked the World Court to answer the following question: "Is the threat or use of nuclear weapons in any circumstance permitted under international law?" While the World Court's answer to this question was not an unequivocal yes or no, in its compliance with the request for an advisory opinion, it did state that "the threat or use of nuclear weapons would generally be contrary to the rules of international law applicable in armed conflict, particularly those of the principles and rules of international law."[93] The official Japanese statement presented to the International Court of Justice on November 7, 1995, by Takekazu Kawamura, director-general of foreign affairs, was as follows:

> The government of Japan believes that, because of their immense power to cause destruction, the death of and injury to human beings, the use of nuclear weapons is clearly contrary to the spirit of humanity that gives international law its philosophical foundation.
>
> Japan, based on the tragic suffering of Hiroshima and Nagasaki, considers the [sic] nuclear weapons must never be used. Japan considers that the international community as a whole should cooperate to make sure that a similar tragedy never occurs again anywhere in the world.[94]

In contrast, the statement by the United States expressed a very different, indeed nearly an opposite, point of view. Presented on November 15, 1995, by John McNeill, senior deputy general council of the Department of Defense, the U.S. statement maintained that

> [t]he argument that international law prohibits, in all cases, the use of nuclear weapons appears to be premised on the incorrect assumption that every use of every type of nuclear weapon will necessarily share certain characteristics which contravene the law of armed conflict. . . . It is the view of the United States that it is not possible in the abstract, without prior knowledge of the precise circumstances of particular uses of nuclear weapons, to determine that such uses would be violative of that body of law. . . . Whether the use of nuclear weapons in any given instance would result in the infliction of disproportionate collateral destruction or incidental injury to civilians cannot be judged in the abstract.[95]

While clearly rejecting the use of nuclear weapons in its official statement to the World Court and although its position contrasts sharply with that given by the United States, Japan does not give a definitive and unambiguous answer to the question asked by the UN General Assembly.

Tokyo did not give a straightforward answer to the question of the illegality of using nuclear weapons for a few reasons.[96] Tokyo could not openly and unequivocally denounce the legality of using nuclear weapons, since this kind of response would jeopardize Japan's position under America's nuclear umbrella, which it still wants. A clear statement by Tokyo officially rejecting the use of nuclear weapons would directly challenge America's international security leadership. Such a statement would also be in direct opposition to the U.S. position on the possible use of nuclear weapons to settle international disputes. Tokyo, in other words, would be directly calling into question the legitimacy of America's nuclear weapons policy. As evidenced by the 2000 review conference on the Nuclear Nonproliferation Treaty, Tokyo has been very reluctant to challenge the United States and the other nuclear powers directly on their positions on nuclear disarmament.

Conclusion

The U.S.–Japan security alliance has existed for more than five decades. For most of this time, the alliance continued because of the politics associated with the Cold War. Since Japan constitutionally decided to renounce war and aggressive military activity, it needed protection during this tumultuous period. Japan's expectation that the United Nations would be able to fulfill its international security objective was strong during the early years of the Cold War; as time went on, however, this sentiment became dormant. Because of the Cold War and the veto power of Security Council members, the United Nations could not provide international security, its principal objective when it was established in 1945. Japan's choices therefore were neutrality, which it rejected, and continuing with the security arrangement it had made with the United States, which it accepted, but not without significant public discontent.

The end of the Cold War and the very visible diminution of superpower tensions briefly rekindled the idea that the United Nations would be able to provide international security. This view not only reemerged in Japan, but there has also been increased discussion about the elimination of nuclear weapons, another historically strong Japanese sentiment. However, Washington policy makers realized that the post–Cold War environment created the opportunity for the United States, which has forthrightly described itself as the world's only superpower, to dominate the East Asia–Pacific region. To this end, it has aggressively sought Tokyo's assistance. Ending the bilateral security arrangement therefore would not be a prudent choice, Washington reasons, since the demise of the alliance or even the loss of a physical American presence in Japan would instantly invite other nations to attempt to dominate East Asia, or at the very least, create unacceptable regional instability.

Tokyo has accepted these U.S. assumptions, concluding that it is easier to continue with the security paradigm that has presumably maintained regional stability for decades than to change it. Tokyo has felt that it is in Japan's best interests to work with the United States, not just to maintain the bilateral security alliance but also to strengthen it. While doing this since 1996, Washington and Tokyo have been constantly evoking the theme of regional instability. Washington maintains that North Korea is still an unpredictable security threat, and because Russia and China are the nations most likely to challenge the military power of the United States in the future, they too are suspect. Washington maintains that China is aspiring to be the dominant regional power in East Asia, while Beijing believes that the U.S. objective is to contain China.[97] Washington recognizes that the strengthened U.S.–Japan security relationship has created angst in Beijing and that Chinese leaders are working to counter this alliance, while expressing opposition to what they see as a resurgence of Japanese militarism.[98] Tokyo continues to assert that besides the missile threat that it poses to Japan, North Korea has "rekindled suspicions over nuclear weapons."[99] The Japanese Defense Agency's 2000 white paper suggests that China is a latent security threat to Japan and to East Asia. The white paper makes specific reference to China's new efforts in the development of intercontinental land and submarine ballistic missiles and stresses that Chinese naval vessels have more frequently been observed near Japanese waters.[100] For Tokyo, exacerbating its frustration relating to Russian reluctance to settle the northern islands disagreement was the alleged September 2000 spying incident, since it helped to justify lingering suspicions of Moscow's intentions.

Thus, Washington and Tokyo have found reasons to rationalize the continuation of the bilateral security arrangement. The centerpiece of this rationalization is the putative instability of East Asia and therefore the continuing need for America's military presence and a strengthened bilateral alliance to forestall regional problems. However, this enduring and strengthened security arrangement is problematic for two reasons. First, because it is a Cold War alliance, it still presupposes that the behavior of some nations is blatantly hostile, surreptitious, and intended to upset the stability of East Asia and perhaps even usurp regional power. In other words, it is built on distrust and suspicion. Second, because it is built on distrust and suspicion, it produces regional tension. The existence of the U.S.–Japan security alliance does this because of its purpose and because of the reciprocation that it prompts from other countries. These enduring problems even cause the genuine efforts by Washington and Tokyo to improve regional relations to be minimized, since their overall objective is interpreted as hegemonic.

Since the end of the Cold War, the continued existence of the bilateral security alliance has meant that Japan must renew and rerationalize its adjustment to the contradictory position of desiring the end of all nuclear weapons and remaining protected by America's nuclear umbrella. At the same time, Japan has relegated its interests in the revitalization of the United Nations, and in particular, its international, collective security mechanisms, to a much less significant policy position than that of continuing the security arrangement with the United States.

3

Consequences of the Alliance

Introduction

As we have seen in chapter 2, Japan continues to sacrifice working for a strong United Nations, which could provide it with protection, so that it can maintain its Cold War security arrangement with the United States. Moreover, because of this bilateral security relationship, Japan cannot move forward assertively at a pace that reflects the historical and current interest of much of the Japanese public in the abolition of nuclear weapons. This type of political activity would call far too much attention to its continuing acceptance of America's nuclear deterrent, not to mention raise the ire of Washington. The continuation of the bilateral security arrangement has one decided advantage for Japan: it remains protected by the United States. But, of course, this protection comes at a price. It is not the price of hosting American troops, which Tokyo is attempting to diminish. Rather, it is the price of *eikyu no gaiastu* (lasting external pressure).

Japan's current security policy largely reflects Washington's East Asian concerns. Militarily, it is highly dependent on the United States; as a result, Tokyo officials must avoid criticism and disagreement with American views, and certainly creating a security controversy is tantamount to an anathema. But these unwritten policy rules are what foreign minister Makiko Tanaka, daughter of former prime minister Kakuei Tanaka, failed to follow in the spring of 2001. Tanaka created a serious problem for Prime Minister Junichiro Koizumi's government when she reportedly made critical comments during separate conversations with German, Italian, and Australian officials in May 2001 that clearly contravened Tokyo's official position that it "understands" the United States' reasons for wanting to develop an NMD (national missile defense) system. She made this matter even worse for the Koizumi government in one conversation when she disapprovingly questioned the bilateral security alliance and Japan's position under the U.S. nuclear umbrella. Tanaka is said to have commented during a late May conversation with the German vice chancellor: "After the end of World War II, Japan was protected by the nuclear umbrella under the Japan–U.S. security structure, but that was the easy way. Japan needs to become more independent. Japan–U.S. relations are at a turning point, and there is a need for careful rethinking in order to smoothly make the transition." In addition to creating an uproar in the Koizumi government, Tanaka's comments worried the United States enough, according to the Japanese ambassador to the United States, Shunji Yanai, to prompt Washington to corroborate the foreign minister's remarks by getting in touch with those governments whose officials were privy to them.[1] As will be shown in chapter 5, Foreign Minister Tanaka is certainly not the only one in Japan who critically questions the bilateral security alliance; rather, it is that such criticisms are considered heretical to many in Tokyo.

This chapter will examine several major cost factors directly connected to Japan's continuing support of the bilateral security alliance with the United States. Hegemony does create privileges. Thus, U.S. Treasury officials do not mince words when it comes to telling Japanese officials precisely what they should do to correct Japan's economic problems. Bilateral trade disputes have long been subjected to exacting American demands, a problem that should be of enormous concern now for Tokyo as Washington attempts to move Japan away from its postwar commitment to pacifism, insisting that to be effective the bilateral security alliance needs to be strengthened. Besides the economic costs that Japan has had to confront as the economy has teetered on recession for the past decade, there are serious political problems associated with the continuation of the bilateral security alliance. Having Japan move incrementally toward a bigger security role has been a major objective of Washington and of many in Tokyo as well, especially since the mid-1990s. However, a bigger security role does not make Tokyo and Washington equal partners. Although it is often said that the bilateral security relationship prevents Japanese remilitarization—it has even been intimated that this is an unofficial part of U.S. policy—today, the alliance breeds disdain, suspicion, and distrust. Serious political costs directly tied to the existence of the bilateral security alliance between Washington and Tokyo today most notably include continuing problems in Okinawa and the exacerbation of regional instability as perceived in Beijing, Pyongyang, and, most recently, Moscow.

Perennial Pressure

Recent discussions of U.S.–Japan relations have commonly underscored two very different points: Some have tended to see Japan becoming an equal partner, or at least something approaching this, in the bilateral alliance, while others have talked about an asymmetrical relationship. But even discussions that emphasize the asymmetrical nature of the bilateral relationship see Japan becoming more nearly equal today. As we will see below, this bilateral partnership cannot be equal under present conditions, for as long as the United States continues to guarantee the protection of Japan it will have the decided advantage in any bilateral relationship.

Equal Partners in an Unequal Alliance

Much of the discussion in the equal-partner position centers on economic matters, although some official agreements between Tokyo and Washington have also stressed the importance of a partnership on issues concerned with global cooperation, such as health, environment, natural disasters, and overpopulation.[2] While this kind of partnership asks for Japan's support, and at times its leadership (e.g., official development assistance), there is cause for concern. Concentration on economic issues and some concerns of the global community, while prodding and encouraging Japan to go along with the United States in regional and international security matters does not make a genuine partnership. Because it purposely minimizes the significant and persuasive pressure of the bilateral security relationship, this kind of equal partnership is much more rhetorical than real. Because of the United States' upper hand in the security alliance, bilateral trade and economic relations cannot resemble an authentic partnership. Although Japan is said to be a "natural partner" because of its economic and political significance,[3] it is a peculiar partnership in that Washington typically outlines its expectations and then demands their realization.[4] Thus, the problem is that

Japan remains the target of continuing pressure from the United States, often to the point that Washington demands structural reform, in bilateral trade and deregulation issues.[5]

Over the years, a number of industries have faced trade pressure from Washington. While it is true that in recent years Japan has been less willing to succumb to American trade and economic pressures, the fact remains that they are constant (e.g., continually trying to increase U.S. automobile exports to Japan). Recent efforts by Japan to move bilateral trade disputes to the World Trade Organization (WTO) notwithstanding (e.g., the Kodak–Fuji film disagreement), this has not put an end to the repeated demands by the United States to accommodate its economic interests. U.S. export trade with Japan is second only to that with Canada. U.S. trade in goods with Japan (exports and imports) amounted to almost $190 billion in 1999, with exports accounting for over $57 billion of this amount.[6] Increasingly greater access to Japanese domestic markets will continue to ensure that U.S. goods and investments[7] will have a place to go. Moreover, the United States has not been reluctant to impose unilateral restrictions on Japanese producers' access to American markets. Failing to account for the facts that many American troops are still in Japan and that the United States has a commitment to protect Japan and ultimately to provide it with a nuclear shield wrongly suggests that bilateral security issues have no bearing on the so-called equal partnership. Japan's worst economic downturn in the postwar period in the 1990s witnessed the emergence of MacArthurian demands from the U.S. Treasury Department, as well as from other parts of the American government, to get the Japanese economic house in order and to do more to end regional economic problems. It is hard to imagine an authentic partnership withstanding this kind of constant pressure—that is, where one partner continuously demands so much from the other—to make adjustments without dissolving the relationship.

Because of the importance attached to the bilateral security alliance by policy makers on both sides of the Pacific, Washington has the freedom to exercise pressure on Tokyo whenever it deems necessary; but this does not work the other way around. Decisions concerning what Japan should do, as Asia's only economic superpower, as well as those relating to the resolution of its domestic economic problems should ultimately be left to Japanese policy makers and to the people. This does not mean that Japan should close itself off from the outside world. However, it does mean that the persistent attempts by American policy makers to gain the compliance of Tokyo, either by demanding access to Japanese markets or by restricting access to U.S. markets, relate directly to the existence of the bilateral security alliance that gives Washington the privilege to act authoritatively and chiefly with America's unilateral interests in mind.

An example of the United States exercising its prerogative in a bilateral trade dispute is the supercomputer controversy that took place during the latter half of the 1990s. Precipitated by NEC's winning bid to the National Center for Atmospheric Research, an organization associated with America's National Science Foundation, Cray Research registered a complaint with the U.S. Commerce Department in July 1996. Part of Cray's complaint alleged that Japanese producer NEC was dumping vector supercomputers in the American market. Siding with the Commerce Department and Cray, the U.S. International Trade Commission (ITC) ruled in late September 1997 that "the domestic industry producing vector supercomputers is threatened with material injury by reason of LTFV [less than fair value] imports from Japan." Cray is the dominant U.S. producer of vector supercomputers, having only one other American competitor; for all intents and purposes, Cray was the only U.S. manufacturer during the period of the dispute with Japan. Because of the ITC determination, NEC and Fujitsu, Japan's largest computer builders, as well as other Japanese producers were slapped with very severe antidumping charges.[8]

The Japanese response to the allegations demonstrated both frustration and great annoyance. NEC called Cray's antidumping charges a "blatant fabrication."[9] NEC tried to contest the ITC ruling before the U.S. Court of Appeals, but the case was thrown out in August 1998. Unsatisfied and deeply disturbed by the federal court's dismissal of the case, NEC brought it before a higher U.S body.[10] Fujitsu made clear that it was opposed to the investigation dealing with material injury to the U.S. market. Showing its deep concern for the unilateral restrictions placed on Japanese vector supercomputers, the government of Japan stated that the U.S. Department of Commerce interfered in this matter before the investigation even started, intervention that it called "opaque and questionable." The Japanese government also pointed out that since "there is some fear that this could be contrary to international [i.e., WTO] rules," it wanted the United States to provide an unambiguous explanation for its unilateral actions.[11] Sometimes known as "trade harassment," the use of unilateral, antidumping measures is a policy stick that has frequently been employed by the United States. The Japanese government notes that "[a]nti-dumping legislation is perhaps the largest source of hidden protectionism in the United States, and many countries have complained about its shortcomings."[12] In December 1998, the U.S. Court of International Trade (CIT) overturned the ITC ruling that Japanese manufacturers had dumped their products in the United States. The ruling by CIT means that ITC had to redo the investigation of dumping alleged to have been committed by Japanese supercomputer producers.[13]

It is important to understand that more was at issue in the ITC ruling than simply insulating Cray Research from Japanese competition. Together, both NEC and Fujitsu have sold only a few supercomputers in the United States. The U.S. government's "buy American" edict effectively locks out foreign manufacturers, particularly when it comes to military-sensitive products like supercomputers. So, while Japanese supercomputer producers did not suffer a terrible financial setback because of the ITC decision, this case demonstrated that the United States is willing to impose severe unilateral penalties to ensure the stability of an American firm deemed critical for defense. That security concerns are still a top priority for U.S. policy makers in the post–Cold War environment, to the point of closing off a section of the American market to an allied country's manufacturers, is clear. Also clear is Washington's determination to safeguard U.S. military superiority and its willingness to sanction foreign producers that threaten it.

Asymmetries in Security

Those who stress the asymmetrical makeup of the bilateral relationship in the present period concern themselves with the imbalances relating to the security alliance.[14] For them, the utilization of American efforts and resources for the protection of Japan still far exceeds the Japanese contribution to the security alliance. U.S. interests in the East Asia–Pacific region, however, require that the United States tolerate this imbalance. Largely as the result of pressure from Washington, bilateral interests have been strong enough that from time to time incremental changes have been introduced to prevent a structural meltdown of the security alliance.[15] Since the mid-1990s, there has been a growing interest in presenting the U.S.–Japan security alliance as approaching a partnership endeavor.[16] Even as the security environment of East Asia began to improve in 2000 (between North and South Korea, the United States and the Democratic People's Republic of Korea [DPRK], Tokyo and Pyongyang, and between Japan and China), there were still calls to strengthen the bilateral alliance.[17] A central tenet of U.S. and Japanese security policy toward North Korea is to get Pyongyang's compliance—and in this way increase the prospect of regional peace—by demonstrating overpowering military capability.

For decades, closing some of the gaps in the security alliance has been a top agenda item for Washington policy makers. But it was in the 1980s that the United States really began applying unmitigated pressure on Japan for it to contribute more to defense. Former prime minister Yasuhiro Nakasone (1982–1987), a conservative who wanted to see the independent development of the Japanese military, was not particularly supportive of the international constraints placed on Japan by the so-called Yoshida Doctrine.[18] For this reason, Nakasone was receptive to U.S. pressure to expand the Japanese defense effort. In January 1987 the Nakasone government lifted the cap on Japanese defense spending, which was set at 1 percent of gross national product in the 1970s.[19] By permitting transfers of some military technology to the United States, the prime minister worked to sidestep the Three Principles on Arms Exports, which were established in 1967 and prohibit the export of military products to communist countries, nations confronting UN sanctions, or any state that is either involved in or appears to have the potential to be involved in activities relating to war. In July 1987, just a few months before Prime Minister Nakasone left office in November, Tokyo signed an agreement with the U.S. Department of Defense permitting Japan's participation in America's Strategic Defense Initiative.[20] To do all of this, Japanese policy makers had to confront strong domestic resistance. Any attempt to change the culture of pacifism in Japan, a way of life that emerged with the adoption of its peace constitution in the early 1950s, would meet with strong domestic resistance. To circumvent this cultural roadblock, the government had to assure the political opposition and the public—as it has done for decades—that changes in the defense structure would not undermine the peace constitution or the nation's position of maintaining only a defensive security system. Thus, the argument that Japan has maintained an "exclusively defense-oriented policy," despite a growing military budget, has served both the interests of Japanese conservatives and the United States.

Driven initially by U.S. criticism, the fact that Japan did not actively participate in the Persian Gulf War turned global attention to the Japanese failure to behave responsibly in support of an international cooperative security crisis. Once again, this culture of pacifism stood in the way of Japan's becoming a "normal" nation, that is, one actively involved in international security missions. Again with ample political assurances in place, specifically those that prevented Japan from creating any appearance of external military aggression, limited Japanese participation in international security missions became permissible with the passage of the 1992 Peacekeeping Operations Bill. In the fall of 2001, Tokyo worked quickly to rectify Japan's image by responding to Washington's call to participate in the U.S.-led international war on terrorism.

The end of the Cold War created a security dilemma for Japan. Because the legitimacy of the bilateral security alliance came into question, Japanese policy makers had to justify its continued existence. During the Cold War the justification for the existence of the security alliance was straightforward: the widespread perception that the Soviet Union was an ever-present threat. So when the Cold War ended, the threat from the north no longer existed, at least not in the same way and especially to the same extent that it did in the past. But new threats quickly emerged. To meet them, East Asian containment policies euphemistically gave way to comprehensive engagement. China—where "politics will almost certainly be volatile"—and North Korea—which "continues to be the most urgent threat to security in Northeast Asia"—were quickly transformed from minor to major actors in the new threat scenario.[21] Although China and North Korea quickly substituted as the principal justifications for the post–Cold War security alliance between Japan and the United States, a watchful eye still needed to be kept on Russia.

While the U.S. Department of Defense provided impetus for a renewed bilateral security alliance in its February 1995 report,[22] it was the U.S–Japan Joint Declaration on Security, signed in April 1996, that unequivocally demonstrated that there was also a strong commitment in Tokyo to an American-led security structure. The Joint Declaration made evident that the end of the Cold War had not eliminated security threats in the Asia–Pacific region and that Japan was prepared to work resolutely with the United States to stabilize the region. At least partly because of prodding by Washington, Tokyo policy makers have been willing to call into question Japan's exclusive defense-oriented policy by openly committing the nation to a symbolically more cooperative security relationship with the United States. The Joint Declaration and especially the

1997 Guidelines for U.S.–Japan Defense Cooperation have created the widespread impression that Tokyo is willing to work more closely with Washington on security matters than with its East Asian neighbors, not only to protect the country but to help stabilize the entire region. While Tokyo could reasonably justify the incrementalism of Japan's defense policy during the Cold War, it is much more difficult to do this today.[23]

The incremental growth of Japan's defense capabilities is precisely the strategy endorsed today by those who are stressing the asymmetrical nature of the bilateral security alliance. Analysts in the United States who stress the asymmetrical structure of the bilateral security alliance support piecemeal efforts on the part of Japan to increase its involvement in security affairs.[24] These analysts understand too that, in addition to the indisputable superiority of America's military, there are strong legal and social constraints than prohibit Japan from becoming a security threat. Reducing or withdrawing U.S. forces from Japan,[25] or having Japan assume a noticeably enlarged security role are structural changes[26] that could severely and irreparably damage the bilateral security arrangement and are therefore generally opposed by those supporting the incremental position. Thus, incrementalism is the latent policy followed by Washington and Tokyo in bilateral security affairs. While those supporting the incremental position in Japan were reluctant to favor abandoning Article 9 (the peace clause) during the 1990s, today it is fair to say that many of them are willing to advocate gradual movement toward this objective. The incrementalist policy at the very least creates the appearance of reducing the bilateral security asymmetries as Japan strengthens its defense capabilities while simultaneously giving the impression that it will not become a regional military threat, as it is constrained by Washington's tutelage. Tokyo understands that there is some sentiment in the United States that the asymmetries in the bilateral security arrangement are too costly for America to maintain.[27] Tokyo also understands that Washington accepts the asymmetries because there are reservations about the autonomous growth of Japan's military capabilities,[28] most especially the effects of this on regional relations.

The existing gap in the alliance between U.S. and Japanese military contributions and capabilities, that is, the asymmetries, legitimates the incremental approach that is embodied in the bilateral security arrangement. This is the preferred policy strategy especially for Washington, since making structural changes in the bilateral alliance, creates an "uncertainty principle" in the relationship: the United States can neither precisely identify the extent of Japan's commitment to assuming the responsibility for its defense nor, if the desire is there, assess how expeditiously Japan would create regionally threatening military capabilities.

It is clear that structural changes will relieve the United States of some of the financial burdens associated with maintaining the alliance. Just as important, structural changes will appease Japanese, and especially Okinawan, discontent with the bilateral security arrangements, which some feel will inevitably strengthen the alliance. Structural changes are intended to bolster a bilateral security alliance that rests on soft political ground. But because of the uncertainty, structural changes potentially undermine U.S. hegemonic interests in the East Asia–Pacific region. In other words, under current conditions structural changes are theoretically defensible but not practical to implement. Thus focusing on asymmetries and seeking to address them by following an incremental approach that is compatible with Japanese constitutional constraints, continue to lead Japan down the road of becoming a military minion of the United States in that it symbolically supports America's hegemonic interests in the East Asia–Pacific region.

Okinawan Problems

Tokyo understands that while Washington complains about the financial asymmetries, Japan must contend with the political asymmetries in the bilateral security arrangement, that is, the problems associated with American bases and troops on Japanese soil. Although never discussed in this way, some of the problems in Japan directly connected to the bilateral security alliance are politically asymmetrical from a Japanese perspective. This is evidenced, for example, in a poll of Okinawans conducted by the *Asahi Shimbun* and the *Okinawa Times* in November 1998. Survey results showed that among registered voters, 65 percent of the respondents did not want the U.S. air station at Futenma to be in the Okinawa prefecture. An earlier poll sponsored by the Japan–U.S. Special Action Committee on Okinawa in December 1996 found that over 60 percent of the respondents thought that a proposal to relocate U.S. military bases needed to be strengthened. More than half of the respondents in the November 1998 survey held the view that the Futenma Base located in Ginowan City should be relocated to American territory.[29]

Precipitated in September 1995 by the rape of a twelve-year-old schoolgirl by three American servicemen, the crisis in Okinawa brought

Figure 3.1 **U.S. Military Facilities in Okinawa**

Source: Okinawa Prefecture (Home Page), Japan.

Figure 3.2 **U.S. Military Facilities Near Okinawa Island**

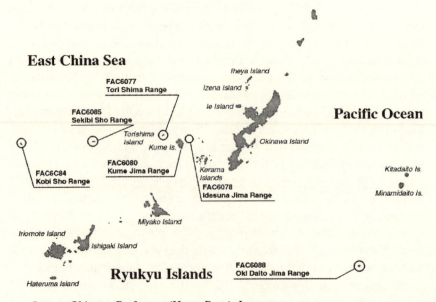

Source: Okinawa Prefecture (Home Page), Japan.

to the fore the uncertainty in Japan that related to the security alliance. In October 1995, approximately 85,000 Okinawans openly demonstrated against the existence of American military bases in their prefecture. Okinawans have felt that while the U.S. occupation of their prefecture formally ended in 1972, occupation conditions still exist.[30] But Japanese incertitude associated with the continuation of the bilateral security alliance existed beyond this prefecture and thus threatened the foundation of the U.S.–Japan relationship.

Figure 3.1 shows that Okinawa Island is literally filled with U.S. military installations—more than thirty all told. There are also six U.S. military facilities in the vicinity of Okinawa Island, as shown in Figure 3.2, bringing the total to thirty-nine. U.S. military troops occupy 558,072 acres in Okinawa, which accounts for approximately 10 percent of the landmass of the prefecture.[31] As it was decades ago, Okinawa remains a very visible symbol of the United States' military presence in East Asia.

Compounding the topographical disturbance to Okinawa, a prefecture that makes up only .6 percent of the landmass of Japan, are daily problems associated with the presence of U.S. military forces in Okinawa. Okinawans have had to grapple with community-wrenching social problems, which eventually find their way to Tokyo as complaints, such as noise, environmental degradation, forced land leases, the constant danger of accidents, and crimes committed by American servicemen. Between 1972, when the United States ended its formal occupation of Okinawa, and 1999 there were 142 air-related incidents, thirty-nine of which involved actual air crashes. Between 1994 and 1999 there were 200 incidents and accidents related to the presence of U.S. forces in Okinawa. These included air-related incidents and problems related to brush fires, waste disposal, and oil spills. At the top of the list for Okinawans troubled by the continuing presence of U.S. forces in their prefecture is crime. Between 1972 and 1999, U.S. troops in Okinawa committed more than 4,900 crimes, an average of over 175 per year. Of the total number of crimes committed during this time, 523 were brutal crimes and 943 were assaults.[32]

Regional Volatility

Perhaps most ironic is that while the major argument supporting the Japan–U.S. security alliance is that, as in the past, it continues to protect Japan and maintain regional stability, there is absolutely no evidence to corroborate this contention.[33] With Tokyo's support, Washington has been very effective in conveying the message that the United States is a proponent of peace and that without its military presence in Japan, Japanese and regional security would be put in jeopardy. Because the advocates of the existing U.S.–Japan security arrangement assume the existence of latent regional instability, for them it follows that the bilateral alliance is still necessary to protect Japan and to deter serious security encroachments in East Asia.[34]

As will be argued below, today the alliance itself is inherently destabilizing, as it maintains the Cold War mentality of distrust, suspicion, and exaggerated reaction to other countries' behaviors and policies. The existing bilateral security alliance pejoratively labels China and North Korea, especially, as *potential* troublemakers that need to be made aware that their actions have consequences. Not only is it wrong to assume that other nations need visible military constraints to act within the confines of sociopolitical decency, but what is ignored is that the bilateral security alliance itself produces consequences such as the lack of transparency and the propensity not to be forthright and fully cooperative. The only major political change discernible in the current bilateral security alliance is that, by asking for Japanese forces to support American troops, the focus has moved from protecting Japan to maintaining regional stability.[35]

China's Discontent

The recent Japan–U.S. reaffirmation of the bilateral security relationship is very disturbing to China. While America's claim of maintaining a "comprehensive engagement"[36] rather than a containment[37] policy toward China sounds politically benign, Beijing remains convinced that the United States is working to maintain regional hegemony.[38] Beijing therefore is very suspicious of Japan's continued military alliance with the United States. Despite recent efforts among Washington, Tokyo, and Beijing to improve bilateral and even trilateral relations,[39] the fact that the United States and Japan are on one side of the security wall while China is on the other is fundamentally problematic. Beijing is very mindful of the military spending differential between China and the United States allied with Japan. China devoted an estimated $63.5 billion to military expenditures in 1995; in this same year, U.S. military spending amounted to $277.8 billion, while Japan allotted $50.2 billion to defense. Thus, U.S. and Japanese military spending—Japan's alone amounted to almost 80 percent of China's in 1985—together totaled over $328 billion.[40] It is true that the United States has military commitments all over the world. Nonetheless, it is clear that America's military power, when supported by Japan's defense resources, creates a very uneasy feeling in Beijing.

American observers state that they are unsure of how Chinese development will unfold, but Beijing is definitely not oblivious to the fact that Washington and Tokyo are watching it very carefully. This condition of unpredictability for the United States helps to justify why it needs to be present in the Asia–Pacific region: the absence of an American security presence would mean an unrestrained China, which *might* lead to Chinese regional hegemony.[41] Thus, the irony here is that even though the end of the Cold War fundamentally changed the political dynamics of the East Asian region, its demise left in place exactly the same security structure, which is built on suspicion, distrust, and the uncertainties directly connected to divergent economies and cultures. Put differently, in the East Asia–Pacific region, the "new world order" is the same as the old world order.

Understand that there are deleterious political repercussions that exist here for Japan. Not accepting Washington's claim to have adopted a comprehensive engagement policy, Beijing believes that the United States still maintains a containment strategy toward China. Given the strengthening of the bilateral security alliance between Washington and Tokyo in recent years, Beijing sees Japan as integral to U.S. military efforts in East Asia. Because of the reaffirmation of the security alliance with the United States, Beijing reasons that Tokyo is making an implicit statement that China should be warily observed, that is, its development, both economic and especially military, pose a potential security threat to Japan and to the entire Asia–Pacific area. That China's recent increases in military spending are being carefully watched by its neighbors, which of course include Japan, is made clear in the 1998 report by the U.S. Department of Defense on the East Asia–Pacific region.[42]

In the back of the minds of at least some observers in Beijing is the suspicion that the ultimate objective of the United States is to undermine and destroy China's communist way of life, since Washington has established the precedent of inducing both political and economic compliance in its strategic policy relations with foreign nations. Most immediately worrisome to Beijing is that it believes that the United States wants to establish indisputable regional hegemony via what China calls "power politics."[43] From Beijing's perspective, under current conditions the growing importance of the Asian economies to the United States makes it imperative for Washington to maintain unequivocal hegemony in the Asia–Pacific region.[44] Tokyo's reaffirmation of the security alliance with the United States increases Chinese angst by bestirring bad memories in Beijing of Japan's militarist past and, specifically, its military aggression against China. Tied to Beijing's concerns about Tokyo's taking significant steps to develop its military is the issue of Senkaku/Diaoyu Islands, the subject of a territorial dispute between Japan and China.[45] In short, Beijing has to entertain seriously the possibility that Japan, allied with the United States, is determined to contain China and reap some of the economic, political, and even territorial benefits of America's regional hegemony. While Beijing favors a multipolar regional and global structure, it sees Washington, with Tokyo's support, working to establish a unipolar or bipolar control.

Washington and Tokyo emphasize that the new guidelines for defense cooperation signed in September 1997 are not directed at China. However, Beijing is far from convinced that this is true. Rather, Beijing sees the new guidelines as directly inimical to Chinese security interests, in large part because Japanese responsibilities in the bilateral alliance have shifted from domestic to regional concerns.[46] Although according to Tokyo officials the new guidelines purportedly suggest that the "area surrounding Japan" is a situational rather than a geographical phrase, Beijing nonetheless is especially concerned about Japan's position on Taiwan. A Chinese white paper on defense published in July 1998 states: "The Taiwan issue is an internal affair of China. Be it directly or indirectly, it would be a violation [of] and interference [with] China's sovereignty for any nations or military alliances to put Taiwan under the sphere of influence of any [other] nation or military alliance."[47]

Not only did China respond critically to the new guidelines, as it saw them as a legitimization of an expanded role for Japan's military in the region, but the NATO attack on Yugoslavia in 1999 made Beijing even more uncomfortable. Former prime minister Keizo Obuchi's visit to the United States in late April 1999 occurred just a few days after the passage of three guideline bills by Japan's Lower House. Beijing stressed that the bills created the danger that Japan would become an accomplice to U.S. aggression and that the legislation passed through the Lower House,[48] despite the opposition and public protestation of many Japanese citizens.[49] With the new guidelines suggesting an expansion of Japan's regional military sphere, Beijing's main concern has been with U.S.–Japanese potential interference in a conflict involving mainland China and Taiwan. However, NATO's aerial attack on Yugoslavia increased Beijing's trepidation, causing officials there to muse with even more consternation about the possibility that the United States, with unimpeded Japanese support, could become involved in any conflict dealing with Taiwan. There is already some suggestion in China that the passage of the new guidelines will cause Beijing to increase the nation's military power.[50] Moreover, Beijing has stressed that the American-fabricated claims of nuclear espionage and furtive political contributions have been used to stir up anti–Chinese sentiment in the United States, ultimately serving to distract attention from America's accidental bombing[51] of the Chinese embassy in Belgrade.[52]

Beijing also views the new guidelines as politically retrogressive for the Asia–Pacific region, particularly in light of the institution of the ASEAN Regional Forum (ARF) in 1994, as well as other recent security developments in the area. Preceded by the 1996 Shanghai agreement, which improved relations among China, Russia, Kyrgyzstan, Kazakhstan, and Tajikistan, the 1997 Agreement on Arms Reductions in Border Areas is seen as a very positive development by officials in Beijing, since it normalizes the security environment and reduces the military forces of the participating countries in border areas until 2020.[53] The July 1998 Chinese white paper on defense expresses great concern about the reaffirmation of the Japan–U.S. security alliance, stating: "Cold War thinking is still alive. Expansion of the military bloc and the strengthening of the military alliance brings instability into international security."

Since March 1997 when Japan's minister of foreign affairs Yukihiko Ikeda visited China and met there with top officials, among them President Jiang Zemin, the two countries have shown increased interest in improving bilateral relations that were normalized with the signing of the Joint Communiqué in September 1972. At the same time, the Chinese and Japanese governments planted the seed for the Treaty of Peace and Friendship. Approved by both the Chinese and Japanese governments, the Treaty of Peace and Friendship was ratified in October 1978. In addition to representing Chinese and Japanese interest in establishing a cooperative and peaceful bilateral relationship, the treaty also contains an antihegemony clause. Included at Beijing's insistence, the clause states that neither country should attempt to establish hegemony in the

Asia–Pacific area, or anywhere else, and that both governments should counter any efforts by other nations to do so.[54] It is because the end of the Cold War has not only not ended the Japan–U.S. security arrangement, but has actually led to the symbolic strengthening of this alliance that Beijing has interpreted as having hegemonic objectives, that a significant wedge remains lodged in the Sino-Japanese relationship. Because current sentiment in Beijing is that U.S. security policy in East Asia is intended to establish hegemony, it is hard to understand how Japan could make the political case that it is living up to the antihegemonic clause within the Treaty of Peace and Friendship.

While Beijing views the Japan–U.S. security arrangement as a destabilizing force in the Asia–Pacific area, Tokyo, like Washington, argues that the alliance is necessary for stability in the region. Tokyo also contends that because its national defense policy is defensive by design, its security alliance with the United States should be interpreted as nothing more than a defensive arrangement. In underscoring the defensive nature of the bilateral security arrangement, Tokyo officials obfuscate two critical points.

First, the United States has consistently justified the need for its bilateral security arrangement with Japan by stressing that this alliance helps to stabilize East Asia, a region that America sees as potentially volatile. It is true that Japan has repeatedly stated that its responsibilities under the new guidelines remain within the parameters of its constitution. However, especially since the crisis in Yugoslavia in 1999, it is not difficult for Beijing to envision a military scenario involving what it perceives as acts of overt military aggression by the United States and supported by Japan, that is, NATO-like intervention—activity that Washington and Tokyo would justify by maintaining the need to stabilize the region. Indeed, this is precisely the scenario that Beijing most commonly envisions with regard to Taiwan.

Second, the perceived expansion of Japan's security obligations precipitated by the new guidelines, most notably its enlarged regional responsibilities, from Beijing's perspective hardly appears defensive. Although China applauds Japan's postwar pacifism, because of its past military aggression and its continuing security relationship with the United States, Beijing is still suspicious of Japanese objectives and is likely to remain so in the immediate future. When Chinese president Jiang Zemin visited Japan in late November 1998, his apparent obsession with Japan's military incursions into China before and during World

War II showed the concerns of a statesman who is not living in the past, but who often reflects on it precisely because he is still very uneasy about the future. Beijing's uneasiness with the existing U.S.–Japan security arrangement partly stems from worries that if Japan abandons its postwar pacifism, which Tokyo policy makers have been more inclined to consider in the last few years, China at some point may have to deal with a recurrence of Japanese militarism.[55] President Jiang articulated some of his concerns about Japan during a speech he gave at Waseda University on November 28, 1998, when he stated that: "Japan should lead young people with a correct view of history and must not allow a revival of militarism in any form."[56]

Currently, Beijing has ample reason to be concerned about the possible recurrence of Japanese militarism. Japan's economy is the second largest in the world, and it has a science and technology and industrial base that arguably is second to none. Already spending copiously on a defensive military system, Japan, in other words, could very quickly become a formidable military opponent to China, or to any other country. In the past, China came to accept the Japan–U.S. security alliance for two reasons. First, it was a regional bulwark deterring Soviet aggression. Second, the bilateral security alliance prevented a full-scale resurgence of Japanese militarism, which included significantly reducing the possibility of Japan's developing nuclear weapons, a point also suggested by Washington. However, China currently believes that the Japan–U.S. security alliance no longer serves to restrain a military buildup by Tokyo.[57] Facing continuous U.S. pressure to modernize its military system, Japan, as Beijing sees it, could move toward constitutional revision and the unrestricted engagement of its troops abroad. Thus, Beijing would prefer that Japan end its security alliance with the United States, while maintaining its postwar commitment to pacifism.

Beijing also emphasizes that historically the Japan–U.S. security alliance has not brought stability to the Asia–Pacific area. China points to the Vietnam War and the Cambodian conflict as two specific examples of serious problems in the past that created regional instability.[58] Similarly, it is difficult to make a strong case that the U.S.–Japan Security Treaty, which took shape during the Korean War, at the time created regional stability. Recent problems on the Korean Peninsula, moreover, do not appear to have been mitigated in anyway by the Japan–U.S. security alliance; in fact, as will be discussed below, the bilateral security relationship has arguably exacerbated regional problems.

Beijing realizes that despite recent improvements in Chinese-American and Sino-Japanese relations, the existing Japan–U.S. security arrangement makes China an outsider that must be carefully watched. Given the demise of the Soviet Union, Beijing is not clear how China has been quickly elevated to the level of a potentially major purveyor of regional instability. Thus, Beijing is currently very much concerned both with Washington's East Asia policy and Tokyo's recent efforts to support it. When it comes to the Japan–U.S. security alliance, what most disturbs China today is their maintenance of a Cold War strategy, which ignores changes in regional politics. Rather than power politics, Beijing fully endorses a multipolar system, a stance it has been effectively using to garner support in Southeast Asia.[59]

Indicative of this anachronistic strategy, from Beijing's perspective, is the concurrence by Tokyo in participating with Washington in joint research on a TMD (theater missile defense) system. Tokyo initially believed that, besides the high cost of the project, its participation in a TMD with the United States would damage its relations with Beijing.[60] The talk of deploying a missile defense system in Asia troubled China so much at one point that the United States gave additional thought to whether or not it was worth going ahead with the project.[61] But Washington quickly overcame its reservations about TMD, as did Tokyo, which, as discussed in chapter 2, the day after the late August 1998 projectile launch by the DPRK, announced its intention to pursue further the study of defensive technologies,[62] despite the large financial commitment and rubbing Beijing the wrong way.

Safeguards

Today, it is clear that Beijing remains highly suspicious of Japan's military objectives and its enduring security alliance with the United States. This, understandably, is especially true of Chinese military officials.[63] While Beijing's perceptions of what Japan might do should a security problem emerge in the East Asia–Pacific region are critical to the Sino-Japanese relationship, presently it is unlikely that Tokyo would respond militarily against China. The Japanese public at this time is not prepared to support military activities in East Asia by their nation's Self Defense Forces. Tokyo would therefore find it very difficult to win popular support for an overseas military conflict with China.

Moreover, economic ties are now very important to the relationship between Japan and China. Still confronted with a troubled economy, it would be imprudent for Tokyo to consider jeopardizing Japan's economic interests by taking military action against China, even if it believed that Taiwan was being bullied by Beijing. China is currently Japan's second most important trade partner, behind only the United States. Japan's exports to China now exceed $20 billion a year. Japan's export trade with China would be put at risk if Tokyo played any role in a military confrontation that Beijing viewed as interfering with Chinese national interests. Also important is that Japanese investments in China have grown since the mid-1980s. Japanese direct investments in China are second only to those in the United States; more Japanese direct investments go to China today than to any other Asian nation. Because of Japan's growing direct investments in China, even its Chinese imports, especially of manufactured goods, would be put in peril. To some extent, Chinese exports to Japan are contracted assembled goods that are related to Japanese direct investments; manufactured imports from China constitute over 75 percent of all Japanese imports from China.[64]

Similarly, it is not likely that Beijing is presently about to order any direct military moves on Japan. Overall, Japan is China's largest trade partner. According to official data from China's General Administration of the Customs, commerce with Japan, that is, both imports and exports, amounted to $66.1 billion in 1999, exceeding trade with the United States by almost $5 billion. Official Chinese data show that in 1999 China's imports from Japan totaled $33.8 billion, far more than imports from any other country. To a large degree, Japanese goods have been attractive to the Chinese. Excluding Hong Kong, in 1999 Japan was China's second largest export market, behind the United States.[65] Beijing would also be dissuaded from taking military action against Japan because it receives financial assistance from Tokyo. Japanese official development assistance (ODA) to China more than doubled between 1997 and 1998. ODA from Tokyo to Beijing amounted to $1.158 billion in 1998, making China the largest recipient of Japanese grant and loan assistance.[66]

More than just economic ties, however, are likely to prevent Japan and China from being involved in a military confrontation today. Chinese president Jiang Zemin's visit to Japan at the end of November 1998 marked a significant moment in Sino-Japanese relations. Not only was this the first official trip by a president of China to Japan, but discernible improvement was made in the Sino-Japanese relationship, despite the fact that President Jiang wanted, but did not get, a written apology from

Japan acknowledging its past military aggression against China.[67] President Jiang and former prime minister Obuchi agreed to the Japan–China Joint Declaration on Building a Partnership of Friendship and Cooperation for Peace and Development. While unsigned, the Joint Declaration established a "partnership" relationship and, more important, emphasized the commitment of both nations to "mutual non-aggression, non-interference in each other's internal affairs" and "peaceful co-existence." The Joint Declaration reaffirmed the value both China and Japan have given to the 1972 Joint Communiqué and to the 1978 Treaty of Peace and Friendship. This important document also stresses that Japan repeats its belief that there is only one China.[68]

Issues in Abeyance

Although there are safeguards that make a serious conflict between China and Japan unlikely today, because of Tokyo's security alliance with Washington, by no means do they completely protect against a deterioration of the Sino-Japanese relationship that could lead to military action. Despite the seeming improvement in Sino-Japanese ties recently, a solid bilateral relationship between Tokyo and Beijing does not exist. This means that relations between Beijing and Tokyo could change quickly because of action taken by either Japan or China.

The use of military force by Beijing against Taiwan, a renegade province in Beijing's eyes, would in all probability precipitate a military response from the United States, which, like Japan, also maintains a "one China" policy. That Tokyo has not specifically ruled out Taiwan as a "situational" problem causes much disquietude in Beijing. Japan's supporting role in an American military response involving Taiwan would, in the best-case scenario, immediately neutralize improvements in the Sino-Japanese relations that have evolved over the past two-and-a-half decades or, in the worse case, destroy the relationship altogether.[69] Equally problematic for Sino-Japanese relations is the realization of what has already been suggested as a possibility: that Taiwan would be protected by TMD.

Apart from Taiwan, several unresolved issues that were addressed in the 1998 Joint Declaration between Japan and China are critical to the security interests of both countries. In the Joint Declaration Japan and China concur "that the United Nations should play an important role in building and maintaining a new international order," and they agree to be actively involved in regional multilateral security structures, such as ARF. Also, in this declaration China and Japan "stress the importance of the ultimate elimination of nuclear weapons," that they are against the proliferation of nuclear weapons, and they "strongly call upon the nations concerned to cease all nuclear testing and [the] nuclear arms race, in order to contribute to the peace and stability of the Asian region and the world."[70]

To prevent a deterioration of bilateral relations, Beijing and Tokyo must soon deal with these issues. That both China and Japan agreed in the 1998 Joint Declaration that the United Nations has a critical role to assume in international security is politically very meaningful. However, during the last several years, the importance that the United States has attached to the role of the United Nations in resolving international security problems can easily be called into question. By the late 1990s, there was good reason to conclude that Washington was willing to respond without international guidance to international security problems. Circumventing the United Nations, Washington independently responded to the terrorist attacks on U.S. embassies in Africa, to problems it was experiencing with Iraq, and, with NATO, intervened in Yugoslavia. Throughout 1998, the Iraqi problem moved progressively away from resolution by consensus within the United Nations and toward a military denouement decided by the United States. By December 1998, the United States, with British support, felt comfortable enough to bypass the United Nations and employ military action to deal with the Iraqi problem. Surely, Tokyo cannot expect to maintain good relations with China indefinitely,[71] as long as it continues to accept American behavior that unequivocally circumvents the consensual security mechanisms of the United Nations. Although the U.S. bombing of the Chinese embassy during the Yugoslavian crisis did not directly turn China against Tokyo, Beijing's opposition to the Washington-led NATO intervention coupled with its deep mistrust of the strengthened Japan–U.S. security alliance kept a chill on Sino-Japanese relations. The Yugoslavian crisis forced Beijing to consider that the strengthened security relationship between Tokyo and Washington was the equivalent of a NATO alliance in East Asia.

Thus, if both China and Japan want to maintain and strengthen bilateral ties and if they are serious about the importance of the United Nations in creating and sustaining a new international system, then Tokyo must do one of two things: convince Beijing that it believes that U.S.

behavior does not contravene international norms, or move to an independent security policy that effectively integrates UN security mechanisms. Falling short on either of these two options means that Tokyo should expect to see little real progress in Sino-Japanese relations.

Nuclear testing is a second pressing issue that could easily alienate China in its relationship with Japan. Although Japan's strong reaction to China's nuclear testing in 1995 indicated an unequivocal disapproval of this type of activity,[72] Tokyo has not been visibly upset with subcritical testing by the United States. The United States conducted its first subcritical nuclear test on July 3, 1997; four years later, on August 18, 2000, it performed its twelfth.[73] But Tokyo has not rebuked the United States for this kind of nuclear testing. A few days after America conducted its fourth subcritical nuclear test in September 1998, the deputy press secretary of Japan's Ministry of Foreign Affairs indicated that Tokyo understood "that the United States undertakes this subcritical experiment to enhance security and reliability of stored nuclear weapons and to maintain a nuclear deterrent without making a nuclear test itself."[74] Just how long Beijing will continue to ignore Tokyo's inconsistent policy on nuclear testing is open to question, particularly since the 1998 Joint Declaration expressly states that Japan and China "call upon the nations concerned to cease *all* nuclear testing and any [*sic*] nuclear arms race."[75] Tokyo stresses that the subcritical nuclear testing does not violate the Comprehensive Nuclear Test Ban Treaty.[76] However, this means that Tokyo must also accept Russia's subcritical nuclear testing.[77] Should China develop the capability to perform subcritical nuclear testing, then Tokyo must also accept this or, alternatively, risk damaging the new "partnership" that it has recently formed with Beijing. Subcritical nuclear testing by China could, of course, be viewed by Tokyo as antithetical to the 1998 Joint Declaration, as it would reflect Beijing's lack of commitment to ending an arms race and the elimination of all nuclear weapons. Thus by denouncing the performance of subcritical nuclear testing by any nation, Tokyo will be acting responsibly, since it will be sending the strong signal that it is very serious about both ending a future arms race and eliminating nuclear weapons.

The tentative commitment to the elimination of nuclear weapons is still another issue that Tokyo must deal with in its evolving relationship with Beijing. It is not just the possibility that Beijing could eventually perform subcritical nuclear testing that could become problematic to the bilateral relationship with China. But the fact that Japan remains protected by the U.S. nuclear shield is also a serious problem. Continued subcritical nuclear testing by the United States to safeguard its nuclear stockpile, along with its resistance to reducing and eliminating nuclear weapons, is a political worry that cannot be ignored by Beijing. Japan's political indifference when it comes to criticizing the existence of America's nuclear weapons, which still serve as a deterrent for Japan despite the continuation of its publicly professed desire to eliminate them, is glaringly contradictory and must therefore soon be addressed by Tokyo if it intends to maintain and strengthen its relationship with Beijing.

North Korea

For Japan presently, a far more complicated security issue than China is North Korea. Before the Bush administration came to power in 2001 there was a noticeable improvement in relations between Seoul and Pyongyang, as well as between the United States and North Korea and Japan and the DPRK. However, similar to the past, today Tokyo, like Washington, sees Pyongyang's behavior as a potential, if not imminent, source of instability in the East Asia–Pacific region.[78] Subsequent to the nuclear tests conducted by India and Pakistan in the spring of 1998, Japan's Defense Agency conjectured in an internal document that North Korea would pursue the development of nuclear weapons—if indeed it did not already possess one.[79] Despite the existence of the 1994 Agreed Framework between Washington and Pyongyang and KEDO (Korean Peninsula Economic Development Organization), arrangements designed to put an end to North Korea's nuclear weapons program (see chapter 2), the East Asia–Pacific region suffered a serious security setback in late August 1998 when North Korea launched a rocket that flew over Japanese territory. Although North Korea repeatedly maintained that the launched projectile was a civilian satellite,[80] Japan continued to disregard Pyongyang's claim that this was the case, and emphasized instead the strong likelihood that it was a ballistic missile.[81]

Prior to the August 1998 projectile launching by North Korea, Tokyo at the very least had been uncertain as to whether or not it would participate in a joint TMD project with the United States.[82] However, the North Korean rocket launch precipitated a renewed Japanese interest in TMD and ultimately was the deciding factor in Tokyo's decision to get involved in the project with the United States. The day after North Korea launched the projectile over Japan, the Japanese chief cabinet secretary,

Hiromu Nonaka, announced that because of the incident Tokyo would suspend aid to the KEDO and that "technical study on the ballistic missile defense system will be further continued."[83] Japan's decision to begin studying TMD served as a confirmation to Pyongyang that Japan has never relinquished its expansionist and militaristic policies of the past.[84] The situation worsened in late October 1998 when the Japanese government announced plans to build and launch four surveillance satellites by the year 2002. Concerned by the fact that it had to rely on U.S. intelligence to get information about the North Korean projectile launched in August, Tokyo decided to fund construction of the satellites.[85] Pyongyang reacted very critically to Japan's announcement about its intention to develop satellites, seeing this as another indication of Tokyo's plan to reinvade Korea.[86]

For several years before the North Korean projectile launch, relations between Tokyo and Pyongyang, albeit far from perfect, had been moving in the right direction. In 1991, Tokyo and Pyongyang made a promising effort to normalize relations. Bilateral discussions fell apart by 1993, however, because of Tokyo's concerns about North Korea's nuclear program and because of a dispute involving the condition of Japanese women allegedly abducted by North Koreans in the 1970s and 1980s. Bilateral relations appeared to be improving in March 1995 when members from key Japanese and North Korean political parties signed an agreement in Pyongyang requesting the resumption of normalization discussions.[87] Tokyo and Pyongyang continued bilateral efforts to resume such discussions. In August 1997, "preparatory talks" between Tokyo and Pyongyang were held in Beijing. Ending on an optimistic note, these talks, along with other friendly overtures, presaged that Japan and North Korea would soon be involved in normalization discussions.[88]

As noted in chapter 2, Tokyo, influenced by Washington, continued to harbor the suspicion that North Korea surreptitiously maintained a nuclear weapons program, notwithstanding the 1994 Agreed Framework, KEDO, and Pyongyang's repeated claim that the suspected underground site was not a nuclear facility.[89] Initially, officials in North Korea wanted the United States to pay $300 million to inspect the site near Yongbyon, the country's nuclear research center. South Korea urged the United States to pay the amount requested by Pyongyang. However, Washington was not about to have the DPRK have its way, demanding instead that no conditions be attached to a U.S. inspection.

Similar to the situation relating to the suspicions that the DPRK was secretly maintaining a nuclear weapons program, the U.S. claim in the wake of the August 1998 launching that Pyongyang was preparing to set off yet another missile with the potential of hitting Japan[90] never took place. Nonetheless, because of this claim, Tokyo became alarmed enough to demand that Pyongyang cancel the second missile launch and avoid creating additional regional instability and worsening its relationship with Japan. Pyongyang insisted that the United States invented the rumor of a second missile launch to satisfy its interests.[91] Pyongyang continued to believe that the objective of the United States—with regard to both the launching of a second missile and the alleged nuclear weapons site—was to rationalize the use of military force against North Korea. Not given to minimizing political rhetoric, Pyongyang consistently charged complicity on the part of Japan and South Korea in that both countries have been willing to support the military "plan" of the United States to take control of North Korea.[92]

Pyongyang was disturbed by the report of the U.S. Department of Defense, published in late November 1998, that announced the American commitment to maintaining a permanent presence of approximately 100,000 troops in the Asia–Pacific area, including forces in South Korea and Japan.[93] A spokesperson for the DPRK's Foreign Ministry responded shortly after the publication of this report that it indicated the intention of the United States to control East Asia by maintaining military domination. Pyongyang further reasoned that a major target of America's deployed forces in the region had long been North Korea and was exasperated when the United States forthrightly rejected the suggestion of troop withdrawal. Pyongyang emphasized that the withdrawal of American troops from South Korea was a critical part of the "four-party talks"[94]—discussions involving the United States, North Korea, South Korea, and China—designed to establish peace and security on the Korean Peninsula.[95]

Even more alarming to Pyongyang than the permanent presence of American troops was the uncovering of "Operation Plan 5027." In 1998 and 1999 Pyongyang believed that Operation Plan 5027 was a detailed war strategy—which included the use of nuclear weapons—designed by the United States and supported by South Korea and Japan, to begin a second Korean War by invading North Korea.[96] Under the leadership of the Untied States, incessant military exercises in the region caused Pyongyang to anticipate an imminent strike on North Korea. Pyongyang viewed the continued demands by the United States for permission to

inspect the underground facility near Yongbyon as a pretext for the abandonment of its appeasement policy. According to leadership in the General Staff of the Korean People's Army: "[I]f inspections of the
underground facilities failed to be realized, they [U.S. conservative hard-
liners] would break the DPRK–U.S. Agreed Framework and take a determined counteraction."[97] Officials in Pyongyang interpreted President
Clinton's visit to South Korea in November 1998 as signifying the "final checkup" of U.S. willingness use military force against North Korea. While DPRK officials emphasized that they did not want war, they
also maintained that they would not back away from it. They maintained that they were ready "to answer fire with fire." DPRK officials
fulminated that their target would not only be "U.S. aggression forces
who chiefly execute the 'Operation Plan 5027' but also south [sic] Korean authorities who are willing to serve as their bullet-shield and Japan
and all others that offer bases or act as servants behind the scenes."[98]
Especially in light of the new guidelines for defense cooperation between Washington and Tokyo, Pyongyang was very concerned about
the U.S.-led NATO bombings in Yugoslavia. Not long after the bombings began, Pyongyang sent a letter to Yugoslavia that stressed the ille-
gitimacy of the NATO attack. Since for some time Pyongyang has feared
being a target of U.S. aggression, Pyongyang found it easy to empathize
with Yugoslavian leaders. Pyongyang emphasized that the NATO attack
violated international law and that it blatantly infringed on the "sovereignty and territorial integrity" of Yugoslavia.[99]

When most of the world's eyes focused on America's continuing
weapons-inspection dispute with Iraq, the security situation in East Asia
was similarly reaching a boiling point. That the United States was considering the use of military force against North Korea for its failure to
permit the unconditional inspection of a suspected nuclear site was not
just a figment of the collective imagination of Pyongyang officials. The
Japanese newspaper *Sankei Shimbun* reported that it had learned from
an anonymous source that during President Clinton's November 1998
visit to Japan he told Prime Minister Obuchi that if Pyongyang does not
permit the inspection of its underground site, "We have to consider military action against the DPRK's threat."[100] At a White House briefing,
President Clinton's press secretary stopped short of mentioning the use
of military action against North Korea when asked a question about the
termination of the Agreed Framework if the United States could not
inspect the suspected facility in North Korea. The press secretary's re-

sponse was: "Well, I think we've expressed in the past the view that we believe that there are some serious questions about the site and we need the ability to inspect and to look for ourselves; and that if there does prove to be something that would violate the rules, that there would be serious consequences."[101] Because the United States still maintained economic sanctions on North Korea, officials in Pyongyang interpreted the use of the words "serious consequences" as a possible military threat.

What largely remained out of the public domain was that the U.S. government had not substantiated the charges related to North Korea's suspected underground nuclear facility at Kumchang-ni. Accusations were made by Washington and accepted by Tokyo. From these accusations the concerned public in the United States and Japan assumed that government officials, who in many cases relied on so-called intelligence reports and policy statements, knew what they were talking about: North Korea had abandoned the 1994 Agreed Framework and was developing nuclear weapons. But Pyongyang has consistently maintained that the DPRK has not violated the Agreed Framework. Rather, it has charged that it has been the United States that is in violation of the bilateral accord, since it has not supplied the light water nuclear reactors nor fully removed economic sanctions[102] on North Korea as promised in the Agreed Framework.

An informative essay written by a former desk officer on North Korean affairs at the U.S. Department of State emphasized that the public perception of Pyongyang's secret underground nuclear facility had been based on "leaks," probably made by some individuals involved in American intelligence work who wanted to see policy shaped to fit their views on North Korea. The author also points out that underground facilities are common in North Korea. Because of extensive losses resulting from bombing during the Korean War, military facilities and factories both are often built underground.[103] Since we have already seen in the previous chapter that the U.S. inspection of Kumchang-ni showed that North Korea had not violated the Agreed Framework, then either the leaked-information hypothesis or misleading policy and intelligence reports, or a combination of both, account for Washington and Tokyo's continuing to suggest that Pyongyang was at work developing nuclear weapons. Indeed, one policy paper published in March 1999 by the National Defense University oxymoronically posits that: "The *discovery of at least one suspect site*—on which the construction began prior to the agreement [the Agreed Framework] reinforces the possibility that Pyongyang has frozen only a portion of its nuclear program or is seeking to develop a covert nuclear weapons program."[104]

In mid-December 1998, the North Korean situation briefly looked promising when Pyongyang suggested that it would permit the site near Yongbyon to be inspected by the United States. Pyongyang suggested that it would drop its demand that the United States pay $300 million to inspect the site and instead requested food for the country's starving population.[105] Yet, the situation was far from rectified, since the United States wanted to be able to inspect other North Korean sites. Pyongyang completely dismissed as unrealistic the carte blanche inspection rights demanded by Washington. Without much public fanfare, perhaps because of the attention given to Washington's preoccupation with the Iraqi crisis, the North Korean situation was increasingly becoming a potentially explosive matter for the United States and thus for Japan and South Korea. Pyongyang's incendiary language made a bad situation worse, as it continued to stress that military action would be used if that were the will of the "imperialists."

Toward the end of December 1998, representatives from the United States, Japan, and South Korea attended a meeting in New York City dealing with the topic of the possibility of Pyongyang's launching another missile. After months of suggestions to the contrary, the U.S. State Department announced at a noon press briefing on December 22 that the claims that Pyongyang was preparing to launch another missile had no basis in fact.[106] Within a few days, however, tensions had once again reached a fiery pitch. Although confronted with the strengthened U.S.–Japan security alliance, Pyongyang was determined to make clear that it was not going to be intimidated by the combined military power of Washington and Tokyo. As a result, Washington and Tokyo continued to call attention to North Korea as the mostly likely source of regional instability and remained highly suspicious of DPRK activities.

An Improving Security Environment and Its Limitations

Although it can be easily argued that the strengthened security alliance between Washington and Tokyo did nothing to quell the East Asian security ambience, other things did. The election of Kim Dae Jung as president of South Korea in 1998 led to the formation of his "sunshine policy," a nonthreatening strategy that emphasized the importance of bringing cooperation and reconciliation to the Korean Peninsula. The highlight of the work by Kim, who won the 2000 Nobel Peace Prize for his efforts, was the historic summit in Pyongyang on June 12–14, 2000, that underscored the importance of rapprochement between North and South Korea.

While South Korea's Kim is widely credited for improving the security of East Asia, other significant events were also important. Kim Dae Jung's North Korean counterpart, Kim Jong Il, realized that the international consequences of continued isolation would not be favorable to the DPRK. North Korea therefore began work to improve relations with other countries. Not only had North Korea already established formal ties with Australia and Italy during 2000, but by the time of the third Asia-Europe Meeting (ASEM) in October 2000, Great Britain, Germany, and the Netherlands, as well as other European countries, made it known that they wanted to establish diplomatic relations with the DPRK, which did not take part in this event.[107] By this time Pyongyang's relations with Washington were also noticeably improving with the two governments having discussed the possibility of opening liaison offices in North Korea and the United States. The climax of the visit to the United States in October 2000 by Jo Myong Rok, first vice chairman of the National Defense Commission of North Korea and Kim Jong Il's special envoy, was a joint U.S.–DPRK declaration made public in Washington.[108] Only days later Secretary of State Albright traveled to North Korea and was able to secure some assurance from Kim that North Korea would not launch any more long-range missiles.

Bilateral relations between North Korea and Japan also improved in 2000. Tokyo approved a 500,000–ton rice-aid package to North Korea in the fall, and the formal normalization discussions that began in the spring of 2000—there had been none for more than seven years—moved along through the year. But similar to discussions between Washington and the DPRK, in the background of discussions between Japan and North Korea most Tokyo officials harbored deep distrust and suspicion of Pyongyang. As in the late 1990s when Washington and Tokyo, as well as many analysts, viewed North Korea as the major source of the security crisis in East Asia,[109] the United States and Japan still see the DPRK as unpredictable and as the region's major source of instability. Thus, despite improving relations, many eyes in Washington and Tokyo have remained guardedly focused on North Korea—and, expectedly, Pyongyang continues to suspect the United States and Japan of having ulterior motives. For example, in the wake of the eleventh round of Japanese-DPRK normalization discussions held in Beijing on the last two days of October 2000, the North Korean government's official news agency published an article stating that Japan's stockpiling of plutonium is compelling evidence of its intention to acquire nuclear weapons and that its space research is a pretext for developing "nuclear capable inter-continental ballistic missiles."[110]

A serious setback to the effort to improve the dialogue with North Korea occurred in the first half of 2001. While the Clinton administration took a hard-line approach to North Korea, it nonetheless was willing to negotiate with Pyongyang. The Clinton administration viewed North Korea as a rogue state but still considered it possible to work with Pyongyang as long as Washington could demonstrate that it clearly was in control and maintained the upper hand in the dialogue. But the Bush administration was quick to send a very different signal to Pyongyang. Actually, even before the Bush administration assumed the reins of power in January 2001, there were suggestions that it was not ready to continue down the path forged by Clinton policy makers in dealings with North Korea. For example, referring to North Korea during his senate confirmation hearings for the position of secretary of state, General Colin Powell stressed that "as long as the dictator in the north continues to field far more conventional military force than any conceivable sense of self-defense would warrant, and develops missiles and unconventional weapons, we and our allies in the Pacific will remain vigilant."[111]

By early March 2001, it became clear that the Bush White House was going to take a considerably tougher approach toward North Korea than the previous administration. During South Korean president Kim Dae Jung's March visit to Washington, the Bush administration played its North Korean card. North Korea's Kim was labeled as untrustworthy. The Bush administration announced that it was suspending discussions with the DPRK. After canceling high-level discussions with Seoul,[112] North Korea lashed out at the Bush administration, vowing to respond to Washington's hard-line policy with a "tough policy" of its own.[113]

Moreover, after concluding his meeting with South Korea's Kim, Bush stressed that, "We're not certain as to whether or not they're keeping all terms of all agreements."[114] Bush's vague statement that Pyongyang had not kept all the terms in agreements presented a problem, because it implied that Pyongyang might be secretly operating its nuclear-weapons program—a program that had supposedly been stopped by the Agreed Framework. Pyongyang stressed that it has not been North Korea but rather the United States that has not been living up to the Agreed Framework. Pyongyang pointed out that there have been scheduling problems related to the delivery of heavy oil to be used to produce electricity and that construction of the light-water reactors has been delayed, making it unlikely for the DPRK to expect completion by the target date of 2003.[115] Seeking compensation for lost electric power, Pyongyang has indicated that the failure of the United States to meet the conditions of the Agreed Framework is causing it to consider restarting the graphite-moderated reactors so that it can generate the power that it needs for the country. It has argued that the U.S. desire for an "early inspection" before meeting the conditions of the Agreed Framework is part of Washington's delaying strategy. Eventually, the Bush administration retreated somewhat from the initial position that it adopted toward the DPRK. By late spring, after nudging from his father, President George W. Bush began to a see reason to respond more favorably to Pyongyang. However, Bush's view of North Korea changed again after the terrorist attacks on the United States in September 2001. In his State of the Union Address in January 2002, Bush infuriated Pyongyang by calling North Korea, along with Iraq and Iran, part of the "axis of evil."

What must be emphasized is that there are self-fulfilling prophecies at work on both sides of the political equation. North Korea is economically depressed, has a starving population, is politically isolated (though less so than in the past), and feels enormously threatened by regional military alliances, especially the arrangement between the United States and Japan. As Pyongyang sees it, the United States is a hegemon determined to establish control over the entire Asia–Pacific area. Tokyo's continuing security alliance with Washington keeps open the possibility of a Japanese-supported American strike on North Korea, which is why Pyongyang continues to denounce statements leveled at the DPRK by what it calls "right-wing Japanese reactionaries." Still fresh in the minds of officials in Pyongyang is Tokyo's December 1998 suggestion that the U.S. military strike on Iraq should serve as a warning to North Korea.[116] Tokyo is very mindful of the historical resentment that Pyongyang holds toward Japan. Tokyo is also very aware of the fact that Pyongyang detests Japan's security alliance with the United States. For these reasons, any threat identified by Tokyo or Pyongyang is likely to be exaggerated and will serve to maintain the chill in Japanese-DPRK relations. Moreover, far too many in Tokyo and Washington still see the potential of malevolence and regional instability coming out of North Korea. Symbolizing U.S. and Japanese suspicions of North Korean volatility is TMD, which Washington and

Tokyo continue to support as overall regional relations improve. Thus, as a consequence of almost any regional event, the continued development of TMD could easily cause Pyongyang to threaten or actually use some military action to bolster North Korea's national image.

Japan appears to be especially sensitive to the North Korean situation and, under present conditions, it has good reason to be. Tokyo knows that Pyongyang has the technological capability to strike Japan. In the event of a military crisis involving the United States and North Korea, with the technology Pyongyang now possesses, Japan would be a target of a missile strike simply because of its security arrangement with Washington. Thus, the argument that the United States would have a reason to end the bilateral security alliance if Japan did not sufficiently support an American military confrontation on the Korean Peninsula[117] is not Tokyo's major security concern.

It must be understood that in recent years, as in the past, Pyongyang has not been an innocent victim. Pyongyang's perennial use of highly inflammatory rhetoric has made bad situations even worse. The launch of a projectile over Japan in August 1998 without any prior notification to either Tokyo or the international community was a very poor decision by Pyongyang, one that it should have known would raise serious security concerns. Whatever Pyongyang's reason, by not providing prior notification, it sent the wrong signal to Tokyo and Washington and provided the rationale for TMD.

Russian Concerns

The end of the Cold War created the sanguine prospect that Moscow's and Washington's views of foreign affairs were converging. But this optimism has proven to be short-lived. Like Beijing and Pyongyang, Moscow opposed the U.S.-led NATO intervention in Yugoslavia. Moscow has also vehemently demonstrated its objections to Washington's proposal to develop NMD and, with Japan, TMD. Moscow argues that deployment of NMD would violate the 1972 Antiballistic Missile Treaty and that TMD could destroy the accord, thereby reasoning that these defensive systems undermine existing disarmament efforts and encourage a new arms race.[118] (In December 2001, Washington formally announced the U.S. intention to withdraw from the ABM Treaty.) Russia has recently given serious thought to what it can do to counteract these defensive shields.[119] Like Beijing, Moscow has endorsed a multipolar international system and is concerned about America's attempt to exploit its status as the world's only superpower and about its propensity to circumvent the United Nations.

As Moscow has done with Pyongyang, it has been reaching out to Beijing. Signed by President Jiang Zemin of China and President Vladimir Putin of Russia in July 2000, the Beijing Declaration points to a converging perspective of international affairs held by Russian and Chinese officials, as does the joint statement denouncing antimissile defense systems. In early November 2000, China and Russia signed a joint communiqué that reasserted support for a multipolar international system. What could easily be interpreted as a reference to the strengthened alliance between Washington and Tokyo, which gives Japan regional security responsibility, Moscow stressed that it recognizes only one China, that it does not support the independence of Taiwan, and that any outside interference in the Taiwan issue would create instability in the Asia–Pacific region.[120]

Moscow watched warily as Washington and Tokyo reaffirmed their security alliance in the mid-1990s. However, suspicions of the bilateral alliance deepened when the United States and Japan announced that they would begin research on TMD. For Moscow, NMD and TMD represent an unnecessary heightening of tensions and create the momentum for an arms race and nuclearization rather than denuclearization. In short, since embracing TMD in the second half of 1998, Washington and Tokyo are nudging Moscow closer to Beijing and Pyongyang—and in ways that will not enhance regional stability. In an early June 1999 meeting in Moscow between Russian defense minister Marshall Igor Dmitriyevich Sergeyev and vice-chairman Zhang Wannian of the Chinese Central Military Commission, the two officials agreed that NMD and TMD would create international and regional instability. The North Korean and Russian Joint Declaration signed in Pyongyang in mid-July 2000 states: "The DPRK and Russia consider that any development of the closed theater missile defense system of bloc style in Asia and Pacific may seriously wreck regional stability and security."[121]

Although Moscow had little reason to move closer to Beijing and Pyongyang prior to the beginning of TMD joint research by the United States and Japan, it really had no other viable alternative once it took place. Facing the two wealthiest countries on earth, Moscow had to make conciliatory gestures to both Beijing and Pyongyang. What is problematic for East Asia is that these gestures have a military foundation and therefore with the Japan–U.S. security alliance have the potential to unsettle rather than enhance regional stability.

Conclusion

Japan has not yet juxtaposed its enduring commitment to its peace constitution with the security relationship with the United States. There is little doubt that Japan must pay for the security arrangement it has with the United States. Host nation support is really only a very small part of the overall cost of the bilateral security relationship. Continuing problems in Okinawa and far less than desirable relations with China and North Korea directly relate the security alliance that Tokyo maintains with Washington. The Japan–U.S. security alliance is even increasing skepticism in Moscow, particularly since the commitment by Washington and Tokyo to study TMD.

Moreover, no matter how hard Tokyo tries to ignore the problem, the existing security relationship with the United States will keep Japan susceptible to American demands to concede on trade and related economic issues. Of course, U.S. demands would exist even without the security alliance, but in its absence, Tokyo would be under much less pressure to comply with Washington's demands. As the world's only military superpower responsible for protecting Japan, and especially by providing it with a nuclear deterrent, the United States has the hegemonic privilege to demand that Japan make the required adjustments—or face the consequences, as in the recent case when Washington imposed antidumping duties on Japanese steel products. True, Japan does not have to accede to American demands, but it must nonetheless listen to them, spend time discussing domestically the problems and costs associated with not conceding, and meet with U.S. officials who see no alternative other than full compliance. These demands from the United States are heard in both good and bad economic times. Getting used to this, one could conjecture, although troubling, is tolerable. But as the second largest economic power in the world, this is not the posture Japan should have to assume. Moreover, Japan increasingly confronts expectations that it will deal with regional and global economic problems. In the twenty-first century being told what it can and should be doing by the United States is a position that Japan most obviously should be working to avoid.

Although Washington frequently demands structural changes in Japan's economic strategies, it is completely satisfied with incremental adjustments to Japanese security policies. As it has done for years, current U.S. policy is urging Japan to accept greater military responsibility—the partnership must be strengthened. In contrast to past actions, however, Japan must now reconcile its political position with the end of Cold War threats. When faced with American pressure to expand its security responsibilities, conservative forces within Japan, most especially feel obligated to support and assist the United States with its policing duties. The demise of the Soviet bear, in other words, gave Japan the chance to raise its political head a little higher; even the mere semblance of a bigger security role for Tokyo raises the specter of Japanese remilitarization in East Asia. Moving too far down this road is very dangerous for Tokyo officials, since it requires not only ignoring the pacifist sentiment still very much discernible in Japan, but it also creates momentum for actual remilitarization.

Steps taken by Tokyo in the last few years—the 1995 National Defense Program Outline, the Joint Declaration on Security Alliance for the Twenty-first Century, the new Guidelines for U.S.–Japan Defense Cooperation, and the decisions to study TMD and to develop surveillance satellites—have been viewed by Beijing and Pyongyang as potentially serious sources of regional instability. However, the worst-case scenario from the perspective of Beijing and Pyongyang is a remilitarized Japan. There is certainly no guarantee that the incremental growth of Japanese security responsibilities will remain contained by the alliance with the United States.

What Tokyo is now ignoring is the opportunity to develop solid bilateral relations with all of its neighbors, most especially China and North Korea. By continuing to align Japan with Washington's policies in East Asia, which some countries view as manifestly ethnocentric, Tokyo is forcing uncertainty and suspicion to remain embedded in the region's security environment. Japan's security alliance with the United States impedes the establishment of genuinely "normal" relations with China. Because Beijing remains skeptical of Tokyo's military ambitions and intentions, it has been very difficult to settle the history issue between China and Japan. The amount of distrust that still exists between Japan and North Korea is even greater than that in the Sino-Japanese relationship. Pyongyang firmly suspects that the United States wants to see the demise of communism in North Korea. Pyongyang sees Japan as a country that supports this U.S. objective. In addition to permitting American bases and troops on its soil, Japan's recent security initiatives have greatly worried Pyongyang, making it even more distrustful of Tokyo's intentions.

4

Debates on the Purpose of
the Alliance

Introduction

The debate related to Japan's current security arrangement with the United States is somewhat diverse. That there are just two major positions associated with this debate certainly does not reflect this diversity. There are also other perspectives within these two major positions, which generally either support or do not support the extant bilateral security relationship.

This chapter will examine all of the different political perspectives that are related to the two positions on the Japan–U.S. security arrangement. There is a general understanding that the Japan–U.S. security relationship has been strengthened during the last few years. This attention, moreover, helps to explain why the most popular position is that the bilateral security relationship is necessary in the post–Cold War environment. What has not been given very much attention, particularly outside of Japan, are the reasons that the bilateral security arrangement should not be maintained.

The following perspectives on the Japan–U.S. security arrangement will be analyzed in this chapter. First, we examine in detail the arguments of those who support the continuation of the security relationship between Japan and the United States. Although this position is the one that most analysts support, this is not to say that there is unanimity among them.

There are, in other words, different perspectives within this position on why there is a continuing need for the existing bilateral security relationship. We will also examine the perspectives of those who at least tacitly believe that the bilateral security relationship should end. Here two very distinct perspectives currently exist: a Japanese viewpoint and the non–Japanese perspective. The latter perspective consists of two disparate views: the first explicitly raises the question of whether there is a need for the existing bilateral security relationship and advocates rearming Japan, and the second, while advocating the termination of the security alliance, does not endorse Japanese rearmament. Rather, this new perspective challenges Japan to fulfill its postwar commitment to a strong United Nations that meets its obligation to maintain international security. But before discussing this new perspective, we will look briefly at the views of the Japanese left.

Preserving the Security Alliance

Most observers of the Japan–U.S. security alliance view it as a requisite arrangement for both political and economic reasons. Despite the different perspectives associated with this position, all advocates of the extant bilateral security alliance base their support on the single assumption, as we saw in chapter 2, that there is a continuing need for the United States to maintain its security commitments to Japan, as both nations benefit from the alliance. It is important to recall that the creation of the bilateral security alliance during the Cold War was due to the fear that the Soviet Union posed a serious threat to Japan and to the region as a whole. But the end of the Cold War and the demise of the Soviet Union did not bring a termination to the security alliance because, Washington argued and Tokyo agreed, instability still prevailed in the region. Thus monumental change in the political atmosphere of the Asia–Pacific area notwithstanding, the preservationist position adjusted the region's condition to new sources of instability.

In the early 1990s, the U.S. Department of Defense (DoD) identified ten (though not necessarily distinct) sources of instability in the East Asia–Pacific region.[1] In a generalized way, the DoD identified the continued existence of several communist states in the region. But at the top of the list was North Korea, which, because it is said to be unpredictable, continues to be the most serious threat to regional stability. Additional sources of potential regional instability, said the DoD, were China, problems involving Taiwan, Cambodia, the Philippines, and Myanmar.

Conflicts associated with several countries' claims to the Spratly Islands in the South China Sea represented yet another potential source of regional conflict. Finally, the DoD expressed its concern that the proliferation of weapons of mass destruction was a serious regional problem, particularly in regard to North Korea.

While there was concurrent discussion in academia, the media, and in policy circles that the end of the Cold War created the prospect that the United States might no longer need to play the role of the world's policeman, the DoD was not at all interested in retreating completely from East Asia. Having played the role of policeman for decades, Washington found it easy to continue the U.S. security commitment to Japan and the East Asia–Pacific region, despite America's withdrawal from the Philippines. However, in Japan the story was a little different. On the one hand, some worried that the United States would withdraw altogether from the region, jeopardizing Japanese security.[2] For the most part, Tokyo did not want to abandon the bilateral security alliance. On the other hand, the end of the Cold War did precipitate some thinking in Japan about the need for an alternative security structure. The emergent policy recommendation was to develop an efficient domestic defense system and maintain the Japan–U.S. security alliance while also remaining open to the formation of a multilateral security structure for the region.[3] The creation of a multilateral security system ultimately would mean that Japan would be less dependent on the Untied States and that America's regional military power would decline. Taking this one step further, some in Japan believed that the bilateral security alliance was no longer needed and accordingly called for its abrogation.[4] Bringing even more attention to this discussion was the rape of a young Okinawan schoolgirl by U.S. servicemen in September 1995 and the military base problems associated with this incident.[5] As we will see in chapter 5, (Table 5.2, Survey 10), a *Nihon Keizai Shimbun* poll conducted in the wake of the Okinawan rape incident showed that 40 percent of the respondents then felt that the bilateral security treaty should end.

Thus, policy makers in both Japan and the United States have had grave concerns about the endurance of the bilateral security alliance. An effective multilateral security structure would be a direct challenge to U.S. hegemony in the Asia–Pacific region; this would be greatly exacerbated should the security relationship end and the United States be forced to play a truncated security role in the region. For some Japanese policy makers, should their worst fears become reality, a reduced U.S. military commitment would precipitate a serious security problem in the region. Because they believe that North Korea, in particular, could act up at any time, Japan would be forced to depend largely on its domestic defense.

Although Washington and Tokyo had been working to strengthen the bilateral security alliance, there were some loose ends in the relationship. The United States' idea—of developing a TMD (theater missile defense) system to include Japan—which emerged soon after North Korea launched a Rodong 1 missile over the Sea of Japan in 1993, had not been finalized in the mid-1990s. In 1997, Japan had intimated that it might not be participating in the TMD system, due to financial costs, domestic and regional resistance, and the potentially deleterious impact on Sino-Japanese relations.[6] A little over a year later U.S. defense officials had also become concerned about the untoward effect the deployment of a TMD system could have on Sino-American relations and considered the possibility of keeping it out of Asia.[7] Not readily discernible even in early 1998 was the fledging Japanese nationalism that became evident after the projectile launched by North Korea in late August 1998. This nationalism calls on Japan to develop a strong defense posture that should be more independent from the United States.[8]

Both Washington and Tokyo took major steps in the mid-1990s to reaffirm the bilateral security relationship. With the publication of its 1995 report, which firmly established America's commitment to the area,[9] Washington eased Tokyo's fears that the United States would withdraw from the East Asia–Pacific region. Before the end of 1995, Tokyo policy makers approved the National Defense Program Outline. This document, among other things, underscored the importance of cooperation on security matters between Japan and the United States by calling attention to the existing bilateral security arrangements (deemed to be "indispensable to Japan's security") and stressed the Japanese need to be protected "against the threat of nuclear weapons" by continuing to "rely on the U.S. nuclear deterrent."[10] Together, Washington and Tokyo subsequently formulated the Joint Declaration on Security (1996) and, most recently, the Guidelines for Defense Cooperation.

Why continue bilateral support for a security alliance formed decades ago? The answer is cultural norms. Coupled with its military power, the United States' bilateral security arrangements in the Asia–Pacific area have given Washington a tactical advantage in the region.[11] From the U.S. perspective, potential threats in the region have to be neutralized to prevent instability, or from an alternative vantage point, to forestall any undermining of Washington's power. Recognizing Japan as its most important ally in the area, as well as having the area's most powerful economy, Washington has long considered its security relationship with Tokyo to be the most critical in the region. The 1978 defense guidelines emerged because of a Soviet military buildup in the 1970s.[12] The new defense guidelines between the United States and Japan are a reaction to regional conditions in a post-Soviet security milieu. The absence of the new bilateral guidelines would suggest that no regional threat exists, since the old order has passed. To continue to exercise its perceived responsibility of maintaining regional security and collaterally to retain hegemonic control of the area, Washington has relied on the same cultural dynamic it used during the Cold War: norms that dictate a unilateral order.

Compared to Washington, Tokyo's accession to the bilateral security alliance is more complicated. Japan adopted, and for several decades fully accepted, norms that support an antimilitarist culture. The Gulf War reflected these norms by demonstrating to the world Japan's resolve not to become involved in an armed conflict that did not directly threaten Japanese national security. However, the Gulf War also revived Japanese nationalism, which had lain dormant for decades. The gradual popularization of nationalist Ichiro Ozawa's phrase "normal country" brought to the fore the idea that Japan had for too long remained a passive international player and that it was incumbent upon Tokyo to change its policy position on security matters. Providing momentum to this emergent nationalism was the fact that the end of superpower confrontation that characterized the Cold War had created the opportunity for Japan to enhance its security role. However, moving decidedly away from an antimilitarist culture would prove to be a difficult task. Still, reaffirming the bilateral security alliance has become the dominant political theme for most Japanese policy makers. It is true that Tokyo's compliance with the reaffirmation of the bilateral security alliance has gotten the attention of its neighbors, especially given Japan's larger security role in East Asia. Although Japan's broadened security role has created angst for many of its neighbors, if there is any good news it is that Tokyo's alliance with Washington helped to keep alive the contention that the resurgence of Japanese militarism would continue to be restrained by the United States.

But while the reaffirmation of the Japan–U.S. security alliance, which was underway by 1996, arguably provided a political safety valve for

Japan's Asian neighbors, nonetheless it inadvertently opened up an avenue upon which nationalist forces could travel to begin developing an independent military system. However, it would be mistaken to argue that the strengthened security alliance has extirpated Japan's antimilitarist and antinuclear culture. Although the bilateral security alliance has been strengthened, currently it has been more symbolic than substantive. As a result, an antimilitarist sentiment remains a visible and important part of the Japanese culture. Japan's current security climate, therefore, is a complicated mixture of continuing support for the security arrangement with the United States, emergent nationalism, which is attempting to create an independent Japanese defense base, and an enduring antimilitarist and antinuclear culture that emanates from the nation's constitution and from the tragedies in Hiroshima and Nagasaki.

Still, Washington and Tokyo's insistence that there is a need to maintain the bilateral security relationship has been of utmost importance in sustaining the support for the alliance. For example, the Japanese Ministry of Foreign Affairs points out that besides the concerns it has about nuclear weapons and large military forces in the region, because defense spending in the Asia–Pacific region is growing faster than in any other area of the world, there is a continuing need to maintain the bilateral security arrangement, which includes American troops stationed in Japan. Moreover, in an effort to demonstrate that Japan, which has one of the largest military budgets in the world, has been contributing to regional security, the ministry emphasizes that Japanese defense spending during the mid-term plan for the years 1996–2000 grew to ¥25.15 trillion, up noticeably from ¥22.17 trillion for the 1991–1995 period.[13] Thus, Tokyo's, as well as Washington's, argument that the strengthened bilateral security arrangement offsets sources of regional instability has helped policy analysts, and others as well, to support the alliance.

The most commonly held view of analysts who support the security arrangement between Japan and the United States is that there is an ongoing need to maintain and strengthen the relationship. Mirroring the position subscribed to by most policy makers in Washington and Tokyo, those who hold this view work to legitimate the continuation of a Cold War security alliance. Advocates of this position, moreover, concede that economic concerns and regional instability both serve as the primary justification for the continuation of the bilateral security alliance.

This preservationist position, however, is not unified; it has two major camps. The first seeks to maintain the existing bilateral security relationship, allowing it to advance slowly.[14] Supporters of this traditional or incremental view of the security alliance argue that instability in the East Asia–Pacific region leaves the United States and Japan with little choice but to retain the bilateral security alliance and that changes to it should occur incrementally. They recognize that asymmetries or imbalances exist in the security arrangement, that is, the United States bears the brunt of the responsibility. Their major concern is not with the immediate elimination of the asymmetries. Rather, their interests generally center on the survival and strengthening of the security relationship.[15] A variant of the incrementalist perspective views America's presence in Northeast Asia as a neutral or benign force, reasons that Beijing sees an increase in Japan's security responsibilities as potentially threatening to China, and therefore advocates that the United States assume as much security responsibility as possible to offset regional discord relating to security perceptions.[16]

The second camp of analysts that support the continuation of the Japan–U.S. security alliance indicates that the relationship is not free of political tensions. To relieve the pressure, they recommend structural changes in the bilateral security alliance.[17] The most important structural change relates to the reduction of U.S. troops in Japan, specifically in Okinawa. Recent tension in Okinawa associated with the presence of U.S. troops there has prompted the idea that the best way to deal with a security relationship that is subject to strain and even to help lessen the intensity of future problems, is to reduce the presence of American forces in Okinawa.[18]

Both camps have serious shortcomings. The incremental view of the security alliance keeps Japan in a subordinate relationship with the United States. Opposed to rapid change in the security alliance, the incrementalists therefore tacitly support a form of bilateralism that maintains Japan's dependence on the United States for security. While currently this may be an easy pill for Japan to swallow, the continued incremental expansion of its military capabilities in an environment devoid of superpower tension is not a politically salubrious development, especially at a time when nationalist voices have been clamoring for a strong and independent Japanese security system (see below). With incremental military growth, it will become increasingly easier in the future for some in Japan to make the case for the need to break free of this dependency status. Even the persistence of the imbalances in the security alliance provides political fodder for Japanese nationalists. Dependent on the

United States, Japan has had to yield to American demands, including too many in the economic realm—a condition that Japanese nationalists unambiguously want to change.

By advocating fundamental changes in the bilateral security relationship, the structuralist camp introduces the prospect of additional uncertainty in the East Asia–Pacific region. The recommendations for structurally correcting the imbalances in the alliance at the same time that the bilateral security arrangement remains in place creates the impression that the United States and Japan are preparing for nothing short of military domination of the entire Asia–Pacific region. For example, an aggressive and enduring push by the United States to get Japan to participate without legal constraint in collective security operations would occasion panic in Beijing, Pyongyang, and even Moscow. Japan's increased security responsibilities accompanying the new bilateral defense guidelines have already created a regional stir; so, under current conditions, unrestrained participation by Japan in collective security would cause even more distrust than now exists. Similarly, pulling U.S. troops out of Okinawa while encouraging Japan to become more security competent in its own right may placate Okinawans, but it does little to ease the worries of some of Japan's neighbors. Even worse is that changes like these in Japan's security policy would play right into the hands of nationalist forces. Once the asymmetries were gone, the argument could be made that there would be little need to retain the existing bilateral security arrangement.

A very serious problem common to both the incrementalist and structuralist perspectives is that neither position adequately explains the necessity for the continuing of the bilateral security treaty and the broader security alliance since the collapse of the Soviet Union. In recent years by relying on the politically fluid argument that has made the transition from viewing the Soviet Union as the prime regional menace to viewing North Korea and China as surrogates in this capacity, both perspectives simply assume that the need for the Japan–U.S. security arrangement still exists.[19]

But this continued "need" is regionally problematic. Seoul, which has recently experienced an improvement in its relationship with Tokyo, still has some serious reservations about an expansion of Japan's security responsibilities. Perhaps even more than Pyongyang and Beijing, Seoul remained unrelenting in its protest against the publication in 2001 of the Japanese history textbook that reinterpreted what have been considered heinous acts of Japanese aggression on the Korean Peninsula during World War II. It has been hard for Seoul to forget the devastation inflicted by Japan on Korea when it colonized the peninsula from 1910 to 1945. The currently improved South Korean–Japanese relationship is an apprehensive one from Seoul's perspective.[20]

Beijing has become very suspicious of the Japan–U.S. bilateral security alliance in recent years.[21] Beijing feels that the continuation of this alliance runs counter to the cooperative security efforts recently formed in Asia, such as the 1996 Agreement on Confidence Building in the Military Field Along the Border Areas (the Shanghai Agreement) and the 1997 Agreement on Arms Reductions in Border Areas (the Moscow Agreement).[22] At the March 1997 meeting of the ASEAN Regional Forum (ARF) Beijing proposed the "new security concept," which calls for increased confidence-building strategies to be developed in Asia. One month later, the "new security concept" became part of the Sino-Russian Joint Statement on the Multilateral World and Establishing a New International Order that was signed by President Jiang Zemin and President Boris Yeltsin.[23] In the wake of the U.S.-led NATO strike on Yugoslavia in 1999, Beijing and Moscow see the need for an effective regional security system to prevent "neo-interventionism" being used on the pretext of the protection of human rights.[24]

Although Russia has generally appeared to accept the United States' security alliance with Japan since the end of the Cold War, the new bilateral defense guidelines and the announced cooperative work to develop a theater missile defense system for Northeast Asia have recently made Moscow very suspicious.[25] In Moscow, America's NATO-led attacks on Yugoslavia have created even more suspicion of the Japan–U.S. security alliance. Moscow, like Beijing, has been unable to comprehend the meaning of the phrase "areas surrounding Japan" in the new defense guidelines. The American-led NATO action had the potential to confirm Moscow's worst fears of the broadened Japan–U.S. security alliance, that is, cooperative intervention in a domestic Russian problem or a joint military response to the Northern Territories/Kurile Islands dispute between Tokyo and Moscow. Russian concerns relating to the insistent American position that the Anti-Ballistic Missile (ABM) Treaty may also need to be altered have further complicated Moscow's perception of U.S. security intentions. (The United States announced its unilateral withdrawal from the ABM Treaty at the end of 2001.)

Pyongyang has asserted that, along with South Korea, "Japanese reactionaries" have demonstrated through their military alliance with the United States that they desire to play a leading role in the implementation of operation plan 5027—an American strategy in place designed to invade North Korea.[26] The political crystallization of this plan, according to Pyongyang, is the Japanese Diet's passage of the bills relating to the new defense guidelines between Japan and the United States. Pyongyang believes that the new defense guidelines, which have the Korean Peninsula as the primary target, reflect Tokyo's retrogressive intention to reinstate the nation's imperialist and militarist past. Pyongyang also maintains that the broadened guidelines permit the United States, with Japanese assistance, to dominate the entire Asia–Pacific region. Especially worrying Pyongyang is what it charges is an attempt by Tokyo to reactivate the "Greater East Asia Co-prosperity Sphere,"[27] a reference to a plan adopted by Japan in 1940 when it was attempting to control Asia and which was in effect during the last few years of its colonization of the Korean Peninsula.

Because of these observations from outside the alliance, it is reasonable to argue that the perceived strengthening of the Japan–U.S. security relationship has heightened the threat ambience in the East Asia–Pacific area. There is little reason to be concerned with the accuracy of these external observations, since it is perception and not precision that matters in international relations. What therefore really matters is that sentiment is growing in Moscow, Beijing, and Pyongyang that the United States is exploiting its position as the sole military superpower and that in East Asia Japan is acquiescing to America's hegemonic plan, perhaps even to the point of readopting its past aggressive behavior.

Western Revisionism

The revisionist perspective shares much in common with the nationalist position that will be discussed in the next section. Western revisionists argue that while the U.S.–Japan security arrangement served its purpose in the past, there is no longer a need for it in the post–Cold War world, at least not in its current form; that while the United States has no other choice but to excuse Japan for "free riding" during the Cold War, the time has come for Tokyo to increase its security capabilities so that the existing bilateral alliance can end. The revisionists generally concede that some type of security relationship between the United States and

Japan will likely still be needed. However, this new security relationship will be nowhere near as costly to the United States as the present bilateral arrangement. This is because Japan will assume considerably more responsibility for security and U.S. military protection of Japan will come only as a last resort. Japan will no longer be largely dependent on the United States for security.

Arguing along the same political line as Japanese nationalists, the revisionists emphasize that it is time for Japan to bear sufficient arms to defend itself. Japan and its Asian neighbors should handle current problems in Northeast Asia, specifically with North Korea, according to the revisionist perspective.[28] There is no need for Tokyo to rely on the United States to resolve a regional problem that primarily affects Japan. It is time for Tokyo to become a truly equal partner with Washington, and this means taking primary responsibility for Japan's defense. For too long Washington has employed "smothering" tactics in its relationship with Japan. This strategy must end, because it is far too costly to U.S. taxpayers.[29]

The revisionist perspective contains four major assumptions. First, advocating the dissolution of the existing Japan–U.S. security arrangement, this perspective assumes that there is no viable alternative to the end of the alliance other than Japanese rearmament. The second important assumption found in the revisionist perspective relates to the "free ride" argument. The revisionists maintain that Japan has consciously exploited the security alliance, saving itself billions of yen each year by having the United States pay most of the bill for its security. The third key assumption of the revisionist perspective is that because Washington still distrusts Japan, it wants to prevent Japanese rearmament. Not only would too many of Japan's Asian neighbors see Japanese rearmament as a regional threat, but Washington does not eventually want to face Japan as a military competitor. Finally, the revisionist perspective assumes that the continuation of the existing security alliance prevents the United States from making significant progress in bilateral trade relations.[30]

The major conclusion that can be easily drawn from the revisionist perspective is that the United States wants very much to retain hegemonic control of the Asia–Pacific region. In other words, because the United States still desires to play the role of global policeman, it must maintain its Cold War security ties in the East Asia–Pacific region, and particularly with Japan. Since the evolving bilateral security alliance continues to place the onus on the United States, this prevents the formation of a genuinely equal partnership between Japan and America.[31]

The problem here is not with the conclusion, but rather that it is drawn from faulty assumptions. To assume that the dissolution of the existing U.S.–Japan security alliance can lead only to Japanese rearmament is faulty, for there is clearly another viable alternative. Since the end of the Pacific War Japan has maintained a culture of antimilitarism. Specifically, in addition to renouncing war, Japan has repeatedly stressed the need for the realization of global disarmament, the total elimination of all nuclear weapons, and the strengthening of the United Nations. Because the revisionist perspective completely ignores the emergence of multilateral security systems, both global and regional, its focus is entirely on shifting military responsibility to Japan to replace the end of the security alliance with the United States.

By assuming that Japan has accepted a "free ride" on security from the United States, the revisionist perspective excludes the contribution that it has made in other areas, most notably in foreign aid. For a number of years, Japan has been the world's leading ODA (official development assistance) provider. But more important than this matter is that Tokyo does not believe that it has been the recipient of a free ride from the United States. Japan believes that it has sufficiently improved its defense capabilities over the years and that the provision of host nation support—currently amounting to about $5 billion—to help defray the costs of American troops stationed on its soil has been more than adequate.[32] If fact, Tokyo sees this host nation support, or what it calls *omoiyari yosan* (consideration or sympathy budget), as a generous reciprocation of goodwill to the United States. Because of its troubled economy, Tokyo has recently announced that it wants to reduce *omoiyari yosan*. Moreover, frustrations related to the presence of U.S. bases and troops in Japan have precipitated political reactions, the most serious of which have come from Okinawa, that point to human and physical costs attached to the presence of American troops in Japan.

Although it is true that several of Japan's Asian neighbors would become very alarmed if it were to rearm without being aligned with the United States, there is no empirical connection between this and the third revisionist assumption that distrust of Japan pervades Washington. While survey data indicate that 89 percent of U.S. opinion leaders feel that the bilateral security treaty with Japan should be maintained, it also shows that nearly all, 97 percent, believe that Tokyo should share the

defense burden with Washington. Most important, survey data show that
nearly two-thirds (64 percent), of U.S. opinion leaders think that Japanese defense capabilities need to *increase*, compared to only 41 percent
of the American public that holds this view.[33] That it is not difficult to
locate some in Washington who distrust Japan does not mean that this
sentiment is an axiomatic part of U.S. policy. That Washington has continued to prod Tokyo to increase its military responsibilities for many
years is a fact that blatantly contravenes the assumption that it deeply
distrusts Japan. It would make little sense for Washington to continue to
press Tokyo to increase its military responsibilities if there was significant distrust of Japan, given the many, and at times quite serious, bilateral trade disputes that have emerged over the years. If there were deep
distrust of Japan, most Washington policy makers would reason that a
serious, ongoing trade dispute could conceivably cause Japan to de-link
from the security alliance. Thus, the argument that efforts by Washington to maintain and strengthen the bilateral security relationship reflects
distrust of Japan, that is, the alliance retains Tokyo's dependence on the
United States by preventing Japanese rearmament,[34] ignores a critical
fact: the security arrangement serves to increase Japanese compliance.
Not only has Washington continued to pressure Tokyo to increase its
military responsibilities over the years, but it has also persisted in making trade and related economic demands.

The final revisionist assumption that the existing alliance prevents Washington from improving its trade relationship with Japan reverses the "reality" of the Japan–U.S. security arrangement. According to the revisionists,
Japan has largely ignored its security responsibility at the same time that it
experienced industrial and technological growth—the free ride argument.
This situation, the revisionist argument intimates, somehow has given Japan more bargaining power than it should have on issues relating to bilateral trade. The 1995 DoD report on security in the East Asia–Pacific
region,[35] say the revisionists, has given Tokyo the assurance that Washington does not intend to change the alliance in a way that would provide it
with the political means or leverage to rectify bilateral trade problems.

Although the revisionists maintain that the existing security arrangement should end or markedly change and that either outcome will enable the United States to bargain more effectively on issues involving
bilateral trade, this position abruptly and inexplicably changes when we
are told that: "A threat to withdraw the [Seventh] fleet might provide
some useful bargaining leverage."[36] It is therefore unclear what the revi-

sionists actually want: Does U.S. bargaining power increase with the end or the major restructuring of the existing bilateral security relationship, or does Washington simply have to produce a threat to get Tokyo to make trade concessions? While the argument could be made that a threat to end the alliance or significantly restructure it could increase American bargaining power, this is certainly not the same as actually following through with the threat. If the existing security relationship were to end or undergo major changes, in other words, what leverage would the United States then have in trade matters with Japan? The revisionists provide no explanation of this critical point.

In any case, the empirical relevance of the revisionist perspective literally collapses in the case involving Japan's decision to develop surveillance satellites. Very shortly after North Korea lobbed a projectile over Japanese territory in August 1998, Tokyo announced its intention to develop surveillance satellites. Initially, Tokyo planned to develop the satellites domestically, exclusively with Japanese research and manufacturing expertise. Washington quickly rebuffed Tokyo's intention by emphasizing that Japan should purchase the satellites from the United States. If the revisionist argument was correct—that is, that the existence of the bilateral security alliance eliminates Washington's leverage when it comes to trade and economic matters—then Tokyo would have either completely ignored Washington's concerns by proceeding to develop the satellites domestically or the United States would have acquired Japanese compliance only by threatening to withdraw American forces. But that is not what happened. Tokyo was able to convince Washington that it was going to build the satellites at home; however, Tokyo also committed Japan to buying eleven different types of sophisticated technological parts from the United States.[37]

As we have seen above, what the revisionists totally ignore is that the existence of the bilateral security alliance has actually *increased* U.S. bargaining leverage when it comes to issues pertaining to trade. The very existence of the bilateral security arrangement has provided the United States with a perennial advantage in trade disputes. Japanese reliance on security from the United States has created a state of dependency, causing Tokyo, much more often than not, to succumb to Washington's trade demands.[38] This is much different than to posit, as the revisionists do, that by announcing its intention to remain militarily committed to the Asia–Pacific region, Washington has forfeited any hope of acquiring Japanese compliance on trade issues.

Analogous in one respect to the revisionist perspective is a variant argument of structural realism—the international relations theory that postulates that states either seek to become militarily powerful or concede to security alliances, for if they fail to do either of these, they must suffer the consequences. Adopting the name "mercantile realism," this argument emphasizes that Japan has consistently placed economic and technological concerns ahead of security matters. Japan's free ride on security, this argument strongly implies, makes it highly susceptible to pressure from the United States. Mercantile realism suggests, in other words, that Washington can leverage Tokyo's compliance because of Japan's inherent reluctance to become a military power not aligned with the United States. Thus, similar to part of the revisionist argument that speaks to the threat of ending the bilateral security relationship, mercantile realism suggests that Japanese compliance on economic, technological, and even military matters can be acquired through political pressure on Tokyo, given its dependence on the existing alliance.[39] However, mercantile realists differ from the revisionists in that they remain staunchly committed to realist propositions, and thus they see no need to end or restructure the existing security arrangements between the United States and Japan.

**The Nationalist View: The Need to Reconsider
the Security Alliance**

The August 1998 launching of a projectile by North Korea that crossed over Japan provided impetus to Japanese nationalism that began to surface after the Gulf War.[40] An important part of the nationalist perspective is the strong suggestion to reassess the security arrangement between the United States and Japan. However, this nationalist call to reconsider the security relationship with the United States is not a categorical rejection of the alliance but rather an appeal to "rethink" it. This perspective is directed at the public's perceptions and doubts of the bilateral security alliance and is therefore considerably more political than analytical. If at least some of the public does not find it appealing, then there is no longer a need to reconsider the dissolution of the security alliance. But as we will see in chapter 5, opinion polls have consistently shown that a notable proportion of the Japanese public has been uncertain about the need for the continuation of the bilateral security arrangement. Thus, this perspective has been able to attract some amount of attention because of its nationalistic appeal. However, there is presently little likelihood that it will gain serious attention, since it directly contravenes Japan's antimilitarist culture.

Because the basis of this perspective is rhetorical, its focus is not squarely on the abrogation of the bilateral security arrangement. The call to reconsider the bilateral security alliance is a way to both criticize the status quo and, if necessary, to accept it. However, the Cold War ended more than a decade ago, and it is hard to understand, as the nationalists do, why there is still a need to reconsider the Japan–U.S. security alliance. Since much time has passed, the decision should have been made as to whether or not a bilateral security alliance is still necessary.

A vociferous advocate of constitutional revision, especially of Article 9,[41] Shintaro Ishihara is the best-known proponent of the nationalist perspective. Formerly a Diet member and prominent figure in the Liberal Democratic Party, Ishihara was elected governor of Tokyo in April 1999. Ishihara previously received international recognition for the best selling book *A Japan That Can Say No.*[42] Originally written with Sony Corporation chairman Akio Morita, this book, as its title suggests, was critical of Japan's place in the bilateral relationship with the United States. According to Ishihara, although the bilateral security treaty has been beneficial to Japan, it does not really need the protection provided by the accord. Still, Ishihara also stresses that it would not be practical to cancel the bilateral security treaty abruptly. This, however, does not mean that Japan should not raise this subject, since the bilateral security treaty is a powerful diplomatic tool that Tokyo can use in its dialogue with Washington.

An important campaign promise made by Ishihara while he was running for governor was the return of the Yokota Air Base, which, he stressed, "well represents Japan's tolerance toward the United States." Not long after taking office, Ishihara announced his intention to seek the return of all eight U.S. military facilities in Tokyo.[43] This recent irksome behavior by Ishihara was not new to officials in Tokyo and Washington. For some time, Ishihara has advocated the view that Japan should be developing a security structure independent of the United States. In 1990, he argued:

> The time has come for Japan to tell the United States that we do not need American protection. Japan will protect itself with its own power and wisdom. This will require a strong commitment and will on our part. We

> can do it as long as there is a national consensus to do so. There may be
> some political difficulties at this point in forming this consensus. From
> both a financial and technological point of view, there are no barriers to
> accomplishing this goal in the near future. We can develop a more effec-
> tive and efficient defense capability at less than we are paying today.[44]

Several years later, during a 1998 interview, Ishihara stressed that
Japan "should move forward from the current situation in which the
SDF (Self-Defense Forces) is merely a support force to the U.S. forces,
and develop a military with an independent self-defense capability. [Ja-
pan] should be resolute and build an independent and strong defense-
oriented military to increase demand, without worrying about any
criticism that may come from outside."[45] Echoing Ishihara's words, another leading politician stressed that "Japan should strive for a more
independent security policy from that advocated by the United States.
There's a sense that we have become too dependent on America."[46]

Suggesting that nationalism has begun to permeate Japanese culture
is that many people recently attending an event at *Yasukuni Jinja* mark-
ing the end of the Pacific War[47] stressed that, while they believed that
Japan's prosperity has been linked to its alliance with the United States,
they abhor the fact that their nation must depend on America for defense. One naval veteran commented that: "My hope is that Japan can
take charge of its own affairs one day and not just be the kind of place
that catches the flu when America sneezes. Most of all I'd like to see
Japan take up its own defenses. But with all of the constraints binding us
today, that just seems impossible."[48]

Because of its militaristic and imperialist past, Japan has to worry about
much more than just verbal criticism from its East Asian neighbors. Japan's
past still raises too many unpleasant memories throughout the region.
Just the appearance of Japan's independent rearmament would send shock
waves throughout parts of Asia. Indeed, if either Beijing or Pyongyang
believed that Japan was fully pursing independent military capability,
existing regional tensions and problems would escalate very quickly. Right
now, any movement by Japan to increase the sophistication of its military
sends shock waves through East Asia and precipitates tension. When the
Japanese government approved the ¥25 trillion ($220 billion plus) five-
year defense plan in December 2000, Beijing and Pyongyang quickly
became alarmed, as ¥90 billion of this had been earmarked for four in-
flight refueling planes. These planes will extend Japanese military capa-

bilities and, as a researcher at the Defense Agency's National Institute for Defense Studies put it, moves Japan to a "more offensive defense [which] creates tension with the Chinese and Koreans."[49]

Tokyo's initial decision to build four surveillance satellites was based on the reasoning that this equipment would enable Japan to learn about the activities of the DPRK (Democratic People's Republic of Korea) without relying on the United States. This not only troubled Pyongyang, but Beijing also became quite upset by Tokyo's decision. Both Beijing and Pyongyang realized that in light of Japan's past military aggression, and given that the new defense guidelines with the United States would shortly lead to an enlargement of Japanese military responsibilities, Japan could eventually become an independent threat in the region. Thus, from the perspectives of officials in Beijing and Pyongyang, Tokyo's announcement that it planned to go ahead and build the surveillance satellites symbolized a decisive move toward military independence.

But Tokyo's decision worried not only Beijing and Pyongyang; Washington also became alarmed for two reasons. Because of the recent reaffirmation of the bilateral security alliance, Washington's major concern related to the procurement orders that American companies would lose if Japan domestically developed most of the surveillance satellites. Moreover, if Tokyo could do this with surveillance satellites, then it was possible that, while not abandoning the bilateral security alliance, it could do this with other defense equipment later.

The other reason for Washington's concern was directly related to security. Over the years, U.S. criticism of the Japanese free ride has been intended to push Tokyo to spend more on the military, not to create the impression that Japan was becoming an independent military power in the region. An official with Japan's Ministry of Foreign Affairs summarized what several observers, including a few in the United States, have seen as fledging Japanese nationalism with these words: "It won't do for us just to be on the receiving end of information if we are to demand that North Korea stop launching missiles. If we have our own satellites it will put us in a stronger position to deal with them."[50] Although not an official part of its Japanese policy, America's protection of Japan has had the benefit of minimizing fears in East Asia that Tokyo would push for rearmament independent of the United States. Washington's concern, then, was not a matter of distrust of Japan, fear of Japanese remilitarization, or worry that Tokyo would become a military competitor of the United States in East Asia. Rather, given Japan's militaristic past, Washington simply did not want to see an unnecessary elevation of trepidation in the region, particularly since, in light of Tokyo's long security association with the United States, this could conceivably spoil America's image as a good hegemon.

Symbolizing the recent surge in Japanese nationalism is the acceptance by the Diet in 1999 of *hinomaru*, the Japanese flag represented by the rising sun, and *kimigayo*, the national anthem. Both *hinomaru* and *kimigayo* existed during Japan's imperialist and militaristic past. For this reason, there is serious concern among the opposition in Japan that the legal recognition of *hinomaru* and *kimigayo* is sending the wrong signal to people, both at home and abroad.[51] There is no doubt that China and North Korea see the recognition of *hinomaru* and *kimigayo* as part of the larger nationalist effort by Japan to retrogress to its past behavior of overseas aggression.[52]

Japanese nationalist groups have been pushing hard for the reinterpretation of recent East Asian history. Proponents of nationalism, which includes policy-oriented groups and scholars, have succeeded in getting the central government to approve a controversial textbook for schoolchildren that depicts past Japanese military assaults against China and Korea in ways that legitimate these actions, rather than malign them.[53] Not only has this controversy upset the people of South Korea[54] and Seoul, which in April 2001 pulled its ambassador out of Japan for a few days to protest this matter,[55] but even more problematic because of untoward regional consequences, it has also strained relations with China[56] and North Korea.[57] For both Beijing and Pyongyang, these efforts represent more than just a reinterpretation of Japanese history; they signify a whitewashing of it and further raise fears of Japanese remilitarization. Adding momentum to revisionist efforts to rewrite history is the pop cultural work of Yoshinori Kobayashi, whose cartoon (*manga*) book, *On War*, has sold almost a million copies.[58] Through the medium of the cartoon, Kobayashi's work attempts to justify Japan's past military exploits.

The biggest concern associated with the nationalist perspective is that it creates the impression that Japan may want to consider developing nuclear weapons. This linkage between the possible Japanese acquisition of nuclear weapons and the need to rethink the security alliance is established by Shintaro Ishihara's argument that the belief that Japan falls under the U.S. nuclear umbrella is a myth. Ishihara stresses that there is no mention of nuclear deterrence in the mutual security treaty, though most Japanese remain misguided by their acceptance of the deterrence myth. Ishihara also argues that since Japan is not part of NORAD (North American Air Defense), a nuclear attack on Japan, and probably even Hawaii, would not be cause for Washington to retaliate. Because a nuclear deterrent for Japan does not exist but the myth does, the United States has been able to use this "illusory deterrent" to its advantage in bilateral economic negotiations.[59]

While it is true that the Treaty of Mutual Cooperation and Security between Japan and the United States of America does not explicitly speak of a nuclear deterrent for Japan, Article V of the treaty makes it perfectly clear that America would react militarily to an armed attack against Japan.[60] The 1978 Guidelines for Japan–U.S. Defense Cooperation and the more recent ones passed by the Japanese government in 1999 specifically address the nuclear deterrence issue. The 1978 guidelines state that: "The United States will maintain a nuclear deterrent capability," the same wording employed in the new defense guidelines.[61]

As the only country in the world to experience the devastation caused by nuclear weapons, Japan has long opposed their existence. However, despite widespread opposition in Japan to the existence of nuclear weapons, some Tokyo officials have at times ignored popular sentiment. In 1950, Prime Minister Shigeru Yoshida stated during a press conference that "Japan should develop atomic and hydrogen bombs to compete with the Soviet Union."[62] A recently declassified document revealed that when the Treaty of Mutual Cooperation and Security was revised in 1960 under Prime Minister Nobusuke Kishi (1957–1960), Tokyo agreed to a secret pact that allowed the United States, without the permission of the Japanese government, to transport nuclear weapons in Japan.[63] A few years later, in 1964, Prime Minister Eisaku Sato (1964–1972) gave some private thought to Japan's acquisition of nuclear weapons in the wake of China's successful nuclear testing.[64] In 1967, Sato promoted and the Japanese government adopted the three nonnuclear principles, which prohibit the possession, manufacture, or introduction of nuclear weapons in Japan. Two years later, according to a now declassified U.S. State Department document, Sato told the American ambassador to Japan, Alexis Johnson, that the three nonnuclear principles were "nonsense." This, however, did not stop Sato from accepting the Nobel Peace Prize in 1974, which he won partly because of his affirmation of the three nonnuclear principles.[65]

Even the adoption of the three nonnuclear principles by the Japanese government did not deter some determined Tokyo officials from rethinking Japan's nuclear weapons policy. During an interview with *Asahi Shimbun* published in September 2000, Yasuhiro Nakasone acknowledged that when he was director general of the Defense Agency in 1970, "I assembled a team of civilians and Defense Agency bureaucrats and had them carry out a study on whether Japan should possess nuclear weapons. I did this secretly. Since I advocated a nonnuclear policy, I wanted to verify whether this was correct or not." Nakasone, who, in addition to serving as director general of the Defense Agency, was prime minister from 1982 to 1987, was also asked during the interview if he knew about the 1960 secret nuclear weapons agreement between Washington and Tokyo when he occupied either of these offices. Nakasone said he did not, but indicated that former prime minister Nobusuke Kishi and former foreign minister Aiichiro Fujiyama probably did.[66] Whether Nakasone knew about the 1960 secret agreement is not as important as what surfaced three months later, in December 2000. An *Asahi Shimbun* article pointed out that a declassified document showed that while serving as director general of the Defense Agency in the Sato government, Nakasone commented during a 1970 meeting with U.S. defense secretary Melvin Laird that nuclear weapons could enter Japan.[67]

Long endorsing constitutional revision, politically conservative Nakasone's position on Japan's nuclear weapons policy privately catered to the nationalist position but publicly has remained consistent with the country's widespread antinuclear sentiment. While Nakasone recently indicated that he "may have made such a statement during my meeting with Laird,"[68] his public comments on nuclear weapons are quite different. In a 1998 article appearing in the *Japan Echo*, Nakasone indicated that "After being appointed director general of the Defense Agency in 1970, I repeatedly and explicitly declared that Japan would not acquire nuclear weapons."[69]

While most nationalists have been extremely careful not to make public statements that openly suggest that Japan should possess nuclear weapons, an exception to this occurred in fall 1999. Parliamentary vice minister of the Defense Agency, Shingo Nishimura, commented during an interview with a Japanese magazine that the Diet should deliberate on the important matter of the acquisition of nuclear weapons for the country. A member of the Jiyuto (Liberal) Party, like the celebrated nationalist Ichiro Ozawa, Nishimura's comment not only deeply offended most Japanese, but it also created angst in Beijing and Pyongyang. Facing significant public backlash, Nishimura, who had been in office for just a little more than two weeks, had little choice but to submit his resignation to Prime Minister Keizo Obuchi.[70]

Japan has the technological competence and enough plutonium to develop nuclear weapons of considerable destructive capability within a very short period.[71] Japan's possession of nuclear weapons—even those far less sophisticated than those now held by the nuclear powers—would immediately destabilize the Asia–Pacific region and literally devastate, perhaps permanently, relations between Tokyo and Beijing and Tokyo and Pyongyang. Because other nations are considerably more technologically advanced today than they were three decades ago, if Japan were to make the decision to become a nuclear power for defensive reasons, the arms race presently unfolding in the Asia–Pacific region would accelerate very quickly. The argument that it is possible that Japan will become a nuclear power is still raised from time to time. Just recently at the fourth UN Conference on Disarmament Issues held in Kyoto in July 1999, delegates considered the possibility that instability in the Asia–Pacific region may move Japan to acquire nuclear weapons.[72]

Thus, the nationalist-security perspective relies on two key reasons for keeping the discussion of Japan becoming an autonomous military power alive. The first is regional instability. North Korea, China, and the recent nuclear tests conducted by India and Pakistan provide "proof" of regional instability and suggest that Japan may need to develop nuclear weapons. The second reason is the assertion that the U.S. nuclear shield does not protect Japan.

We have already seen that it is not correct to argue that Japan does not fall under the U.S. nuclear umbrella. A decision by Japan even to begin studying the possibility of developing nuclear weapons would immediately be interpreted as a serious act of brinkmanship and give the appearance that it would soon violate its antinuclear norms. Similarly, a decision to reconsider the necessity of the bilateral security alliance in conjunction with a plan to develop independent military capability would quickly destabilize the entire Asia–Pacific region. Japan's historical record of military aggression would unleash an inordinate amount of regional suspicion and tension. Should it ever be made into policy, the nationalist perspective on security would give the immediate impression—and impressions do matter—that Japan has decided to abandon its nonmilitarized culture based on nonnuclear and nonaggressive norms and instead rely on the threat of settling its differences by employing sophisticated military solutions.

Policy moves recently made in Tokyo to consider constitutional change further raise regional suspicion of Japan's inchoate nationalism. In 1999, Tokyo authorized two committees in each parliamentary house to begin the study of prospective constitutional changes in the year 2000. The principal target of the nationalists is the revision of Article 9, the war-renouncing clause in the Japanese constitution.[73] Nationalists want to revise Article 9 so that Japan can participate more fully in UN peace-keeping operations, thereby becoming a "normal country" and, of even greater immediate concern, because they want Japanese forces to be permitted to cooperate with the United States in regional military activities without constitutional constraint. While many Japanese have supported the revision of the Japanese constitution, most have not advocated amending Article 9, since this would be a big step taken in the direction of Japanese remilitarization. Nonetheless, the important matter of constitutional change is admittedly receiving more attention today than it was in the past.[74]

Fear of constitutional change extends beyond the geographical perimeters of Japan. Serious discussions in the Japanese Diet on the topic of revising Article 9 could easily become a catalyst for a precipitous deterioration in Sino-Japanese relations. In addition to recent efforts to revitalize the Japan–U.S. security alliance, Beijing remains very troubled by Tokyo's reluctance to provide the Chinese people with a full apology relating to Japan's past military aggression against their nation.[75] As we have already seen, Beijing is paying very close attention to the emergence of conservative politics in Japan, fearing that it is attempting to "whitewash history."[76] Any change in Article 9 would immediately be perceived in Beijing as a clear signal that Japan has succumbed to nationalist forces, making Japanese remilitarization a fait accompli.

Concern is also running very high in Pyongyang on the important matter of constitutional change in Japan. Pyongyang is closely monitoring any movement in Japan that it suspects would lead to constitutional revision. Pyongyang has at least tentatively concluded that there is currently a concerted right-wing effort in Japan to remove Article 9 from the constitution so that there will be no legal restriction to Japanese overseas aggression. Pyongyang stresses that Article 9 "has become a cumbersome and unnecessary thing for the Japanese reactionaries [nationalists] now that they have become a military power through militarization and rounded off preparations for overseas aggression in a bid to realize their old dream of 'Greater East Asia Co-Prosperity Sphere' at any cost."[77] Moreover, Pyongyang regularly lambastes Tokyo for failing to acknowledge past Japanese aggression and crimes on the Korean Peninsula. Indeed, part of the reason for the stalling of normalization talks between Japan and North Korea during 2000, according to Pyongyang, was Tokyo's reluctance to provide a full apology for its colonization of the Korean Peninsula.

Security Policy and the Japanese Left

Japanese socialists' and communists' positions on Japan's security alliance with the United States have not been uniform. The following is meant to serve as a brief look at where the Japanese left stands today on key security issues.

The Social Democratic Party

Despite its long postwar opposition to both Japan's Self Defense Forces and the bilateral security treaty with the United States, advocating "unarmed neutrality" in the place of the latter, the Social Democratic Party officially changed its position on these issues in 1994. For years, the socialist party was Japan's major opposition to the Liberal Democratic Party, which had controlled Japanese politics since the 1950s and which had strongly supported the bilateral security alliance. After playing a leading part in forcing the Liberal Democratic Party out of power in 1993, the socialist party successfully maneuvered to get its chairman Tomiichi Murayama into the prime minister's office in June 1994. Perhaps in response to its waning public support, indicated by the significant loss of seats held by socialists in the lower house as a result of the July 1993 election, the socialist party radically changed its position on both the legality of the Self Defense Forces and Japan's security treaty with the United States. In September 1994, just a few months after Murayama became prime minister, the socialist party's platform recognized the constitutionality of the Self Defense Forces and declared its support for the bilateral security treaty.[78] The Social Democratic Party, however, has remained consistent in its support for Article 9. As it has in the past, the party sees a continuing need to prevent Japan from becoming involved in aggressive military activities and believes that preserving Article 9 is the best way to do this.

The Japanese Communist Party

Like the socialists, the Japanese Communist Party, which became a legal organization after the Pacific War, remains committed to Article 9. Unlike the socialists, however, the communists' position today is that Article 9 makes clear that the Self Defense Forces are unconstitutional. It is because of Article 9, say the communists, that Japan has been kept out of foreign wars for years, despite the political efforts by other Japanese parties to undermine it. The Japanese Communist Party's position is that Article 9 still serves as a model for peace and nonaggression to the rest of the world. The party argues that no further violation of Article 9 should be tolerated today, that is, recognition of an interpretation of it that permits Japanese forces to be sent overseas. The Japanese Communist Party opposes Japan's security treaty with the United States, arguing that its abrogation will free the Self Defense Forces from the control of Washington. Once this occurs, the communists maintain, Japan will be free in time to disband the Self Defense Forces "based on the people's consensus," since it will be a nonaligned nation literally posing no armed threat to foreign countries.[79]

A Primer: Global Disarmament and the Bilateral Security Alliance

The very existence of the bilateral security alliance puts Japan in a contradictory position. Decades-old Japanese arguments concerning the need for global disarmament and the complete abolition of nuclear weapons manifestly contravene the fact that Japan still stands underneath the U.S. security umbrella. Japan's postwar history has been one in which a decided culture of antimilitarism has prevailed. Integral to this culture has been the incontrovertible norms that have sustained an antinuclear sentiment.[80] Although it could have easily attained the status of a nuclear weapons power, Japan has unreservedly rejected this choice.

But at the same time, Tokyo has consistently decided to remain in a security alliance with the United States. Renewed in 1960, despite significant public opposition,[81] the U.S.–Japan Security Treaty has survived the Cold War. Because of Japan's economic power and technological prowess, when the Cold War ended it became internationally evident that it had to assume a larger global role. Refusing to shed its pacifist past and beset by problems related to the bilateral security relationship,

Japan simultaneously gave attention to the importance of a stronger and revitalized United Nations, including the implementation of its collective security mechanisms, in the aftermath of the Cold War.[82] As a result, Japan now faces the problem of retaining its pacifist principles—which most prominently include its antimilitarist and antinuclear culture that has existed simultaneously with the belief that the United Nations should become a functional international security organization —and continuing to succumb to the forces of remilitarization, at least some of which comes from the United States.

For Japan to accept a significant international leadership responsibility in the present period and realign with its historical commitment to renounce war, encourage a strong UN security system, and help in the abolition of all nuclear weapons, it must move away from its security alliance with the United States. Similar to the way the security alliance caused Tokyo to follow Washington's foreign-policy lead throughout the Cold War, more recently it has prevented Japan from giving serious attention to bona fide UN security and the elimination of all nuclear weapons. The security alliance keeps Japan in a follower status, leaving very little room for it to develop an international position that is compatible with a large part of its cultural disposition.

Moreover, Japan's security alliance with the United States has prevented it from forming stronger relationships than it presently experiences with some countries in East Asia. Certainly Chinese and Japanese public perceptions of bilateral relations between China and Japan have not grown stronger in recent years. Despite mutual state visits by high-level Japanese and Chinese leaders in 1998 that somewhat improved communication ties between Beijing and Tokyo, most people in China and Japan do not believe that bilateral relations between their countries are strong—a feeling that has actually increased from the recent past. A 1999 Gallup-*Yomiuri Shimbun* survey showed that only a third of the Japanese respondents think that China and Japan have a good relationship; for Chinese respondents, the figure was 17 percent. This represented a significant decline for both groups (34 percent for Chinese respondents and 32 percent for Japanese respondents) from a survey conducted in 1988. The 1999 survey also showed that one-half of the Chinese respondents held an unfavorable view of Japan, compared to 46 percent of the Japanese respondents who felt this way about China. These figures on unfavorable beliefs relating to the Sino-Japanese bilateral relationship, compared to a similar poll conducted in 1995, represent an increase of 12 percent for Chinese respondents and over 10 percent for Japanese respondents.[83] The unfavorable perceptions between China and Japan are especially interesting, given that both nations rely very heavily on each other for trade—Japan is China's biggest trade market and, after the United States, China is Japan's next largest trade market. Although it is true that the Japan–U.S. bilateral security alliance is not the only obstacle to a stronger Sino-Japanese relationship, it has certainly been a major one, particularly since 1996. To argue that the recent steps taken by Washington and Tokyo to strengthen their bilateral security alliance have played no part in the opinion that the Chinese now have of Japan is tantamount to completely discounting its adverse effects on regional perceptions.

The bilateral security relationship has a constraining effect on Japan for two major reasons. First, the bilateral security alliance prevents Japan from realizing an independent foreign policy, most especially one that is consistent with its historical and present interests in global disarmament and a strong UN security system.[84] Japan's continuing interests in global disarmament and its post–Cold War commitment to strengthening the United Nations, including expanding the Security Council, cannot be effectively implemented as long as it remains connected to a regional security arrangement with the United States, which has been increasingly distancing itself from this organization for the past several years. Japan's defense policy rests on three interrelated pillars: (1) its peace constitution, (2) the charter of the United Nations, and (3) the security treaty with the United States.[85] The bilateral security alliance, which includes keeping Japan under America's nuclear umbrella, ostensibly interferes with any serious and sustained global leadership responsibilities Tokyo would choose to undertake that are completely consistent with the amalgamation of the first two pillars of its defense policy.

Another problem is that because the United States continues to prod Japan to strengthen its commitment to the bilateral security alliance, Japanese remilitarization continues to evolve. Especially in the last few years, this incremental remilitarization has given some momentum to nationalist forces, which would prefer the development of Japanese military power independent of the United States. Thus, the longer the bilateral security alliance remains in place, the more difficult it will be to dissipate Japanese nationalism. Incremental remilitarization combined with nationalist forces attempting to persuade the Japanese public of the need for constitutional revision portends the prospect of a substantial alteration in the norms sustaining Japan's antimilitaristic and antinuclear culture. Protestation by nationalists appeared, of all places, on August 6, 2001, at the memorial service commemorating the fifty-sixth anniversary of the atomic bombing of Hiroshima.

Second, the bilateral security alliance makes it exceedingly difficult for Japan to develop close and enduring relationships with all of its Asian neighbors. The threat structure symbolized in the Japan–U.S. security alliance means that distrust and uncertainty continue to pervade parts of the Asia–Pacific region. The Japan–U.S. security relationship is a *military alliance* that is perceived as a threat by China, North Korea, and increasingly, Russia. The security alliance is obviously exclusionary and assumes the existence of oppositional parties that wrongly perceive and interpret regional affairs. The security alliance between Tokyo and Washington appears formidable to the opposition. Japan's defense spending in 1998 amounted to $36.99 billion. This was about the same as China's military spending in 1998,[86] which was $36.71 billion and well above North Korea's $6 billion military budget. That only a part of the United States' $266 billion military budget is directly invested in Northeast Asia does not address the fact that more could be easily transferred to this region.[87] Typically ignored by those supporting the continuation of the bilateral security alliance is that both Beijing and Pyongyang feel threatened when looking at the reality of Japanese and U.S. power, a force that is augmented, at least in some scenarios, by South Korea's $14 billion military budget.

This final perspective discussed in this chapter emphasizes the immediate need to end the Japan–U.S. security alliance. This perspective has not been created out of thin air. Rather, it is based on existing Japanese antimilitarist and antinuclear sentiments and positions on defense and foreign policy sans the security alliance with the United States. This perspective seeks the effective activation of international and regional security institutions, such as the United Nations and ARF (ASEAN Regional Forum), to promote security. Paradigmatically, therefore, this perspective moves security up the evolutionary scale, since it eliminates hegemonic ambitions and the inclinations of states to settle disputes by utilizing realist responses.

5

How the Japanese Public Views Security

The vast majority of analysts of the Japan–U.S. security alliance have relied on the assumption that it continues to be politically beneficial for Japan and its people. The assumption that a Cold War security relationship needs to be maintained in a post–Cold War environment is unreasonable and inconsistent with current political conditions. It is inconsistent with current conditions because the end of the Cold War signified the demise of the Soviet Union, the military superpower that was the political catalyst for the creation of the Japan–U.S. security alliance and therefore eliminated the putative raison d'être of the relationship. Simply to shift the security alliance's justification, as Washington and Tokyo did in the 1996 Joint Declaration and then later with the 1997 Guidelines for Defense Cooperation, introduces the plausible criticism of an American attempt, with Japanese support, to establish regional hegemonic control over the East Asia–Pacific area. This assumption is unreasonable because it has led to the derivation of four propositions that are then parochially examined to justify why the Japan–U.S. security alliance must continue to exist. These propositions are as follows:

- The United States is the world's only superpower, which necessitates its maintaining, under existing conditions, Japan's protectorate status
- Japan is a pacifist country, which means that it should be afforded protection by a righteous superpower

Table 5.1

Japanese Views of Threat from Soviet Union/Russia, 1990–1993
(numbers represent percentage of respondents)

	A great deal	A fair amount	Not very much	None at all
May 1990	14	49	21	3
June 1991	12	49	22	3
September 1991	16	40	34	5
November 1991	6	43	34	2
May 1993	6	41	34	4

Sources: Survey data were obtained from the Roper Center for Public Opinion Research, University of Connecticut.

Notes: All surveys were sponsored by the United States Information Agency. Interviews for the May 1990 survey were conducted by Central Research Services between May 16 and May 23, 1990; for the June 1991 survey, interviews were conducted by the Shin Joho Center between June 6 and June 12, 1991; for the September 1991 survey, interviews were conducted by Video Research on September 8 and 9, 1991; for the November 1991 survey, interviews were conducted by the Shin Joho Center between October 3 and November 6, 1991; and for the May 1993 survey, interviews were conducted by Central Research Services between May 18 and May 25, 1993.

Interviewers asked respondents one of two questions: (1) How much danger do you think the military power of the Soviet Union poses to Japan's security? a great deal, a fair amount, not very much, or none at all; or, (2) How much of a threat, if any, do you think the Soviet Union now poses to the national security of Japan? a great deal, a fair amount, not very much, or none at all. In these five surveys, an average of approximately 13 percent responded "don't know."

- It is imperative that the United States remain militarily committed to the East Asia–Pacific region, because this area of the world is potentially unstable
- A fully rearmed Japan would jeopardize regional stability, as its neighbors would become immediately suspicious of its intentions

Proposition 1. While the United States is now the only military superpower in the world, it does not ipso facto have to maintain Japan's protectorate status. The only obligation that the United States has in this regard comes from the mutual security treaty and other bilateral security arrangements. These arrangements reflect a formalized security relationship designed by policy makers in both countries. If Japan were invaded, attacked, or had its sovereignty seriously threatened, then the United States *and* other nations would have an obligation—indeed, a moral responsibility—to help Japan, similar to the way the world community responded to Iraq's invasion of Kuwait in 1990. Thus, formal security arrangements should not be depicted as tantamount to the responsibility of a superpower, since the two are quite separate.

Proposition 2. While it is true that Japan is a pacifist nation, it cannot be considered pacifist in an absolute sense. Having one of the largest military budgets in the world does not make Japan an absolute pacifist nation. For these reasons, Japan does not require military protection provided by the United States. Japan's constitution has been interpreted as preventing it from adopting an offensive military posture but not from providing an adequate defense of the nation.[1] Japan is considerably stronger than the majority of countries in the world, therefore its defense capabilities are adequate for the nation's protection. What the United States provides over and above Japan's domestic defense capabilities is a nuclear shield. However, because of the prodding effect that nuclear weapons create, that is, by encouraging other nations to acquire them, a nuclear shield provided by the United States to Japan in the post–Cold War period does not amount to good political sense, especially if the concern is with international peace and security.

Besides Japan's domestic defensive capabilities, changing global conditions since the end of the Cold War have virtually eliminated the need for Tokyo to depend on the United States for protection from either Russia or China. Public opinion surveys conducted in Japan between mid-1990 and mid-1993 show a clear trend of decreased concern about a military threat from the Soviet Union, and later from Russia. (See Table 5.1.) In the fall of 1998, *Asahi Shimbun* conducted a national survey on Japanese perceptions of a Russian military threat. Although answer selections were a little different in this more recent survey from those in previous ones, the results were very similar. Fifty-two percent of the respondents said that Russia posed some military threat to Japan (roughly equivalent to the categories "a great deal" and "a fair amount" listed in Table 5.1), 39 percent indicated no threat, and 9 percent gave another answer or did not reply.[2] We can reasonably conclude from these surveys that compared to the time when a Cold War environment prevailed, today fewer Japanese believe that Russia is a military threat to Japan and more think that it does not represent a danger. Moreover, in recent years Russo-Japanese relations have generally improved. For example, Japan has been playing a leading role in helping Russia dispose of nuclear weapons and materials from the Cold War and has helped displaced Russian military scientists to convert their talents to useful civilian purposes.[3]

While China poses no realistic military threat to Japan in the foresee-able future, Beijing does feel threatened by the Japan–U.S. security alli-ance, specifically in regard to how Japan will react to a confrontation between the United States and China that involves Taiwan. Responding to the passage of bills related to the new Guidelines for Defense Coop-eration by Japan's Lower House in late April 1999, the Chinese Foreign Ministry stated that they could "adversely affect regional security."[4]

Despite the strengthening of the Japan–U.S. security alliance in recent years, Sino-Japanese relations have shown some symbolic improvement.[5] However, this does not mean that there is not much more room for growth between Tokyo and Beijing. Indeed, the Japan–U.S. security alliance it-self is a major impediment to a better Sino-Japanese relationship.

Very important to Japanese security is the fact that Beijing officially has maintained that "As early as the 1960s, China unilaterally under-took not to be the first to use nuclear weapons and not to use or threaten to use nuclear weapons against non-nuclear states."[6] Japan finds it reas-suring that China has recently commended Germany and Canada's de-cision to encourage NATO to relinquish the policy relating to the first use of nuclear weapons.[7] But there remains some lingering distrust in Tokyo, among military and nonmilitary officials alike, about Beijing's objectives. This distrust helps legitimize Tokyo's security alliance with the United States, which in turn causes Beijing to see Japanese pacifism today as little more than fading symbolism, a remnant of its defeat in the Pacific War. Still, the Japanese public does not see China as a major threat to their country. While 9 percent of the respondents to a 1998 *Asahi Shimbun* survey indicated that they viewed China as a major threat to Japan, 55 percent believed that it was a minor threat and nearly one-third (31 percent) said that it was not a threat at all to their country.[8]

The biggest security threat currently perceived by Japan is North Korea. A *Yomiuri Shimbun* survey conducted in the fall of 1997 found that 69 percent of Japanese respondents, the largest proportion, believed that North Korea could become a military threat to Japan, followed by 32 percent, China; 23 percent, Russia; and the United States and the Middle East, 15 percent.[9] The Japan–U.S. alliance does not eliminate perceived threat and therefore does not make the Japanese people feel secure, particularly in regard to North Korea. Although North Korea could possibly develop nuclear weapons, there is currently no evidence that it has such a capability. However, this is not what the majority of the Japanese public believes. Since at least the early 1990s, much of the

Japanese public has felt that the development of nuclear weapons in North Korea was imminent. Opinion surveys conducted in Japan between 1991 and 1993 indicated that over 60 percent of the respondents in each poll believed that North Korea would develop nuclear weapons within three years.[10] An opinion survey conducted in Japan in 1994 revealed three interesting findings: 60 percent of the respondents thought that North Korea was a threat to Japanese security; 94 percent of the respondents believed that North Korea already possessed nuclear weapons; and 78 percent said that even if North Korea has nuclear weapons, they would still oppose Japan's developing nuclear weapons.[11] Thus, despite the widespread belief that North Korea is a threat to Japan, the Japanese public still does not support the country's possession of nuclear weapons.

This is in large part due to the existence of the three non-nuclear principles. The Japanese public's support of these principles—that Japan will not develop, possess, or introduce nuclear weapons into the country—remains strong. A 1991 survey showed that over 80 percent of the Japanese public gave their support to the three non-nuclear principles, 63 percent of the respondents strongly agreed with them, and another 18 percent somewhat agreed with them.[12] A *Yomiuri Shimbun* survey showed that 80 percent of the respondents indicated that they believe that Japan will not possess nuclear weapons in the future.[13] Indicative of the Japanese sentiment about extending the effects of these principles internationally, an *Asahi Shimbun* survey conducted in the fall of 1998 found that 78 percent of the respondents felt that all countries that possess nuclear weapons should destroy them and that there should be no exceptions to this.[14]

The major threat that Japan faces from North Korea today stems from the fact that Pyongyang believes that Japanese defense policy blindly supports U.S. hegemonic objectives. This makes Tokyo, like Washington—with which it is aligned in a security alliance—a potential aggressor that intends to undermine DPRK socialism.[15] Not only does North Korea perceive itself as vulnerable to military aggression from the United States, Japan, and South Korea, it is also consumed by the belief that U.S. nuclear weapons in South Korea have made the DPRK susceptible to nuclear attack for many years.[16] Pyongyang has also emphasized recently the "double standard" evident in the American-led security policy in the East Asia–Pacific region, a policy it sees as fully acceptable to Japan. Pyongyang has argued that while the United States complained loudly in August 1998 when North Korea launched a missile that flew over Japanese territory, it failed to rebuke South Korea when it fired off a Hyonmu missile in April 1999.[17]

It is important to emphasize that Pyongyang is not likely to rebuff what it sees as well-meaning Japanese efforts to improve bilateral relations. Expanding economic relations would benefit North Korea as well as Japan. An expansion of bilateral economic activity would open the door for Japanese technology transfers to North Korea, especially if security relations between the countries improved to the point of mutual trust.[18] Under these conditions, Japanese Official Development Assistance could be used to promote North Korean disarmament. In this kind of regional environment, Pyongyang would welcome a cooperative effort between Tokyo and Beijing to initiate a global disarmament process that most prominently included the complete elimination of all nuclear weapons. Pyongyang has recently emphasized its desire to see a nuclear-free world. Pyongyang has even encouraged Japan to pay attention to the pacifist desire of its people to eliminate nuclear weapons.[19]

However, because of both the security alliance between Tokyo and Washington and the strained Japanese-DPRK relationship, Pyongyang largely dismisses Japan's pacifism, seeing it merely as a way to deflect attention from its real objective: to rearm and reinvade the Korean Peninsula. From Pyongyang's perspective, the existence of the bilateral security alliance hardly makes Japan a pacifist nation, given the size of its defense budget and its command of advanced technologies. Adding even more to Pyongyang's uneasiness with the security alliance, since it presumably has strengthened Japan's military responsibilities in the East Asia–Pacific region, is the memory of the atrocities committed in Korea by Japanese troops in the past.[20] By remaining under America's nuclear shield, Japan is arguably prodding North Korea to develop advanced weapons systems, specifically those that will enable it to counteract TMD (theater missile defense). Thus, like Beijing, Pyongyang remains suspicious of Japanese pacifism and maintains that the U.S.–Japan security alliance has no place in the post–Cold War world, save to promote regional hegemony.

The argument that because of its national commitment to renounce war Japan needs American military protection does not really correspond to what many Japanese people think about this issue. Since the end of the Cold War, many Japanese have not been convinced that the U.S. military would defend their country in the event of a national security problem. Three surveys sponsored by the United States Information Agency during the early 1990s each showed a large proportion of Japanese respondents lacking some amount of confidence in the American commitment to defend Japan. This is important, because the United States' military commitment to Japan had been formally established for four decades by this time. A 1990 survey showed that when asked how sure they were about the United States' willingness to defend Japan if a security problem arose, 42 percent of the respondents expressed a lack of confidence (35 percent indicated not very much and 7 percent answered none at all). Given also that 11 percent of the respondents said that they did not know, this uncertainty combined with the expressed lack of confidence that the U.S. military would defend Japan is not too different from the 47 percent who felt sure that Washington would assist their country in a time of crisis (43 percent indicating a fair amount of assurance and 4 percent a great deal).[21] Similarly, a 1991 survey found that 39 percent of the respondents were not especially confident that the U.S. military would defend Japan (34 percent answering not very much, and 5 percent saying not at all). Although 51 percent of the respondents did express some amount of confidence in American military assistance (6 percent indicating a great deal and most, 46 percent, replying a fair amount), the survey also showed that 8 percent answered that they did not know.[22] A 1993 survey showed that 40 percent of the respondents were not convinced that America would be willing to defend Japan in a security crisis (34 percent saying that they were not very confident and 6 percent indicating no confidence at all). While 52 percent of the respondents expressed some amount of confidence in America's willingness to defend Japan (5 percent answering a great deal and most, 47 percent, indicating a fair amount), 8 percent did not know.[23] Recent survey data indicate that Japanese confidence in the United States' commitment to defend Japan is far from overwhelming. A 1999 *Asahi Shimbun* survey showed that only 31 percent of Japanese respondents believe that U.S. troops are in Japan to protect their country.[24]

Proposition 3. The end of the Cold War created a huge problem for U.S. policy makers in the Asia–Pacific region. With the Soviet Union gone, and with it the presumption of Soviet military adventurism, the bilateral security alliances the United States had with Australia, the Philippines, Thailand, South Korea, and Japan appeared to be in jeopardy. By 1992 the Department of Defense had officially identified the justification for the continuation of these bilateral security alliances: "Of the

five remaining Communist regimes in the world, four are in East Asia—
the People's Republic of China, Vietnam, North Korea and Laos."[25] Only
Cuba is outside the East Asian region. In its 1998 report, the Department
of Defense once again stressed the continuing need for the security alliances that it has had in the Asia–Pacific region, the most important of
which is the U.S.–Japan security relationship. At the same time, the
United States made a commitment to maintain approximately 100,000
military personnel in the Asia–Pacific region, the same number that it
had retained in the area in previous years.[26] Approximately two-fifths of
these U.S. troops are in Japan. According to recent *Asahi Shimbun* data,
38 percent of Japanese respondents think that American troops are in
their country to fulfill U.S. global military objectives and, different from
the views held by Americans, as will be shown below, 19 percent believe the purpose is to prevent Japan from becoming a military power.[27]
With less than a third of the respondents to this survey thinking that
American military forces are in Japan to defend the country, as indicated above, it is likewise hard to argue convincingly that the people of
Japan overwhelmingly view the bilateral alliance as guaranteeing the
security of the East Asian region. In fact, a *Yomiuri Shimbun* survey that
asked only those individuals who thought the U.S.–Japan Security Treaty
was beneficial to their country (57 percent of the total) to choose three
selections from a list of six found that the most commonly identified
answer, which was acknowledged by 54 percent of the respondents, was
to maintain solid relations with the United States. This hardly conveys
the meaning that the treaty brings security to East Asia or Japan. While
the answer to help to maintain regional stability was the second most
commonly made selection, with 50 percent of the respondents making
this choice, the point is that just as many people did not see any connection between the security treaty and regional stability.[28] What is more,
there is no way of knowing how many people who believe the alliance
has brought stability to the region have been influenced by Tokyo's position on this issue and by the fact that the security treaty has been an
integral part of Japanese culture for decades. Inextricably connected,
both of these facts support the impression that regional stability is syn-
onymous with the security treaty.

Perhaps to a greater degree than Tokyo, Washington has been more
suspicious of China's military objectives. Academics have not been reluctant to warn U.S. policy makers of the potential security problems
that loom in China.[29] Some arguments—for example, China's rapid eco-

nomic growth creates the potential for it to pursue military options that it could not consider with a slower growing or a stagnant economy—have caused U.S. policy makers to listen attentively. An economically powerful China with a well-developed military may begin to pursue hegemonic objectives, which could lead Beijing to challenge the U.S. presence aggressively in the East Asia–Pacific region. Accordingly, China must be carefully watched, because it is possible that Beijing may feel compelled to test the strength of the Japan–U.S. security relationship in the future.[30] Allegations that China stole U.S. nuclear secrets in 1999 further strained Sino-American relations and led to additional speculation that Beijing is seeking to challenge the United States.

President Jiang Zemin's visit to Japan in late 1998 provided a reasonable amount of optimism that bilateral relations between Beijing and Tokyo had now been put on a smoother track than in the past. A few months later President Jiang called on statesmen from both China and Japan to avoid being critical of the other nation's policies so that a strong and permanent friendship could be built and maintained well into the following century.[31] The Japanese people have a positive view of China second only to their view of the United States. According to a survey supported by the prime minister's office, 43.2 percent of the respondents "have generally positive feelings" toward the United States, while 36.3 percent felt this way about China.[32] Still, too many Japanese have an unfavorable view of China today, something that can change in the future only by responsible government action. The territorial dispute between China and Japan over the Senkaku/Diaoyu Islands is not likely to erupt into a major problem, at least not by itself, anytime soon. Apart from the failure to come to a satisfactory resolution on the history issue, currently the only significant bilateral problem between China and Japan is the Japanese security alliance with the United States. Beijing cannot understand how both the United States and Japan can make a commitment to a one China policy but supposedly be willing to use the bilateral security alliance to protect Taiwan.

To argue that the stability of the Asia–Pacific area depends on the Japan–U.S. security alliance, as most analysts do,[33] dignifies the military horse but ignores the cartload of political problems that have beset the region since the 1950s. Today, by unnecessarily exacerbating mistrust between nations, the Japan–U.S security alliance compounds regional problems. Since China and North Korea feel that each has been targeted by the security arrangement, the alliance itself is responsible for regional instability. Military spending in the East Asia–Pacific area has been high. There has been much concern about China's growing military budget and North Korea's missile development. The possible introduction of a U.S.–Japan TMD system into the East Asia–Pacific area has been interpreted by China and North Korea as a catalyst for a regional arms race. TMD will not make Beijing and Pyongyang politically docile; rather, they will become even more inclined than they are presently to seek ways to circumvent what they perceive as an arms buildup by the United States and Japan. Although Moscow did not make much of a fuss about the continuation of the Japan–U.S. security alliance after the end of the Cold War, the strengthened military arrangement and especially TMD have made it highly suspicious of Washington and Tokyo's objectives in East Asia.

Proposition 4. There is a widespread, albeit repressed, opinion in the United States that without the Japan–U.S. security alliance, Japanese rearmament would be inevitable. For this reason, it is assumed that the bilateral security alliance must be maintained and that an American military presence in Japan is necessary. Contrasting sharply with the Japanese respondents' views indicated above, a survey conducted jointly by the *Asahi Shimbun* and Louis Harris and Associates in March 1999 revealed the following about the opinions of Americans on U.S. military presence in Japan. Forty-nine percent of the Americans interviewed in the survey said that U.S. troops need to remain in Japan to prevent it from becoming a regional military threat once again (compared to 19 percent for the Japanese respondents); 34 percent thought that troops in Japan are necessary to help the United States fulfill its global military strategy; and just 12 percent think that the troops were there to protect Japan.[34]

Given its aggression in Asia in the past, many of Japan's neighbors also do not want to see it rearm. For many countries in the Asia–Pacific region, Japan's security alliance with the United States prevents the reemergence of a Japanese military threat. Even though China and North Korea oppose the continued existence of the bilateral security relationship, there is an unstated understanding that Japanese military restraint is a possible outcome of the alliance. But Beijing and Pyongyang also recognize that the alliance has been encouraging incremental Japanese rearmament and that it is conceivable that at some point Japan could choose to break from the security alliance with the United States. An independent and rearmed Japan would be unacceptable to Beijing and Pyongyang, since to them it would portend serious security problems in East Asia.

What matters almost as much as whether a militarized Japan would break from the security alliance is the perception that it is rearming. Tokyo's recent efforts to renew its commitment to the security alliance with the United States have already alarmed China and North Korea. Lurking in the background is the dialogue that is being advanced by Japanese nationalists about considering constitutional revision that would alter Article 9—the war-renouncing clause. But concern about a Japanese military buildup is not peculiar only to Beijing and Pyongyang. The Asia–Pacific area as a whole would become very uncomfortable if it were clear that Japan was attempting once again to become a regional military power, even if allied with the United States. Russia, for example, would have to rethink its improved relationship with Japan. Moscow would be unwilling to accept Japan as a growing regional power, since its relatively strong technology base used for military development would pose a threat to its neighbors, including Russia. Moscow would be sure to reason that unrestrained military development by Japan would precipitate an arms race. Given its current economic problems, an arms race is definitely something that Moscow wants to avoid.

While there is strong sentiment in the United States and in the Asia–Pacific region that the bilateral security alliance serves to check Japan's military ambitions, ironically it is not restraining Japanese rearmament. Rather, the alliance has been encouraging increased Japanese involvement in regional security affairs and helping to advance the position of nationalists in Japan who have long sought a stronger military apparatus for their country. The more Japan commits itself to the security alliance with the United States, the more it will become involved in developing its military. Increasing involvement in the bilateral security alliance will make it difficult for Japan to convince Beijing, and certainly Pyongyang, that its military efforts are innocuous. Creating much angst in North Korea is Tokyo's recent effort to raise the status of the Japanese Defense Agency to a ministry, something that Pyongyang sees as inconsistent with Japan's commitment to the renunciation of war. A deeper Japanese involvement in the bilateral security alliance is likely to engender additional military response by Beijing and Pyongyang.

Shaping Japanese Views on Security

The major problem that all industrialized countries face in the area of national security, which is saturated with patriotism, is that it is formulated almost exclusively by policy makers.[35] People want security; however, policy makers may also be interested in power and party ideology. While the citizens of a country have opinions on national security and may occasionally protest a detested policy, the normal mode, even when there is noticeable public disagreement, is for them to accept the state of affairs as defined by officials. This is partly because it is hard for people to assess the external threat that their nation faces and partly because of the political anomie that pervades life in modern industrial societies. Citizens are largely—and for too many, totally—dependent on the domestic media, which rely heavily on policy makers, for their views on national security. Given the strategic positions that policy makers hold and because of the information that they have access to, they directly and indirectly affect—and when necessary attempt to manipulate—public opinion related to national security. Dialogue relating to national security therefore typically occurs among policy makers and among political parties and factions. Serious dialogue does not take place between the people and policy makers. Moreover, most policy makers too often opt for the status quo in matters of national security, or at least they are unwilling to move too far from traditional positions.

This was evident when Tomiichi Murayama, a leading socialist party statesman, became prime minister of Japan in 1994. While in office, Murayama and his party acknowledged the constitutionality of Japan's Self Defense Forces (*nihonjieitai*) and accepted the Japanese bilateral security treaty with the United States—two issues that socialists had opposed for years but which remained central to the political position of the long-dominant Liberal Democratic Party. What Murayama confronted was the deeply embedded national security culture, which had existed for decades. Two generations of Japanese people had experienced the effects of the existing security arrangements. The most recent generation had not been directly exposed to the resentment and turmoil associated with Japan's bilateral security arrangement with the United States as the previous one had three decades before.

Japan's security relationship with America began as a temporary arrangement; in time, the United Nations was expected to relieve the United States of the responsibility of protecting Japan. Because this never happened, the people of Japan came to accept the generally held position of most of the nation's policy makers that the country must maintain the security treaty and a broader alliance with the United States. Yet a major discordant point is discernible: although accepting the security relationship with the United States, Japan's postwar pacifism, along with the people's disinterest in rearmament, have remained evident in the public's view of national security issues.

Japan's defeat in the Pacific War caused the nation to adopt a constitution that renounced war as a way of resolving international disputes.[36] Later, Japan's acceptance of the security treaty with the United States reinforced the pacifism that had initially become apparent in its postwar constitution. Japan needed security, and after the Occupation, it was willing to rely on the United States for this. But while support for the pacifist constitution remained widespread, there was hardly a national consensus on this matter. Early on there was substantial revisionist interest in amending the constitution's war-renouncing clause.

Prime Minister Nobusuke Kishi was an advocate of both adjusting the security treaty with the United States to make Japan's position more nearly equal and of amending the war-renouncing clause in the constitution to permit Japanese rearmament.[37] But constitutional revision did not take place. Instead, in 1960 there emerged significant pacifist opposition in Japan to the bilateral security treaty with the United States and to the prospect of rearmament.[38] With the passing of this public opposition, many Japanese came to accept the security alliance with the United States. But when the Cold War ended, the question briefly emerged concerning whether Japan needed to maintain its security alliance with the United States. The government of Prime Minister Ryutaro Hashimoto answered this question by moving with Washington to strengthen the security alliance.

Japanese Views on Strengthening the Security Alliance

One of the major outcomes of the 1996 Joint Declaration on Security was that Tokyo and Washington agreed to begin a review of the 1978 Guidelines for Defense Cooperation. What is evident is that in formulating recent policy on the security relationship with the United States, Japanese legislators ignored the public opinion that existed *before* the appearance of the Interim Report on the Review of the Guidelines for U.S.–Japan Defense Cooperation in June 1997. An NHK (Japan Broadcasting Corporation) survey conducted in March 1995 found that 42 percent of the respondents felt that if any revisions to the U.S.–Japan Security Treaty were to take place,[39] the degree of cooperation between the two nations should be decreased. Only 24 percent of the respondents believed that that amount of defense cooperation between Japan and the United States should be increased; another 30 percent said it was difficult to say (5 percent either did not know or had no response).[40] This same NHK survey also pointed out that 61 percent of the respondents thought that the power of Japan's Self Defense Forces should stay the same and 20 percent felt that it should decrease.[41]

Almost two years later, in January 1997 (five months prior to the publication of the Interim Report), a *Yomiuri Shimbun* survey presented two important questions on security to the Japanese public. The first question asked respondents whether, based on the mutual security treaty, they thought that there was a need to strengthen the amount of military cooperation between the United States and Japan. Only 7 percent of the respondents felt that the amount of cooperation should be increased. The majority of respondents, 57 percent, said the amount of cooperation should remain the same, while 28 percent thought that it should be decreased (8 percent had no response). The second question asked respondents whether they felt that revisions to the security treaty that would strengthen the bilateral security relationship would either increase Asian stability or exacerbate regional tensions. Although the security treaty had been in place for over four decades, the responses to this question did not show that the Japanese public supported revisions that would strengthen the bilateral security alliance. An equal number of respondents, 12 percent, thought that revisions would either help "stabilize" Asia or "heighten tension" in the region. While 30 percent felt that revisions would "somewhat stabilize" Asia, 28 percent believed that they would "somewhat heighten tension" (8 percent had no response).[42]

By the time the Interim Report on the Review of the Guidelines for U.S.–Japan Defense Cooperation appeared in June 1997, Japanese public opinion on security enhancement measures with the United States reflected indifference. Perhaps because they realized that policy makers had ignored their concerns, disinterest had taken hold of a large part of the Japanese public. After interviewing over 2,500 Japanese adults, a survey sponsored by NHK found that the majority of the respondents were not especially interested in the new guidelines. All told, 54 percent of the respondents said that they were "not very interested" or "not interested at all" in the guidelines.[43]

However, by late August, just a few weeks before the signing of the new guidelines, a survey conducted by the *Yomiuri Shimbun* indicated that 64 percent of the Japanese public now supported them and that only

18 percent felt that they were unnecessary (17 percent had no response).[44] How in about eight weeks did Japanese public opinion move decisively from where the majority had little or no interest in the new guidelines to the point where nearly two-thirds of the public supported them? Some part of the answer may very well be that the form of the question produced the intended results. The question asked by the conservative-leaning *Yomiuri Shimbun* is really a very good example of what survey researchers call a leading or biased question. The newspaper's question was as follows: "The guidelines for Japan–U.S. military cooperation are being revised on the assumption that a war or conflict could threaten Japan's security. The revisions focus on the roles Japan and the United States will play in such situations. Do you think these revisions are necessary or not?" The phrase on the assumption that a war or conflict could threaten Japan's security unambiguously represents a bias.[45] The phrase leads respondents to consider their answers based on the belief that a war or conflict is inevitable, or at least nearly so, and that the threat Japan faces is currently grave enough to produce either of these outcomes.[46] But most of the answer to this question lies in the fact that many Tokyo policy makers wanted very much to strengthen Japan's military alliance with the United States. So, these policy makers, joined and assisted by some of the media, worked to convince the public of the looming security problems in the region.

In any case, less than two years later there was survey evidence of public opposition to the new guidelines in Japan. This is important, considering both the support for the new guidelines that had existed for some time among many Japanese policy makers and the national commotion in Japan that the North Korean satellite-missile launch caused in late August 1998. An *Asahi Shimbun* opinion poll conducted in March 1999 showed that the largest proportion of respondents, 43 percent, expressed opposition to the bills then being considered by the Diet; 37 percent of the respondents supported the legislation. Over half of the respondents who opposed the bills felt that they would cause Japan to become involved in a war.[47] This fear that Japan could be involved in a war being fought by the United States in the region has long been a concern of the Japanese public.[48] When a *Yomiuri Shimbun* survey asked respondents their views on the bilateral security treaty in October 1995, among those who believed the accord was not very beneficial or not beneficial at all (23 percent), 47 percent felt that the treaty could lead to Japan's involvement in a war.[49]

With the passage of the new guidelines, it does not appear that the Japanese public feels any more secure. A 1999 *Yomiuri Shimbun* survey asked respondents whether they thought the new guidelines would help to secure Japan or threaten its safety. While 33 percent of the respondents believed that the new guidelines would add to Japan's security, 28 percent thought that they threatened the nation's security, and 35 percent answered that it was too difficult to say.[50] A 1999 *Asahi Shimbun* survey showed that 59 percent of the respondents were worried that the use of U.S. military power in the region and Japan's enlarged geographical responsibilities mandated by the new defense guidelines would affect Japanese peace and security, while 34 percent said that they were not worried.[51] In this survey 67 percent of the respondents felt that Japan should have the option of refusing to assist the United States, should there be a military problem in the region; only 19 percent said that Japanese cooperation should occur in any security situation.[52]

Views on the Constitution and War-Making Activities

There has been increasing discussion in Japan during the last several years about changing the nation's constitution. A survey conducted in 1993 by NHK asked respondents whether they thought it was necessary to revise the nation's constitution. Then, respondents were almost equally divided, with 38 percent answering yes, 34 percent saying no, and 16 percent believing that it was too difficult to say.[53] A *Nihon Keizai Shimbun* survey conducted in the spring of 1997 showed that the Japanese public was still divided on the issue of revising the constitution, with about 46 percent endorsing amendment, approximately 44 percent supporting its current form, and the remaining 11 percent saying they were unsure.[54] Although surveys conducted in 1997 by both the *Yomiuri Shimbun* and the *Asahi Shimbun* showed about the same amount of support for revising the constitution as the *Nihon Keizai Shimbun* poll, they also indicated that smaller proportions of respondents wanted to leave it unchanged. In the *Yomiuri Shimbun* survey, while 45 percent supported constitutional amendment, 37 percent did not, and the remaining 18 percent did not respond. In the *Asahi Shimbun* survey, 46 percent supported amending the constitution, 39 percent did not, and 15 either did not respond or gave another answer.[55] A 1998 *Yomiuri Shimbun* survey showed increased support for constitutional revision: 52 percent of the respondents favored amending the constitution, 31 percent were opposed, and 17 percent did not respond.[56] A 2001 *Yomiuri Shimbun* survey indicated that 54 percent of respondents supported amending the constitution, down from 60 percent in 2000. This same survey showed that 28 percent opposed changing the constitution, an increase of 2 percent from 2000.[57]

Surveys conducted during the last few years make clear that the people of Japan endorse a public discussion of their constitution. A *Yomiuri Shimbun* survey showed that 72 percent of the respondents felt that it was good for both knowledgeable citizens and politicians to discuss the constitution; only 11 percent thought this was not good.[58] When queried in a 1999 *Nihon Keizai Shimbun* survey about constitutional amendment, 58 percent of the respondents stressed the importance of thorough discussion; 20 percent supported revision (without discussion), and 15 percent believed that neither discussion nor revision is necessary.[59]

The *Yomiuri Shimbun* has been attempting to ascertain both why and how the Japanese people think the constitution should be revised. Survey results on the "how" and "why" of constitutional revision are ambiguous.[60] Concerning the question of how to revise the constitution, 42 percent of the respondents said that new amendments should be added when necessary and obsolete issues should be deleted, 32 percent felt only that obsolete issues should be removed, and 11 percent favored just adding amendments. Regarding the question of why the constitution should be revised, respondents were able to choose from several selections and provide as many answers as they desired. Half of the respondents indicated that the constitution does not deal with international cooperation, 32 percent said that it provides too many rights to people but does not clarify individual responsibilities, 30 percent replied that flexible interpretations of the constitution create confusion, and 22 percent answered that it had been written by and forced on Japan by the United States. Receiving relatively little support, with the endorsement of only 12 percent of the respondents, was the selection that Japan must establish its right of self-defense so that it can officially maintain military forces.[61]

Interest in expanding Japan's military activities has not been especially popular among the Japanese public. Survey data strongly suggest a Japanese affinity to limiting the nation's defensive posture, as required by the constitution. A *Yomiuri Shimbun* survey shows that 53 percent of the respondents believe that Japanese cooperation with U.S. military forces should be limited to defending Japan's homeland, territorial waters, or airspace. Ten percent of the respondents said that Japanese cooperation should be extended outside of the territorial waters and into open airspace. Just 5 percent believed Japanese forces could cooperate with the U.S. military in other nations' territories, but even then only if there was no combat, and 6 percent felt that cooperation could be extended to areas where there was fighting.[62] In this survey, the overwhelming majority of respondents felt that Japanese cooperation with U.S. military forces in the region should be limited to helping civilians and refugees and to offering medical care to soldiers.[63] Similarly, an *Asahi Shimbun* survey conducted about two months prior to the Diet's approval of the new guidelines points out that they permit Japanese forces to cooperate with the U.S. military on the open seas by providing arms, ammunition, and other requisite materials. However, in this survey only 13 percent of the respondents thought that Japanese forces could transport anything, 49 percent answered anything except arms and ammunition, and 29 percent said that Japan should not assist the United States to transport military material.[64] Thus, both of these surveys suggest a preference among the public for maintaining constitutional restrictions relating to the renunciation of war and explicitly indicate an aversion to extending Japan's military responsibilities by assisting the United States should security problems emerge in the region.

During the post–Cold War years, the Japanese public has unequivocally maintained its support for Article 9. In addition to looking at the issue of constitutional change, the 1993 NHK survey cited above asked respondents whether they thought that Article 9 needed to be revised. Respondents' answers were as follows: 49 percent opposed revision of Article 9, 38 percent supported it, and 8 percent said that it was difficult to say.[65] Japanese conservatives and some policy makers have recently been pushing harder than in the recent past to revise Article 9 so that the military can react more effectively to international security problems, which would include active cooperation with the United States. This initiative has been at the top of the Bush administration's priority list. Before the Bush administration assumed the reins of power in 2001, Richard Armitage and Paul Wolfowitz, who subsequently became deputy secretary of state and deputy secretary of defense, respectively, had indicated in a policy paper that it is important for the United States and Japan to have a "mature partnership."[66] For them, this meant revising Article 9 to permit cooperative military operations with the United States. Members of the Bush administration have since been encouraging the revision of Article 9. Recently, Howard Baker, U.S. ambassador to Japan, infuriated Pyongyang when, referring to Japan's involvement in TMD research with the United States, he reportedly remarked that "the reality of circumstance in the world is going to suggest to the Japanese that they reinterpret or redefine [A]rticle 9 of their constitution."[67]

But the current campaign to amend the constitution's war-renouncing clause must still overcome strong public antipathy in Japan. An *Asahi Shimbun* survey, conducted in April 1997, asked respondents what they thought about the renunciation-of-war clause in the constitution. The overwhelming majority of respondents, 82 percent, said that they thought it was good that their nation's constitution renounces war and rejects the use of force to resolve international problems; only 10 percent felt that this was not good.[68] When asked by NHK survey interviewers in fall 1997 to make three choices from a list of seven selections concerning the principles most strongly established by the Japanese constitution, 63 percent of the respondents picked the renunciation of war, second only to respect for fundamental human rights, which was supported by 74 percent of the survey's participants.[69]

While the *Yomiuri Shimbun* has surveyed the Japanese people on the question of security and constitutional change, its poll data do not provide nearly enough evidence of public support for revising Article 9. In one survey question, after setting up the hypothetical situation of war breaking out in the region and military action taken by the United States, the *Yomiuri Shimbun* asked respondents their views on constitutional revision. While 26 percent of the respondents favored amending the constitution, 42 percent felt that Japan should deal with the crisis by relying on the existing interpretation of the document. This survey also showed that 14 percent of the respondents believed that the existing constitution should be interpreted differently and 11 percent felt that Japan should not cooperate with American military forces.[70]

Poll data from *Asahi Shimbun* show that when asked a simple straightforward question with only three possible selections, proportionally more respondents supported the existing constitution than disapproved of it. This survey indicated approval from 48 percent of the respondents, while 34 percent disapproved; the rest, 18 percent, either did not answer or gave another answer.[71] In this same survey, another short, straightforward question with only three possible sections—this one inquiring about whether to revise the constitution's war-renouncing clause—showed overwhelming public support for Article 9. Only 20 percent of the respondents favored amending Article 9, while 69 percent believed that it should not be revised.[72] Recent survey data show even more support among the Japanese people for maintaining the constitutional war-renouncing clause. *Asahi Shimbun* survey data for 2001 indicate that 74 percent of the respondents want to preserve Article 9, 5 percent more than in the newspaper's 1997 poll.[73]

Although the intentions of many Tokyo policy makers, most especially those predisposed to conservative views, now appear to be leaning in the direction of revising the constitution, the Japanese public is currently showing much more concern for the discussion of this issue rather than for the amendment of the document. The Japanese public has accepted the idea that there should be discussions on constitutional change, but this is very different from implementation. What is unambiguous from the survey data is that the people of Japan overwhelmingly want to retain Article 9; they are not prepared to forsake the nation's war-renouncing constitutional clause.

Although discussion of constitutional issues is healthy, in the next few years there will be a danger of explicit attempts by powerful government officials and some of the influential media to try to manipulate public opinion in favor of amending Article 9. The goal of those who support revising the constitution's war-renouncing clause is to enable Japan to establish international credibility. For them, Japan has not achieved its recognition as a major international force because it has maintained a lame security policy. To attain this recognition and establish international credibility, Japan must uproot embedded national sentiment and be permitted to use its forces in international security operations, which include cooperative military activities with the United States.

In the forefront of constitutional change has been Japan's largest newspaper, the *Yomiuri Shimbun*. Since 1994, it has published two proposed revisions to Japan's constitution, the most recent draft appearing in 2000. Establishing Japan's international credibility is the major objective of the *Yomiuri Shimbun*. Omitted from the newspaper's proposal to revise the constitution are the words in the original preamble that the Japanese people are "resolved that never again shall we be visited with the horrors of war through the action of government." The newspaper also replaces the words, "We desire to occupy an honored place in international society striving for the preservation of peace," with the phrase we "respect the spirit of international cooperation and pledge to use our best efforts to ensure peace, prosperity, and security of the international community." [74]

But most important to the conservative pursuit of Japan's international credibility is the revision of the constitution's war-renouncing clause. The *Yomiuri Shimbun's* recent proposal to this clause replaces paragraph one, which reads:

> Aspiring sincerely to an international peace based on justice and order, the Japanese people forever renounce war as a sovereign right of the nation and the threat or use of force as a means of settling international disputes.

Instead, the newspaper wants the first paragraph of the renunciation-of-war clause to state the following:

> Aspiring sincerely to an international peace based on justice and order, the Japanese people shall never recognize war as a sovereign right of the nation and the threat or use of force as a means of settling international disputes.

The significant proposed change to this paragraph is replacing the words *forever renounce war* and replacing them with *shall never recognize war*. Paragraph two in the original Japanese constitution states that

> In order to accomplish the aim of the preceding paragraph, land, sea, and air forces, as well as war potential will never be maintained. The right of the belligerency of the state will not be recognized.

The *Yomiuri Shimbun* proposes to change paragraph two to read as follows:

> Seeking to eliminate from the world inhuman and indiscriminate weapons of mass destruction, Japan shall not manufacture, possess or use such weapons.

Yomiuri Shimbun's proposal for paragraph two commendably inserts much of the spirit of the nation's nonnuclear principles into the constitution. But the combination of changes to paragraph one and the elimination of the original paragraph two from the constitution means that the newspaper has removed those words that have been interpreted to prohibit Japan's active military participation in international security operations. The *Yomiuri Shimbun* also proposes that Article 14 of a revised constitution read:

Japan shall lend active cooperation to the activities of the relevant well-established and internationally recognized organizations. In case of need, it may dispatch public officials and provide a part of its armed forces for self-defense and for the maintenance and promotion of peace and for humanitarian support activities.[75]

Thus, with the Japan–U.S. security alliance firmly in place it appears that Article 14, in particular the words "relevant well-established . . . organizations," along with the proposed revisions to the original war-renouncing and internationally recognized clause, clears the way for Japanese military cooperation with U.S. military forces in international disputes.

It is indeed important for Japan to acquire international credibility. However, credibility is not tantamount to revising Article 9 so that the Japanese military can join with the United States in forming a NATO-like security force in East Asia. Suffice it to say now that Article 9, while renouncing war, does not expressly proscribe the active involvement of Japanese military forces in international peacekeeping efforts. But since such an initiative would unsettle other East Asia countries, Tokyo would have to be simultaneously and demonstratively committing the nation to a nonthreatening security policy.

Japanese Views on the United Nations

In the past, the Japanese people envisioned the United Nations playing a very important role in international peace and security. This United Nation's optimism still exists today. For example, recent *Asahi Shimbun* poll data reveal that, among the more than 2,000 Japanese respondents interviewed in a multinational survey, a popular selection was strengthening the United Nations so that it can effectively employ diplomacy to resolve problems and maintain peace and security in Asia during the twenty-first century.[76]

Not only have the Japanese people long believed that the United Nations has an important part to play in international security, but for some time, Japan has wanted to become a permanent member of the UN Security Council. This is especially true since 1993.[77] Polling results consistently show that the majority of the Japanese people want their country to be a permanent member of the Security Council of the United Nations. Two NHK surveys conducted in 1993 found considerable public support for permanent membership for Japan in the UN Security Council. In the first survey 59 percent of the respondents believed that Japan should become a permanent member of the UN Security Council, 25 percent did not think so, and 15 percent either said that they did not know or gave no answer. Results from the second NHK survey found that 48 percent of the respondents supported the idea of Japan's becoming a permanent member of the UN Security Council, 20 percent opposed this, and 31 percent said that they did not know or did not reply.[78]

In 1994, NHK again conducted two surveys on this same question. The first survey showed that 46 percent felt that Japan should become a permanent member of the Security Council, 24 percent opposed this, and 29 percent either said that they did not know or did not reply. The second survey found that 45 percent supported the idea, 23 percent opposed it and 32 percent either said that they did not know or did not give an answer.[79]

A 1995 *Yomiuri Shimbun* survey similarly showed that 47 percent of the respondents believed that Japan should become a permanent member of the Security Council, 25 percent did not think so, 20 percent said that they were not interested in the issue, and 7 percent did not provide an answer.[80] A 1995 *Nihon Keizai Shimbun* survey found considerably more public support for Japan's assuming the position of a permanent member of the Security Council; 62 percent of the respondents favored this idea, 22 percent opposed it, and 16 percent either said that they could not tell or did not know.[81]

Surveys sponsored by the prime minister's office in 1995 and 1996 also showed that the Japanese public wanted Japan to become a permanent member of the Security Council. Interviewing respondents for the prime minister's office in the fall of 1995, the Shin Joho Center found that 61 percent of the respondents felt that Japan should become a permanent member of the Security Council (23 percent agreed and 38 percent somewhat agreed), 16 percent disagreed (12 percent somewhat disagreed and 4 percent disagreed), and 23 percent did not know. In this survey, of those who agreed that Japan should become a permanent member of the UN Security Council, the largest proportion of respondents, 34 percent, said that they felt this way because they believed that their nation's pacifist principles combined with the fact that their country does not possess nuclear weapons would help bring about world peace. Twenty-five percent of the respondents—the next largest highest proportion—said that since Japan is an economic power it has an obligation to contribute to global peace.[82] The 1996 survey sponsored by the prime minister's office indicated that 65 percent of the respondents thought that Japan should have a permanent position on the Security Council (27 percent agreed and 38 percent somewhat agreed), 13 percent expressed disagreement (10 percent somewhat disagreed and 3 percent disagreed), and 22 percent answered that they did not know. Similarly, the 1996 survey indicated that of those supporting the idea of Japan's becoming a permanent member of the Security Council, 32 percent thought that the country's pacifism and refusal to possess nuclear weapons would permit it to contribute to world peace,[83] and 29 percent believed that because of their nation's economic power, it should contribute to global peace.

The surveys of the prime minister's office show that much of the Japanese public thinks that Japan should be involved in international security affairs. A 1997 prime minister's survey showed that, second only to helping to deal with global environmental problems (43.3 percent), more than one-third of the respondents believed that Japan should be contributing to international peace and security by being involved in the resolution of regional conflicts. A slightly different question in this survey indicated that the largest proportion of respondents, 60.8 percent, felt that Japan should cooperate with the United Nations in international efforts to maintain peace and security.[84] Results of these two questions from the 1998 prime minister's survey indicate that 40 percent of the respondents thought that Japan should play a role in resolving regional conflicts and 67 percent felt that it should actively cooperate through the United Nations in maintaining international peace and security.[85] The prime minister's 2000 survey shows increased public support for Japan's helping to settle regional conflicts and for it to cooperate actively with the United Nations to maintain international peace and stability—41.8 percent and 67.6 percent, respectively.[86]

However, answers to specific questions relating to the important matter of Japan's role in international security show a continuing reluctance on the part of the Japanese people during the post–Cold War years to permit the Self Defense Forces to be involved militarily in settling conflicts. A 1994 survey conducted by *Asahi Shimbun* asked respondents three questions relating to this issue. The first question asked respondents what they thought of Japan's becoming a permanent member of the UN Security Council, as long as it did not have to assume military responsibilities: 70 percent approved, 16 percent disapproved, and 14 percent gave another answer or none at all. When asked whether they believed that Japan would be required to assume military responsibilities as a member of the Security Council, 69 percent said yes, 21 percent said no, and 10 percent gave another answer or did not reply. Of the three questions asked respondents, the most important was whether they agreed or disagreed that Japan should become a member of the Security Council even if it had to assume military responsibilities. Only 29 percent of the respondents said that they agreed with Japan's becoming a member of the Security Council even if it had to assume military responsibility; the majority, 57 percent, indicated disagreement; and 14 percent gave another answer or did not reply.[87] A 1994 NHK survey found that 57 percent of the respondents said that they approved of Japan's becoming a permanent member of the Security Council provided it does not have a military role. Only 15 percent supported Japan's having responsibilities like those of other permanent Security Council members, 11 percent said they were unable to generalize, and 18 percent did not know or did not reply.[88]

An answer to a question in a 1999 survey conducted by the *Yomiuri Shimbun* indicates that the public is still reluctant to see Japan's Self Defense Forces involved in international military operations. Although not inquiring about permanent membership in the Security Council, the newspaper found that after being reminded that Japan's involvement in UN peacekeeping activities consists of building roads and assisting with the transportation of goods, 42 percent of those surveyed thought that current policy should not be changed to permit involvement in ceasefire and disarmament efforts. Only 26 percent of the respondents said that policy should be changed, another 26 percent felt that it is too difficult to say, and 6 percent did not answer.[89]

Security Treaty Surveys

It has become commonplace to aver that the Japanese public largely supports the U.S.–Japan Security Treaty.[90] However, this conclusion is typically reached without thorough analysis, that is, it is drawn by looking only *prima facie* at the survey results. Those who draw this conclusion ignore critical historical and demographic information that casts an entirely different light on this important issue. Moreover, this conclusion discounts the fact that military security is generally not the foremost concern of the public. People ordinarily do not regularly attempt to weigh the advantages and disadvantages of a security treaty that has been around for decades. That their country is not at war or on the brink of one is for most a sufficient reason to affirm—however tentatively—a security accord, especially one with a military superpower.

It is important to understand that opinion polls attempting to assess the amount of public support for the bilateral security treaty rely on Japanese adults who are of voting age, that is, at least twenty years old. Demographic data indicate that a sizable percentage of Japanese adults were not even alive when the Treaty of Mutual Cooperation and Security was first signed in 1951, or even when it was renewed in 1960. Japanese census data show that in 1998 more than one-third of voting-age adults in Japan were born after 1951.[91] Another 8 percent were either not born yet or were only two years old in 1951. In other words, in 1998 approximately 42 percent of the Japanese voting-age population either had not yet been born in 1951 or had only reached the age of two at about the time of the initial signing of the security treaty. Still another 7.5 percent of the Japanese voting-age population was between the ages of three and seven in 1951. Thus, when American and Japanese officials signed the Treaty of Mutual Cooperation and Security in 1951, close to half of Japan's 1998 voting-age population either had not been born or was below the age of eight.

At the time of the signing of the revised 1960 security treaty, 28 percent of the 1998 Japanese voting-age population had not yet been born or was no older than one. Another 14 percent were between the ages of two and eleven. Still another 7.5 percent of the 1998 Japanese voting-age population were between twelve and sixteen years of age in 1960. Thus, almost half of the 1998 Japanese voting-age population was below the age of seventeen in 1960.

Although the opinion surveys on the security treaty discussed below were conducted a short time before 1998, the major point remains true, that is, a very large part of Japan's voting-age population was either not born or was quite young when the 1951 and 1960 treaties were signed. This raises a very important sociological question: to what extent does the current support for the U.S.–Japan Security Treaty by a large proportion of the Japanese population indicate that culture and tradition account for the endurance of security norms? It is certainly arguable that, having experienced peace since the time of the Pacific War, the Japanese people are somewhat reluctant to conceptualize a security system that is different from that of the past. Much of the Japanese public

Table 5.2

**Japanese Public Opinion on the Japan–U.S.
Security Treaty, 1991–1997**
(numbers represent percentage of respondents)

Survey 1

Question: Is the Japan–U.S. security treaty useful, somewhat useful,
somewhat useless, or useless in maintaining the peace and safety of
Japan?

Useful	26
Somewhat useful	44
Somewhat useless	12
Useless	4
Don't know	15

Source: Prime Minister's Office, interviews were conducted between February 6 and
February 16, 1997.
Note: All survey data in Table 5.2 on the bilateral security treaty were accessed from
the Roper Center for Public Opinion Research, University of Connecticut.

Survey 2

Question: Do you think it is necessary for Japan and the United States
to maintain a security treaty at all, or not?

Necessary to maintain treaty	76
Unnecessary	13
Other/no response	11

Source: *Asahi Shimbun*; interviews were conducted between April 20 and April 21,
1997.

Survey 3

Question: What do you think of the Japan–U.S. security treaty? Choose
one from the list.

It should be maintained	56
It should be abolished	33
Can't tell/don't know	11

Source: *Nihon Keizai Shimbun*; interviews were conducted between April 25 and
April 27, 1997.

Survey 4

Question: Do you think that the Japan–U.S. security treaty is very useful, somewhat useful, or not useful at all with regard to providing Japan with national security?

Very useful	22
Somewhat useful	45
Not useful at all	12
Difficult to say	17
No response	4

Source: *Yomiuri Shimbun*; interviews were conducted between August 30 and August 31, 1997.

Survey 5

Question: What do you think of the Japan–U.S. security treaty? Choose one from the list.

It should be maintained	56
It should be abolished	32
Can't tell/don't know	12

Source: *Nihon Keizai Shimbun*; interviews were conducted from April 19 to April 21, 1996.

Survey 6

Question: Do you think it is necessary for Japan and the United States to maintain a security treaty at all, or not?

Necessary to maintain	70
Not necessary	13
Other/no response	17

Source: *Asahi Shimbun*; interviews were conducted between May 12 and May 13, 1996.

Survey 7

Question: Do you think the Japan–U.S. security treaty is useful or not useful with regard to providing the Asia and Pacific region with security?

Useful	63
Not useful	24
Other/no response	13

Source: *Asahi Shimbun*; interviews were conducted September 16 and September 17, 1996.

Survey 8

Question: What do you think of the Japan–U.S. security treaty? Choose from the list.

It should be maintained	40
It should be maintained after it is revised	36
It should be abolished	6
Don't know/no response	18

Source: NHK (Japan Broadcasting Corporation); interviews were conducted between March 4 and March 5, 1995.

Survey 9

Question: What do you think of the Japan–U.S. security treaty? Choose one from the list.

It should be maintained	60
It should be abolished	29
Can't tell/don't know	12

Source: *Nihon Keizai Shimbun*; interviews were conducted between August 4 and August 6, 1995.

Survey 10

Question: What do you think of the Japan–U.S. security treaty? Choose one from the list.

It should be maintained	44
It should be abolished	40
Can't tell/don't know	16

Source: *Nihon Keizai Shimbun*; interviews were conducted between October 13 and October 15, 1995.

Survey 11

Question: Do you think maintaining the Japan–U.S. security treaty is beneficial, somewhat beneficial, not very beneficial, or not beneficial at all to Japan?

Beneficial	19
Somewhat beneficial	38
Not very beneficial	15
Not beneficial at all	8
No response	20

Source: *Yomiuri Shimbun*; interviews were conducted between October 28 and October 29, 1995.

Survey 12

Question: Do you think the Japan–U.S. security treaty is very useful, somewhat useful, or not useful at all with regard to providing Japan with national security?

Very useful	23
Somewhat useful	43
Not useful at all	11
Difficult to say	18
No response	5

Source: *Yomiuri Shimbun*; interviews were conducted September 24 and September 25, 1995.

Survey 13

Question: To what extent do you think the Japan–U.S. security treaty contributes to the peace and security of Japan? Very much, somewhat, not very much, or not at all.

Very much	16
Somewhat	55
Not very much	19
Not at all	2
Don't know/no response	8

Source: NHK; interviews were conducted on March 1, 1992.

Survey 14

Question: Japan has signed a security treaty with the United States. Do you think the Japan–U.S. security treaty has been good for Japan?

Been good	52
Not been good	21
Difficult to say	18
Other/no response	9

Source: *Asahi Shimbun*; interviews were conducted on April 1, 1992.

Survey 15

Question: Do you think that maintaining the Japan–U.S. security treaty after the end of the Cold War is very beneficial, somewhat beneficial, not very beneficial, or not beneficial at all for Japan?

Very beneficial	12
Somewhat beneficial	40
Not very beneficial	29
Not beneficial at all	4
No response	15

Source: *Yomiuri Shimbun*; interviews were conducted on September 1, 1992.

Survey 16
Question: Is the Japan–U.S. security treaty useful, somewhat useful, somewhat useless, or useless in maintaining the peace and safety of Japan?

Useful	27
Somewhat useful	37
Somewhat useless	13
Useless	5
Don't know	18

Source: Prime Minister's Office; interviews were conducted between January 31 and February 10, 1991.

Survey 17
Question: Japan has signed a security treaty with the United States. Do you think the Japan–U.S. security treaty has been good for Japan?

Been good	50
Not been good	23
Difficult to say	17
Other/no response	10

Source: *Asahi Shimbun*; interviews were conducted on November 1, 1991.

may accept the security status quo because—to paraphrase a useful adage—as long as it works, there is no reason to fix it. It is also important to reemphasize that a substantial part of the Japanese public sees the maintenance of strong bilateral relations as the principal purpose of the security treaty.

The results of several opinion polls in which Japanese respondents were asked to give their personal view of the U.S.–Japan Security Treaty are given above. All seventeen of the surveys from 1991 through 1997 in Table 5.2 show more support for the treaty than opposition to it. However, all opinion surveys in Japan since the end of the Cold War show that some proportion of respondents, ranging from small to substantial, flatly oppose the existence of the bilateral security treaty.

What is discernible from these surveys is that there is disagreement among the Japanese public about the benefits that the bilateral security treaty provides to Japan. Perhaps an even better way to describe the results of these surveys is that they reflect some public uncertainty. Typically, there is a large category of people who have responded that the treaty is "somewhat useful," or "somewhat beneficial," or has "not been good" for Japan. Moreover, these surveys attempting to assess Japanese public support for the bilateral security treaty often have a modest proportion of people who "don't know," "can't tell," give "no response," or find it "difficult to say" whether the accord is of any value to Japan. What should be most alarming to Japanese policy makers is the substantial proportion of people questioned in the *Nihon Keizai Shimbun* surveys who have consistently responded that they believe that the security treaty should be abolished. One-third of the respondents in the newspaper's spring 1997 poll believed that the bilateral security treaty should be abolished. This was down seven points from the 40 percent of respondents who favored the treaty's cancellation in the fall 1995 survey conducted by the *Nihon Keizai Shimbun* (see Table 5.2, Survey 10) in the wake of the tragic September 1995 incident when three servicemen raped a young Okinawan schoolgirl.

Considering all that has been said here, there is not enough evidence to draw the unequivocal conclusion that because the largest proportion of respondents express some support for the bilateral security treaty, the people of Japan are comfortable with it. To infer hastily that there is solid public support for the treaty based on the available survey data is to generalize beyond all of the facts associated with this issue. It is indeed very important that the security treaty between the United States and Japan has been in place for nearly half a century. Could the tentativeness evident in the public opinion polls on the security treaty largely or even partly relate to political tradition? How many Japanese adults aged forty-five and under when asked in 1996, for example, whether the bilateral security treaty was useful or not would be inclined to indicate their support for the accord, because during their lifetimes Japan had not experienced war. Are they really affirming the treaty or the fact that Japan has not experienced war? Not only is there no evidence that the bilateral security treaty has stabilized the East Asia–Pacific region, but there is also none whatsoever that shows that the accord has brought peace to Japan. How many more Japanese people understand the value of the treaty to Washington and to its regional and global military goals and are therefore more concerned about sustaining the overall bilateral relationship than with anything else? Japan's huge trade surplus with the United States would be perennially under attack by Washington were it not for the bilateral treaty and the more inclusive security alliance.

As sociologist William Sumner pointed out many years ago, a "strain for consistency," is commonly found in society. Even though change could improve their lives, what people get used to too often fashions their beliefs and behavior. Nowhere is this seen more clearly than in the Japanese cities of Nagasaki and Hiroshima. Having experienced the human and physical destructiveness of atomic warfare, people who live in both these cities understandably have vehemently opposed the existence of nuclear weapons, all forms of nuclear testing, and, more recently, Japan's remaining under America's nuclear umbrella. Yet, a recent *Asahi Shimbun* opinion poll in Hiroshima and Nagasaki found that 44 percent of the respondents in the former city and 39 percent of those surveyed in the latter city felt that Japan should no longer accept America's nuclear protection but that it should retain the bilateral security treaty.[92] Just how this would work is not particularly clear. The leading proposal in this debate is to create a nuclear-free zone in the Northeast Asian region. But as long as the bilateral security treaty remains in place it is difficult to envision the United States involved in a conflict in the Asia–Pacific region and agreeing not to use nuclear weapons, which can be launched from anywhere, in the conflict.

Opposition to U.S. Military Presence in Japan

While some discernible ambiguity exists in Japan's relating to the existence of the security treaty with the United States, there is little uncertainty associated with the issue of how the Japanese people feel about the continued presence of the large number of U.S. military forces and bases in their country. Opposition to the existence of the U.S. military in Okinawa has received a large amount of public attention since 1995. Many Okinawans want to see the U.S. military removed from their island prefecture. A 1998 survey jointly conducted by the *Asahi Shimbun* and the *Okinawan Times* leaves little doubt of this. A clear majority of Okinawans reported that they wanted to see the removal of the Futenma

Base, a U.S. marine facility, from their prefecture. This is consistent with a survey performed by the Japan–U.S. Special Action Committee on Okinawa in December 1996, when poll data showed that 60 percent of Okinawans then believed that the plan to relocate Futenma facility out of Okinawa needed additional political support. In the 1998 survey, when Okinawans were asked where the facility should be relocated, 52 percent responded by saying American soil. Only 12 percent endorsed a site in the northern part of the prefecture, and 13 percent answered somewhere in mainland Japan. Just 7 percent of the Okinawans surveyed favored Tokyo and Washington's plan to relocate the base to an offshore facility in Nago Bay.[93]

A more recent survey, conducted by *Asahi Shimbun* in March 1999, indicated widespread disapproval throughout Japan of the presence of U.S. bases. Surveying more than 2,000 Japanese voters, this poll found that 63 percent of the respondents wanted to see a reduction of the number of American bases in Japan. Support for maintaining the present number of U.S. military bases in Japan was noticeably smaller; only 28 percent of the respondents felt that American facilities should not be reduced.[94]

One should not disregard the connection between the Japanese opposition to the U.S. military presence in Japan and the bilateral security treaty. The two issues are intimately related. As we have already shown, opposition to the bilateral security treaty noticeably increased in the aftermath of the 1995 rape incident in Okinawa. Opposition again increased after the tragic sinking of the Japanese training vessel *Ehime Maru* off the coast of Hawaii in February 2001. To many Japanese the sinking of the vessel was the antithesis of their expectations of the security treaty, because rather than harm Japanese, the treaty is supposed to protect them. While there may not appear to be a connection between the security treaty and the sinking of the *Ehime Maru*, especially given where the ship went down, to many Japanese the event created a baneful association between the tragedy and the U.S.–Japan military alliance, a visible part of which is the American presence in Japan.

On the one hand, the Japanese people want security. On the other hand, there is a controlled hostility to the continued presence of the American military in Japan, particularly in Okinawa. Serious problems relating to the U.S. military presence in Japan that crop up from time to time incontrovertibly jeopardize support for the bilateral security treaty. The Japanese people tolerate the presence of the American military for three reasons: they want security, they do not want to undermine Japan's relationship with the United States and, perhaps most important, this is the official position of the central government. The fact that survey data show that the Japanese people are not generally supportive of the extent of the American military presence in their country strongly suggests that they are not wholly convinced by Tokyo's position.

Conclusion

This chapter has argued that the basic propositions derived from the assumption that there is a continuing need for the Japan–U.S. security alliance are not especially strong when they are scrutinized empirically. In fact, survey data indicate an appreciable amount of public uncertainty and opposition to some specific parts of the bilateral security alliance, most ostensibly the presence of U.S. troops and bases in Japan at the current levels. As the world's only superpower the United States is not obligated to provide protection to Japan in the form of a formal security alliance. Japan's commitment to the renunciation of war has not made it an authentically pacifist society. The fact that it has one of the largest military budgets in the world and a very advanced science and technology base means that Japan's defensive capabilities are more than sufficient to protect the country under most circumstances. The probability that Beijing would hurl nuclear weapons at Japan, a nonnuclear state, is utterly remote and, as we have seen in this chapter, unequivocally against China's stated foreign policy. Rather than meeting a perceived threat from North Korea with an even bigger one that is inherent in the Japan–U.S. security alliance, Tokyo could easily demonstrate to Pyongyang that it has chosen undisguised diplomacy and the complete normalization of bilateral relations as the preferred course.

There is also no evidence that the East Asia–Pacific area would degenerate into regional chaos without the Japan–U.S. security alliance. Despite the strengthening of the Japan–U.S. security alliance, Pyongyang refuses to abandon indefinitely what it sees as its right to maintain an active missile-development program, and Beijing currently plans to utilize more science and technology to bolster the nation's military capabilities.[95] These two current issues alone provide poor testimony to the regional stability created by the bilateral security alliance.

The survey data in this chapter show that the Japanese people were initially reluctant to see an expansion of the Japan–U.S. security alliance in the years prior to the appearance of the new guidelines for defense cooperation. However, the data also show that this reluctance began to weaken about the time when it was clear that the national government was seriously considering the adoption of the new guidelines. Here there are two major possibilities: first, because there was a generalized perception that Japan needed more security, the views of the Japanese people changed during the 1990s to accommodate this understanding by strengthening the security alliance with the United States; or second, that through the much publicized need to strengthen the military alliance, a position promoted strongly by Washington and many officials in Tokyo and then endorsed by some of the major Japanese media, public perception shifted in the direction of more support for the bilateral security arrangement. Whereas the first possibility allows for the people of Japan to arrive at a conclusion on this matter more or less on their own volition, the second points to the manipulation of public opinion—first by disregarding popular sentiment and then by trying to reshape it—to strengthen the security alliance.

Since the Japanese public's perception of the military threat from Russia is not now as high as it was at the end of the Cold War, and because the people of Japan do not necessarily see China as a direct and imminent danger, North Korea is generally recognized as being the biggest potential threat to the nation. The problem is that the perceived North Korean threat is not new and, incontrovertibly, during the Cold War Moscow could have inflicted considerably more harm on Japan than Pyongyang could today. This said, it is hard to place too much weight on the first possibility stated above; rather, it is more likely the case that public views changed on the question of whether to strengthen the bilateral security alliance because this was the position adopted by many Tokyo officials who were prodded by Washington. Somehow, policy makers in Tokyo and Washington knew better than the Japanese people and decided to strengthen the bilateral security alliance symbolically. That revising Article 9 is a high priority for the Bush administration, as well as for some policy makers and others in Japan raises the question of the extent to which a concerted effort will be directed at winning public compliance for changing the constitutional war-renouncing clause.

Survey data indicate that a substantial proportion of the Japanese people have felt that the U.S. military will not come to Japan's defense in a crisis, something that many still believe today. Many Japanese suspect that U.S. forces are in their country to meet Washington's global military objectives, and a large number believe that the strengthened bilateral alliance either threatens Japan's peace and security or will increase the prospect of their country being pulled into an American war. Survey data leave little doubt that much of the Japanese public wants, at the very least, to see a reduction of the U.S. military presence in Japan.

Constitutional change has become an important discussion topic in Japan since 1994. While survey data show that the Japanese public is willing to discuss revising the constitution and perhaps even to amend it, this is unambiguously not the case with Article 9. There is overwhelming public support for maintaining Article 9. Whether or not the Japanese people see Article 9 as providing other countries with the example of the need to renounce war is not nearly as important as the point that much of the public still believes that this clause is worth preserving.[96] Indeed, one of the most important conclusions reached in this chapter is that the survey data strongly suggest that the Japanese people have retained the pacifist sentiments that emerged after the Pacific War. This is evident in their continuing commitment to Article 9 and in their strong belief that all nuclear weapons should be eliminated from the world.

Surveys relating to the bilateral security treaty between Japan and the United States show that a large part of the Japanese public endorses the accord. But survey data also indicate that generally a smaller but still significant proportion of the public believes that the treaty should be abolished. Perhaps it is just as important that many of these surveys indicate that, other than simply not supporting the accord, there is additional public uncertainty about the bilateral security treaty. This uncertainty shows up in these surveys in ambivalent answers, such as "don't know," "can't tell," or "no response." Given that the treaty's main purpose is to provide Japan with security, the fact that very discernible uncertainty and even opposition to it exist raise the question of why so much of the Japanese public feels the way it does about the accord.

It is important to stress that the bilateral treaty is different from other security issues. Unlike the military troops and bases, the security treaty is generally not visible. Unlike the new defense guidelines, it has been around for decades. These differences make the treaty a cultural appendage to Japanese security. The security treaty, it should be noted, is also very different from Article 9. Unlike Article 9, which represents a national predilection for a way of life, the bilateral treaty is the political manifestation of an alliance that, although coexisting with the reality that Japan's peace and security have not been disrupted in decades, creates the prospect that the Japanese commitment to the renunciation of war could be shattered by Washington's military initiatives.

The Japanese have remained sanguine about the importance of the United Nations in dealing with international security. Much of the Japanese public believes that Japan should become a permanent member of the UN Security Council; however, because of the high level of distrust that still pervades East Asia, Pyongyang, Beijing, and even Seoul do not currently support this belief.[97] As this chapter makes clear, the problem in Japan is that public opinion does not favor the nation's Self Defense Forces being active militarily in international security operations. Just as Article 9 and the national recollection of the death and destruction associated with the Pacific War has nurtured Japan's strong antinuclear sentiment,[98] so it is that the peace constitution and the war have restrained Japanese enthusiasm for military activities.

6

Security Options: Staying the Course or Implementing an Alternative

Choices in Security Evolution

Japan currently has two major security options. The first is that it can continue to move along its present security trajectory, which is to remain aligned with the United States and incrementally increase its defense capabilities.[1] On this trajectory, Tokyo must be prepared to endure constant pressure from the United States, even in bad economic times,[2] to expand its defense contributions.[3] Remaining on this trajectory is the easier of the two major options available to Japan, as it requires only periodic, minimal adjustments to the status quo. This option therefore does not require dramatic changes in Tokyo's political and diplomatic efforts; nor does it require the assumption of leadership responsibilities in either regional or global security initiatives. This option allows Tokyo to insist on the importance of the United Nations and the ASEAN Regional Forum (ARF) to global and regional security, to stress the need for these multilateral bodies to be strengthened so that they can effectively deal with security problems, and to call repeatedly for nuclear nonproliferation and worldwide nuclear disarmament. However, Japan's present trajectory does not encourage officials in Tokyo to work continually and assertively to frame policies that would markedly increase the prospects that these proclamations become the foundation of a viable security regime. Moreover, by remaining on the current trajectory, Tokyo will continue to ignore what often has been significant public uneasiness about the bilateral security alliance, a problem reflecting a serious deficiency in Japan's democratic process and one that undermines it efforts to bolster the United Nations.

The second major security option available to Japan is for it to begin developing international and regional policies that link directly to its war-renouncing constitution and enduring interests in nuclear disarmament. To do this will require more democratic input from outside government, that is from civil society, so that political subcultures with shared sentiments can help shape the policy-making process. Public opinion clearly supports Japan's contributing to international peace and security through the United Nations. Appreciable movement on this path would take Japan back to its early postwar security roots. Although the expectations of the United Nations security obligations are still an important pillar of Japan's defense policy, they have remained dormant because of the alliance with the United States.

Option One: Staying the Course

Because an incremental defense policy is evolutionary in design, it has the propensity to fulfill the realist expectation that eventually Japan will become a major military power, perhaps even possessing nuclear weapons. One could conceivably argue that Japan's possession of nuclear weapons is constitutionally permissible, since they would serve as a deterrent and be for defensive purposes only. In Japan's situation as one of the two parties in a security alliance, an incremental defense policy is inherently precarious, since it permanently exposes the nation to political transitions that, given its militarist past, are or can be perceived as steps toward remilitarization. In the most extreme form of remilitarization Japan would sever its security ties with the United States and develop an independent military capability. However, this is not likely to happen in the immediate future.

Another form of remilitarization—and the one that is currently the most problematic—relates to the policy steps taken by Tokyo since 1996 when, working with Washington to reaffirm the bilateral security alliance, it committed the nation to the Joint Declaration on Security. China, North Korea, and more recently even Russia have categorically perceived these initiatives as destabilizing because of Japan's expanded involvement in regional defense.[4] The prospect that Japan might undertake more security responsibilities, however, also troubles other people in the Asia–Pacific area, who are occasionally reminded of past Japanese aggression in the region. While some may see Tokyo's security relationship with Washington as a restraint on Japan's potential for military aggression, more worrisome to Beijing, Pyongyang, and Moscow is that a strengthened bilateral alliance establishes, or at least portends, Japanese support for an American-instigated regional arms race.[5]

Any critically forthright evaluation of this trajectory cannot avoid emphasizing that Japan's alliance with the United States leaves little room for the development of a relatively independent security policy that specifically draws on Japanese norms relating to the renunciation of war and opposition to the existence of nuclear weapons. To argue the contrary would be to overlook the fact that these norms are still very evident in Japan. Tokyo's reluctance to develop regional and international security policies corresponding to these norms and to work so that they can infuse other political cultures suggests that it is not prepared to assume a dynamic leadership role and that it is ignoring public sentiment that has been shaped by these norms.

The continued existence of these norms is very evident in Japan's political culture. That Article 9, the war-renouncing clause, has existed for more than fifty years, despite appeals for change, is a political testimony to Japan's continuing repudiation of war. For some time, many Japanese have feared that Tokyo's security alliance with Washington could pull Japan into an American war or at least endanger the safety of their nation. Much of the controversy directly connected to the new bilateral guidelines for defense cooperation stems from the guidelines' words "areas surrounding Japan," which have been generally interpreted as expanding Tokyo's responsibilities from domestic security (defending the homeland) to involvement in regional problems. As indicated in the previous chapter, recent survey data show that much of the Japanese public is concerned about what could result from the new guidelines for defense cooperation between Washington and Tokyo. The source of their worry is obvious: a security problem in the surrounding area that the United States determines warrants intervention could now more easily draw Japan into a regional war—a political behavior that is prohibited by the Japanese constitution.

That the Japanese public still overwhelmingly supports the three nonnuclear principles indicates unambiguously that antinuclear sentiment endures in Japan. The 1999 resignation of Shingo Nishimura, the parliamentary vice minister of the Defense Agency who was effectively forced out of office because he publicly commented that Japan should consider developing nuclear weapons, was a political repercussion of Japanese antinuclear sentiment. By introducing the subject of Japan's acquisition of nuclear weapons in a society that abhors them, Nishimura was attempting to undercut a cultural taboo. Survey data show that that 81 percent of Japanese respondents support the three nonnuclear principles[6] that prevent Japan from developing or possessing nuclear weapons or introducing them into the country.

Consistent with public sentiment, Tokyo supports the three nonnuclear principles. However, they are part of Japan's national policy (*kokuze*) rather than the law (*houritsu*) infrastructure. This difference is problematic for Tokyo. When calling on the international community to abolish nuclear weapons on August 6, 2001, at the memorial commemorating the fifty-sixth anniversary of the atomic bombing of Hiroshima, Prime Minister Koizumi also stressed that Japan has adhered to Article 9 and to the three nonnuclear principles.[7] But since national law does not back the prime minister's words relating to the three nonnuclear principles, this significantly reduces Tokyo's will and capacity to thoroughly monitor the entrance of U.S. warships into Japanese ports. Moreover, should a nuclear-free zone in Northeast Asia be established, as some disarmament advocates now propose, its effectiveness would be in constant jeopardy. Not only is there a growing suspicion in East Asia that Japan may be moving away from the constraints of its war-renouncing constitution, but there is also distrust directly related to its nuclear intentions. Establishing the three nonnuclear principles as law would help to diminish regional tension and add credibility to Japan's commitment to a nuclear-free zone for Northeast Asia.

In 1960 when Tokyo renewed the U.S.–Japan Security Treaty, it permitted ideology to shape policy; in doing this, it ignored the position shared by much of the public that the accord should not be extended. Tokyo is doing something very similar today. As Tokyo has moved in the direction of strengthening the security alliance with the United States it has ignored the public's position. As we have seen in chapter 5, some survey data show either that the Japanese public does not support the new guidelines for defense cooperation or that it is concerned about the possible adverse effects on Japan's security. Moreover, the vast majority of Japan's constitutional scholars believe that the new guidelines violate the constitution.

When ideology that shapes policy becomes institutionalized, policy is maintained and continually influenced by tradition, as it has been in the U.S.–Japan security relationship. This makes it quite easy for policy makers to be insensitive to public sentiment. When government officials overlook the will of the public because they feel that they know what is in the best interests of the country, democracy atrophies; decisions made in this way also diminish public trust and support of the policy-making process. To the extent that Tokyo relies on ideology and tradition to maintain and shape the nation's security policy, it cannot be as attentive as it should be to public sentiment. This willingness to comply with Washington's wishes while ignoring sizable parts of the Japanese citizenry encourages public dissatisfaction with government officials, which is quite high in Japan. A January 2001 *Asahi Shimbun* survey showed that 63 percent of the respondents did not support the Mori government.[8] According to a recent *Yomiuri Shimbun* survey 75 percent of the respondents reported that they were dissatisfied with Japanese politics (51 percent somewhat dissatisfied and 24 percent very dissatisfied). Dissatisfaction this pervasive should not be trivialized, as this same survey showed that 62 percent of the respondents expressed interest in Japanese politics (20 percent very interested and 42 percent somewhat interested).[9] Disapproval of Prime Minister Obuchi's foreign and defense policies stood at 44 percent in May 1999; this was well above the 34 percent approval that he and his cabinet got from the public.[10]

Presently, Tokyo gingerly handles the contradiction between the continuation of the security alliance with Washington and the position of many in Japan who maintain the sociopolitical norms that reject militarism and oppose the existence of nuclear weapons. Tokyo does this by presenting the nation with policies that fall short of expectations but do not completely jeopardize its domestic legitimacy or its security relationship with Washington. Thus, to a large degree Tokyo must practice "mediation politics," attempting to cater to Washington's interests and those of large sections of the Japanese public at the same time. This is evident, for example, when Tokyo officials appeal to the world community through the United Nations for the complete abolition of nuclear weapons. As they do this, they acknowledge the public's expectation that nuclear weapons should be eliminated, yet at the same time they are not seriously and persistently encouraging Washington to adopt and implement a disarmament policy, remaining content to keep Japan under America's nuclear umbrella. Still another example is the relocation of the Futenma base in Okinawa. Survey data indicate that 45 percent of Okinawan respondents, a plurality, are against the relocation of the U.S. Marines' Futenma base from Ginowan to Nago. To help win some support in Okinawa for Futenma relocation, Tokyo has had to promise economic support.[11]

Option 2: Forging a New Security Trajectory

There is security for Japan beyond its alliance with the United States. But before Japan can realize this security, it has to deal with the issues that preclude its movement to a new trajectory. Tokyo needs to reexamine the post–Cold War security environment in the Asia–Pacific region. In doing this, Tokyo must fully reassess the rationale for the bilateral security alliance and understand that more serious threats emerge because of the alliance than its existence eliminates. Recognizing the promise of this new security trajectory is not as hard as adopting it and remaining on it. The latter requires that Tokyo resolve the contradictions in Japan's security policy.

Reminiscent of the Cold War, the most commonly used justification for the continuation of the bilateral security alliance is that instability still exists in the Asia–Pacific region. Today, Washington and Tokyo identify North Korea and China as the principal sources of potential instability in the region.[12] The justification for the existence of the alliance is that it provides some assurance to Japan that it will not have to contend alone with foreign threats that jeopardize its national security. Moreover, it is often said that Japan's neighbors would be enormously uneasy if the bilateral security alliance did not exist, for, sans the U.S. restraint, they would fear impending Japanese rearmament. After weaving together these diverse threads, observers typically draw the specious conclusion that the U.S.–Japan security alliance is necessary to stabilize the Asia–Pacific region.

However, there is no valid reason for Japan to maintain the Cold War security alliance with the United States. To assume that Japan needs the protection afforded by the United States is erroneous, as is the reasoning that without the bilateral alliance Japanese rearmament would be imminent. Japan's military capabilities are good enough to provide the nation with an adequate defense during most times. Moreover, multilateral security, especially over time, could develop into the chief form of defense for Japan and other nations as well. An effective multilateral security system, when combined with both regional and international mechanisms, would eliminate the need for Japanese rearmament. Such a system would also eliminate any need for revising or recklessly reinterpreting Article 9—Japan's war-renouncing constitutional clause—and with the dissolution of the bilateral security alliance, would markedly reduce regional tension and threats. But Tokyo insists that multilateral security cannot sufficiently provide for the real-world security threats that Japan currently faces.

Today, the existence of the security alliance between the United States and Japan sets in motion a self-fulfilling prophecy: the repeated suggestion that the Asia–Pacific region is not stable and that the bilateral security arrangement brings about some stability actually creates an observable amount of instability. Just in the last few years, despite the U.S.–Japan alliance, China tested nuclear weapons in 1995 and fired missiles near Taiwan in 1996; North Korea launched a Taepo Dong satellite missile, which flew over Japanese territory in late August 1998, and both India and Pakistan conducted nuclear tests in the spring of 1998. Because China and North Korea interpret the renewed interest of Washington and Tokyo in the bilateral security alliance as problematic and promise to work to counteract the resulting perceived threats, even more instability finds its way into the region.

A sober assessment of its current security relationship with Washington can easily bring Tokyo to the realization that the bilateral alliance is incompatible with two of Japan's major security objectives: strengthening the United Nations—including this institution's international security mechanisms—and global disarmament, specifically the elimination of all nuclear weapons. Facing the security challenges of the twenty-first century without maintaining the alliance with the United States and without rearming itself, especially to the point where it develops nuclear weapons, is a serious and viable alternative that Japan has not yet fully considered. Tokyo's preoccupation with traditional postwar security and the Japanese population's uneasy acceptance of peace since the Pacific War have caused too many in Japan to minimize the importance of change and to overlook the serious contradictions that exist in their nation's security policy. These contradictions are as follows:

- opposing the existence of nuclear weapons, but remaining protected by America's nuclear shield and not formulating the three nonnuclear principles into law;

- valuing norms that support an antimilitary culture and that encourage diplomatic solutions to international problems, but retaining the security alliance with the United States, which to some countries of the world is seen as a nation much too inclined to suggest the threat of or actual use of military force to solve problems;
- having a deep concern for promoting nuclear nonproliferation and nuclear disarmament, but remaining much more rhetorical than substantive on this issue;
- having an enduring interest in the United Nations as the reconciler of international disputes, but continuing to look first to the United States for answers to how to evaluate global security problems; and
- maintaining a war-renouncing constitutional clause, but financing one of the largest military budgets in the world.

Having recognized the necessity of undertaking international responsibilities, including those related to global security, it is incumbent upon Japan to resolve these contradictions. Resolving them in a way that eliminates any perception of hegemonic interests or intentions means that Japan needs to design a new security trajectory for itself that centers on nurturing confidence-building measures that provide the foundation for developing an international disarmament regime.

Resolving the Security Contradictions

Least worrisome in the immediate future is the last contradiction listed above. Japan is a wealthy nation, so maintaining relatively high military expenditures need not necessarily be threatening to other nations now. Moreover, Tokyo is unlikely to do significant damage to the Japanese economy as long as it keeps military spending at about 1 percent relative to gross domestic product. Since Japan's neighbors have become used to its relatively high military budget, it would be much more problematic for regional relations if Tokyo were to abandon the nation's purely defensive policy. Tokyo's continued commitment to a military for defensive purposes only, including retaining Article 9 in its current form, establishes a far less threatening environment than would be the case if this restraint did not exist.

Putting the nation on a new security trajectory, however, will require that Tokyo expeditiously resolve the other four contradictions. In doing this, Japan would also be identifying an important international role for

itself. Instituting this role will entail Japan's assumption of the leadership position in the design of a new international security paradigm. But
it is very unlikely that this new trajectory can materialize as long as
Japan remains tied to a security alliance with the United States. Thus,
the resolution of the contradictions in Japan's security policy is contin-
gent upon abrogating the bilateral security alliance. Otherwise, Japan
will remain far too susceptible to pressure from Washington to follow
the security course it has laid out.

Tokyo has refused to acknowledge that there is a contradiction in
Japan's policy relating to nuclear weapons. Specifically, Tokyo does not
recognize that, while denouncing the existence of nuclear weapons, remaining under America's nuclear umbrella is a contradictory policy
position. Tokyo rationalizes this policy anomaly by arguing that Japan
still faces serious security threats and intimates that being protected by
the U.S. nuclear shield does not violate the three nonnuclear principles.[13]

Top Japanese officials have routinely presented their case to the global community indicating the necessity of eliminating nuclear weapons.[14] Japan's formative role in the Tokyo Forum, a recent multilateral
initiative, although commendable, leaves far too much room for the
nuclear weapons states, especially the United States, to ignore the imperative of nuclear disarmament. Moreover, both China and North Korea have serious criticisms of the Tokyo Forum's final report. Among
some other things, Beijing strongly objects to the report's suggestion
that China is promoting a regional arms race in the Asia–Pacific area.[15]
Pyongyang's criticism is that although the Tokyo Forum's report meaningfully and directly addresses the issue of eliminating nuclear weapons, it suspects that Japan has the ulterior motive of becoming a
full-fledged military state and a nuclear power.[16] Tokyo has been working to convey the image that it wants to see nuclear weapons abolished—
for example, Japan has hosted the UN Conference on Disarmament Issues
every year since 1989—but remaining under America's nuclear umbrella
prevents Tokyo from making a convincing case to skeptics, particularly
in Beijing and Pyongyang.

To deal with this contradiction, Tokyo has two choices; however, they
will afford markedly different results. Tokyo could decide that it no longer
wants to be protected by America's nuclear shield.[17] Such a decision
would substantially increase the credibility of Japan's endorsement of a
nuclear-free world. Skeptics would be forced to consider Tokyo's official policy statements on nuclear weapons as representing something

other than rhetoric. An important confidence-building measure that To-kyo could initiate would be to abandon its gradualist position on the elimination of nuclear weapons, since today it calls for their reduction by employing a "realistic and incremental modus operandi."[18] Although this choice would send a positive signal that Tokyo recognizes that its past contradictory position prevented it from placing the nation on a security trajectory designed ultimately to promote nuclear disarmament, this decision has limitations. Specifically, suspicious observers, of which there are many, would reason that because Tokyo still maintains its security alliance with Washington, a de facto U.S. nuclear shield still exists. To them, Tokyo's active promotion of nuclear disarmament would be seen as hollow. In other words, as long as the bilateral security alliance exists there will be enough uncertainty in the minds of skeptics to burden the process of global nuclear disarmament with unnecessary suspicion. This suspicion would make it extremely difficult to move the disarmament process forward.

The other choice available to Tokyo to resolve the nuclear-shield contradiction is to declare an end to the security alliance with the United States. This declaration not only is much more convincing than the first choice, since it demonstrates Japan's security autonomy, but, just as important, because it reduces the amount of international suspicion, it would substantially mitigate the risk that the disarmament process would go awry. Japan's decision not to develop nuclear weapons, even though it has long possessed the physical resources and technological know-how to do so,[19] is generally accepted as the correct one within the country.[20] However, it is neither enough for Japan not to develop or possess nuclear weapons nor for it to reject America's nuclear shield. To build the trust and to establish the credibility that are necessary to afford Japan recognition as a leader in the global disarmament process, Tokyo must relinquish the Japanese connection to the bilateral security alliance.

Since the end of the Cold War, Beijing and Pyongyang have increasingly viewed the U.S.–Japan security alliance as having hegemonic designs. Moreover, since the Yugoslav War in 1999, Russia has reconsidered its security threats, now seeing the United States as potentially more aggressive than it had earlier.[21] Just how a strengthened American-Japanese security alliance in the East Asia–Pacific region can prevent apprehension in Moscow, particularly in light of Tokyo's decision to participate in TMD (theater missile defense) research with the United States, is unclear. The recent signing on February 9, 2000, of the Treaty of Friendship, Good Neighborliness, and Cooperation between Russia and the Democratic People's Republic of Korea is quite possibly a harbinger of increased tension in Northeast Asia. Although Pyongyang wanted the treaty to include a clause that specified mutual military support, Moscow prudently chose to reject the anachronism associated with such an alliance. In its current form, the treaty stipulates that in the event of a security problem, immediate contact will take place between Russia and North Korea.[22] Any increased tension in Northeast Asia could easily prod Moscow to ratchet up its current treaty with Pyongyang to the point of solidifying a bilateral military alliance.

Moscow has also been working hard on rapprochement with Beijing since 1999. Former Russian president Boris Yeltsin's visit to China in December 1999 produced a discernible renewal in the relationship between Moscow and Beijing. Discussions between Yeltsin and Chinese president Jiang Zemin successfully resolved historical border disputes between China and Russia. The two-day meeting between Yeltsin and Jiang resulted in a Sino-Russian joint statement, which demonstrated the shared bilateral interests of Russia and China. The joint statement forthrightly opposed any violation of the 1972 Anti–Ballistic Missile Treaty.[23] The document stressed that Beijing and Moscow would support each other's efforts at national unification, specifically emphasizing Russia's rejection of a "state-to-state" relationship with Taiwan while endorsing Russian activities in Chechnya. The joint statement also underscored the importance of establishing a multipolar world that rests on international laws and the charter of the United Nations, with the expectation that this institution can evolve into an effective international body and addresses the shared desire to have peace and stability in the Asia–Pacific region.[24]

By withdrawing from the military alliance with the United States and declaring its intention to proceed on a security trajectory that identifies nuclear disarmament as the objective, Japan can establish the basis for multilateral trust- and confidence-building that is necessary so that it can take meaningfully consistent steps toward this goal. In the present global situation several countries possess nuclear weapons: the five previously declared nuclear states, plus Israel and more recently India and Pakistan. Very troubling is that other countries may be clandestinely developing nuclear weapons. Therefore, it is incumbent on Japan to represent itself in the disarmament process as a credible leader that completely disavows any connection to nuclear weapons, including protection by a nuclear power.

Actually, the continuation of the security alliance with the United States prevents Japan from adequately resolving all of the contradictions that have been listed above. The security alliance is an ever-present threat to Japan's renunciation of war, its antimilitary norms and values, and even the national desire to find diplomatic solutions to regional and global problems. The strengthened security alliance with the United States places Japan in a more readied military position than it occupied in the past, and this increases pressure to drive up the defense budget. A substantial number of Japanese currently recognize that this strengthened alliance puts their nation at risk. Any regional conflict in which Japan participates is likely to undermine antimilitary norms and values and provide momentum to nationalist forces that want to bring about constitutional change, most especially the amendment of Article 9. To the extent that Tokyo follows Washington's lead, Japan also sacrifices the national desire to promote multilateral solutions to international problems. If Washington deems it necessary to implement a military response to a regional problem, the Japanese desire for diplomacy and a multilateral resolution to the conflict will not mix well with Tokyo's broadened commitment to the bilateral security alliance.

Dissolving the bilateral security alliance will also permit Tokyo to overcome its apparent hesitancy to promote nonproliferation and nuclear disarmament in a more determined manner than it has done in the past. An indication of Japan's continuing interest in nuclear disarmament is that it was the first nation to both sign and ratify the Comprehensive Test Ban Treaty (CTBT), of the states required to do so before it could come into force. In three recent instances, Tokyo has used its foreign assistance program to sanction nations—China, India, and Pakistan—that have conducted nuclear tests. Well recognized is Japan's leadership role in the Tokyo Forum, whose report calls for nations to end and "reverse the unraveling of the Nuclear Nonproliferation Treaty" and stresses both the need to abolish all "nuclear weapons through phased reductions" and the importance of bringing "the nuclear test ban into force."[25] But despite the Japanese interest in nonproliferation and disarmament, the security alliance with the United States has caused it to institutionalize its gradualist approach to nuclear disarmament. Abstaining from voting on a UN resolution in 1998 that called on the nuclear weapons states to abolish nuclear weapons expeditiously and completely, Japanese ambassador Akira Hayashi stressed that it "went just a little too far and contained some elements that are a little bit premature."[26] Tokyo's reluctance to design and launch a nuclear disarmament agenda, aside from the very unlikely possibility that it wants to keep open the option of developing nuclear weapons, can only be reasonably explained by the continuation of the bilateral security alliance and the protection of the U.S. shield.

Without the security alliance with the United States, Japan will be in the position to design disarmament initiatives that will add consistency to its bilateral relationship with China and Russia and, perhaps very soon, with North Korea. Beijing has recently drawn attention to the contradictory nature of the Sino–Japanese relationship, emphasizing that despite bilateral cooperation in social and economic areas, Japan's approach to security and politics follows U.S. policies far too closely. This, says Beijing, makes Tokyo an accomplice in secretly working to contain China.[27] Although there is an obvious compatibility between the positions of Japan and China regarding the existence of nuclear weapons— that is, both nations have officially appealed for their abolition[28] and have even jointly stressed the need to eliminate them[29]—distrust on security issues is still very evident in the bilateral relationship. To dissociate much of this distrust and the accompanying tension from Japan's security alliance with the United States is to miss the significance of Beijing's opposition to hegemony. Similarly, Moscow and Pyongyang have to be cognizant of the potential for this contradiction to exist in their bilateral relationships with Tokyo, specifically, cooperation in social and economic areas being offset by the concerns they have about the U.S.–Japan security alliance.

Tokyo also needs to resolve the contradiction associated with Japan's UN policy. From the time it became a member of the United Nations in 1956, Japan has taken the position that this multilateral body should play a leading role in the resolution of international conflicts. Since the end of the Cold War, Tokyo has been forthright in its position that the United Nations needs to be strengthened so that it can fulfill its mission of maintaining international peace and security.[30] Tokyo has even argued that because the United States cannot alone attend to global security problems today, it is important that multilateral solutions become the way to resolve international conflicts. Therefore, says Tokyo, there are increasing expectations that the United Nations will become effective in bringing about world peace.[31] As we saw in chapter 5, the Japanese public stands solidly behind their country's desire to become a permanent member of the UN Security Council, although it does not support an active military role for Japan when performing its duties.

Despite its antimilitary norms and the belief that the United Nations has the potential to maintain global peace, Japan's security alliance with Washington tempers its enthusiasm for the emergent international interest in multilateral security.[32] Because the United States' relationship with the United Nations has become tepid since the mid-1990s, it has created a policy time warp for Japan. Thus, as Tokyo builds on the security relationship with the United States, which has shown an increased propensity to circumvent the United Nations, it is forced to marginalize the generalized interests of the Japanese people who strongly support this multilateral body and its potential to realize global peace and security.

The major policy rub that Tokyo faces as a consequence of the failure to resolve the contradiction between its alliance with Washington and its position that the United Nations needs to develop into a viable international security institution appears in its relationships with Russia and China. Both Moscow and Beijing have emphasized the multipolar composition of the post–Cold War world and that U.S.-led initiatives undermine the changed security environment. While their interest in a multipolar world is fully compatible with a strengthened UN security system, Beijing and Moscow have become increasingly suspicious that the United States may be harboring hegemonic objectives. Beijing and Moscow reason that Tokyo is more concerned with bolstering its alliance relationship with the United States than it is with strengthening the security mechanism of the United Nations. Beijing and Moscow therefore remain apprehensive about Tokyo's objectives. Suspicions are running high in Moscow and Beijing about Japan's new responsibilities and initiatives associated with its security alliance with the United States.[33] The one-two punch of U.S. and Japanese military power is a difficult blow for Beijing and Moscow to defend themselves against.

Add to this the following questions that Moscow and Beijing must now consider: Is the recent strengthening of the U.S.–Japan security alliance merely the beginning step in an ongoing process? Is Tokyo considering the adoption of an independent military posture in the near future? Does Tokyo plan to shift the nation's science and technology competency to the development of offensive military systems? Will Japan's stockpiling of reactor-grade plutonium and strong science and technology infrastructure be combined to make Japan a nuclear weapons state? Or, perhaps the most ruminated question, Does the United States, with Japan's assistance, really intend to establish hegemony in the East Asia–Pacific region, and perhaps elsewhere as well?

This last question is particularly important, as the way nations answer it directly influences the security ambience of the entire East Asia–Pacific region. China's foreign policy officially "opposes hegemonism."[34] Beijing maintains that any country that attempts to establish hegemony—ideologically, physically through direct intervention, or both—will be challenged by China. When former Russian president Boris Yeltsin visited China in December 1999, he made a point of denouncing any single country's attempt to shape outcomes in the global order by proclaiming: "Major issues concerning the future and destiny of the world can only be determined with extensive participation by the entire international community."[35] Thus, the common thread in Beijing and Moscow's position is the need to foster and sustain multilateral security structures to obviate the efforts of any nation to establish hegemony. What is incontrovertibly the major source of tension today in the East Asia–Pacific area is the shared perception in Beijing and Moscow that Washington, with assistance from Tokyo, is assiduously working to establish regional hegemony. Tokyo is cognizant that a potentially serious rift in relations between Washington and Moscow links directly to Russia's unwavering efforts directed at "neutralizing unipolar dominance," given that its objective is to establish a multipolar international order. Moreover, Tokyo has been working hard to try to convince a disbelieving Beijing that the new U.S.–Japan guidelines for defense cooperation are transparent and are intended to be situational rather than geographic.[36]

Although it is often argued that a strong U.S. military presence in the region is a critical stabilizing force, this is increasingly being viewed as a specious contention. Advocates of America's military presence in the region frequently maintain that the United States is a good or benign hegemon.[37] This argument is nearly identical to the official line propounded by Washington. During discussions in Southeast Asia in the 1990s, the Clinton administration described America's military presence in East Asia as "an anchor of stability amidst the storm."[38] However, the problem is that those nations that feel dominated by the hegemon never see it as benign. Because hegemonic efforts are always subjectively interpreted, simply claiming for the United States the status of benign hegemon does mean that this coincides with the conditions in the East Asia–Pacific area as perceived by Beijing and Moscow, which are very leery of America's regional strategy and objectives.

What is apprehensiveness in Moscow and Beijing is actually paranoia in Pyongyang. North Korea unequivocally believes that the primary objective of the United States in the East Asia–Pacific area is to establish regional hegemony.[39] The breakup of the Soviet Union, economic malaise, and an ongoing food shortage all contributed to the past reclusion of the Democratic People's Republic of Korea (DPRK). While the DPRK has been accused of maintaining an anomalous negotiating style,[40] it has not been sufficiently emphasized that its economic conditions, national ideology, independent foreign policy, and determination that history should not be allowed to repeat itself, together create Pyongyang's propensity to be enormously distrustful of the United States and its security alliance with Japan. Improving relations between Tokyo and Pyongyang beginning in late 1999 notwithstanding, North Korea is still very suspicious of any move by Japan that can be associated with military activities. Pyongyang is not yet convinced that Japan does not intended to reinvade the Korean Peninsula.[41] On one hand, Pyongyang welcomes recent movement toward establishing normal bilateral relations with Tokyo; on the other hand, the DPRK continually mistrusts Japan's motives. Moreover, since Pyongyang believes that North Korea is the explicit target of the U.S.–Japan security alliance, it tends to perceive Tokyo's UN position as a political smokescreen. In the eyes of Pyongyang officials, Japan's proclaimed commitment to pacifism, to avoiding becoming a military power, and to global disarmament including the elimination of all nuclear weapons are incongruous with its willingness to proceed with new military initiatives and to maintain and strengthen the Cold War security alliance with the United States. Thus, for Pyongyang, Tokyo's position concerning the potential of the United Nations to become the steward of international security deflects attention from Japan's desire to establish itself as a regional military power.[42] Pyongyang's suspicion of Tokyo's objective of making Japan a dominant military power also causes it to oppose the Japanese acquisition of a permanent seat on the UN Security Council.[43]

Moving Forward without the Bilateral Security Alliance

Some analysts still argue today that the chief purpose of the bilateral security arrangement is to prevent independent Japanese remilitarization, as this would immediately make Japan a regional threat.[44] This argument is even taken one step further. At least one analyst contends that Japan's antimilitary culture would be eroded without the bilateral security alliance.[45] Many Americans also appear to believe that there is an association between the bilateral security alliance and minimization of the possibility of Japanese rearmament. This is certainly suggested in the Ministry of Foreign Affairs survey of Americans' opinions about Japan. The Ministry of Foreign Affairs 2000 survey shows that 84 percent of American respondents support the continuation of the U.S.–Japan security treaty and that 87 percent think that the accord is still important to American security. However, 51 percent of the American respondents do not want Japan to increase its defense capabilities, which is slightly more than the 49 percent who felt this way in the 1999 survey.[46] In other words, while Americans support the security treaty, more than half do not want to see Japan become a more capable military power.

Some analysts speculate that without the security alliance with the United States, Japan may very well be inclined to abandon its nuclear allergy and develop nuclear weapons.[47] What analysts minimize is the manifestly strong antinuclear sentiment that pervades Japan. In addition to the fact that antimilitary norms are easily ascertainable in Japan, the Japanese people overwhelmingly believe that their country should not possess nuclear weapons.

While it is true that the cities of Hiroshima and Nagasaki show an especially heightened disdain for the existence of nuclear weapons and nuclear testing, including the subcritical nuclear testing still performed by the United States and Russia,[48] strong antinuclear sentiment continues to suffuse the Japanese culture.[49] As we have seen, this strong antinuclear sentiment quickly became evident when the public overwhelmingly rejected the suggestion made by Shingo Nishimura, parliamentary vice minister for defense, when he declared in October 1999 that Japan should consider developing nuclear weapons. Japanese outrage at Nishimura's comment was so intense that he had little choice but to resign from the Obuchi government.[50]

Despite substantial economic development over the years and even the realist prediction that this growth would persuade it to become a military power that possesses nuclear weapons,[51] Japan has thus far largely retained its aversion to excessive militarism, its strong antinuclear sentiment, and its support for the United Nations. The Japanese public wants to see the United Nations become a strong and viable force in international security. Both the Japanese public and Tokyo have also demonstrated a continuing interest in Japan's becoming a permanent member of the UN security council. There is increasing frustration in Japan relating to the disparity between Japan's financial support of the United Nations and the amount of influence that it has within this institution.

The Japanese public's endorsement of the United Nations security objectives does not make it an outlier on this issue relative to Japan's Asian neighbors. An *Asahi Shimbun* survey conducted in 1999 indicates that the majority of the respondents in several Asian nations feel that the United Nations should be strengthened and that use of dialogue to resolve disputes between countries will be the best way to ensure international peace and security in the twenty-first century.[52] What is interesting is that this regional public endorsement of multilateral solutions to disputes among nations is directly at odds with Washington's position in recent years, which has been to deliberately circumvent UN involvement in international security matters. Discussions pertaining to the need to develop a multipolar international order based on the United Nations that resound from Beijing, Moscow, and elsewhere are antithetical to the recent efforts by Washington and Tokyo to strengthen their bilateral security alliance.

What is more, Tokyo is arguably dismissing public sentiment so that it can maintain a good relationship with Washington. This is most apparent in the continuing problems that Okinawans must contend with because of the disproportionately large share of U.S. bases and troops in their prefecture. It appears to many Japanese and certainly to Okinawans that Tokyo is succumbing to Washington's security policy. They believe that Tokyo is more inclined to support Washington's military strategy for Northeast Asia and for the entire Asia–Pacific region than to address the public's concerns seriously.

An interesting political irony evident in the Bush administration relates to its "new" security perspective. While attempting to justify the development of missile defense, the Bush administration has often stressed that the Cold War is over and that a new security mind-set needs to take hold; the 1972 ABM Treaty is an anachronism that does not reflect post–Cold War conditions. However, when it comes to the U.S.–Japan security alliance—formed at the onset of the Cold War—this new mind-set does not apply: the bilateral security treaty is immutable and the Status of Forces Agreement (SOFA), which authorizes and manages U.S. forces in Japan, is as relevant today as it was decades ago. Thus, while Okinawans have repeatedly called for changes in SOFA so that they can cope with the serious and continuing problems associated with U.S. troops in their prefecture, a concern that Tokyo has related to Washington, the Bush administration maintains that the agreement should remain unaltered.

Catalysts of Change

The security policy that Tokyo maintains is not altogether consonant with Japanese popular sentiment. Japan remains heavily burdened by U.S. troops and Tokyo has not determinedly moved to incorporate into substantive policies either the nation's antinuclear sentiment or its perennial interest in a strong United Nations. The longer Tokyo remains committed to the current security trajectory to which it is bound by Washington's military strategies, the more difficult it will be to nurture these now-marginal security interests into national policy. External pressure from Washington coupled with conservative domestic forces increases Tokyo's alienation from public security concerns. This problem is exacerbated by the constant promotion of some exogenous threat, which superficially legitimizes Tokyo's efforts in shaping public perception of national security.

Therefore, the most immediate way for an alternative Japanese security policy to come to the fore is for one of two developments to take place. The first is that some very significant event could occur relating to U.S. bases in Japan. Given the widespread belief that the U.S. military presence places an excessive burden on Japan, a major development pertaining to American forces that is perceived as further undermining or jeopardizing Japanese culture is very likely to put an enormous amount of political pressure on Tokyo to make a fundamental change in the nation's security relationship with Washington. The second is the development of a national movement that stresses that the disadvantages of the bilateral security alliance outweigh the advantages.

In addition to holding discussions in Japan about creating nuclear free zones and moving the country out from under the U.S. nuclear umbrella,[53] some local Japanese communities have rejected the intrusion of American ships into their waters because of the fear that they are carrying nuclear weapons. In March 1975, Kobe passed a formal resolution proclaiming that its port was a nuclear weapons–free zone.[54] In February 1999, Kochi prefecture governor Daijiro Hashimoto, brother of former prime minister Ryutaro Hashimoto, angered Tokyo officials. Hashimoto introduced a bill in the prefectural assembly stating that Japan's foreign ministry would have to provide documents certifying that military ships entering the prefecture do not have nuclear weapons on board.[55] Hashimoto's bill, however, was not successful due to opposition from both the local government and Tokyo.[56]

A recent example of local resistance to a port visit by a U.S. military ship comes from the city of Tomakomai in Hokkaido. In January 2001, Tomakomai initially rejected a U.S. Navy request for the Seventh Fleet's flagship, the *Blue Ridge*, to make a three-day stop in February in the city's port. The city's mayor claimed that the U.S. Navy visit would interfere with what is already an extremely busy commercial port. Resisting pressure from Tokyo for several days, Tomakomai's mayor indicated that should the ship be permitted to make a port call, presumably by permission from the central government, the city must be given unambiguous assurance that there are no nuclear weapons on board.[57] After intense pressure from both Tokyo and Washington, Tomakomai's mayor agreed to allow the port call by the U.S. warship. The mayor indicated that the Japanese Ministry of Foreign Affairs had not attempted to find out from the U.S. military whether the ship would be carrying nuclear weapons. He further stressed that because the visit by the U.S. vessel could be a violation of the three nonnuclear principles, he promised to seek a Kobe-like ordinance for port calls by foreign ships.[58]

Another aspect of local resistance is the perceived threat to the nation's pervasive antimilitary norms that many Japanese associate with the recently enacted guidelines for defense cooperation between Japan and the United States. Both Washington and Tokyo worry about the very real possibility that should there come a time when the guidelines need to be implemented because of a regional security emergency, they will encounter severe opposition from civilian port communities in Japan. The new guidelines give Japan's Self Defense Forces and the U.S. military the right to plan for regional security emergencies. But Tokyo has been unwilling to name specific Japanese ports that would be needed in such emergencies, because it fears that, once identified, local communities will manifest their opposition.[59]

It is, of course, conceivable that these two developments could be sufficiently intertwined so that the first could not be distinguished from the second. For example, the amalgamation of the antinuclear sentiment—which is especially strong in Hiroshima and Nagasaki—with the popular dissension relating to the problem of U.S. bases. Recent official efforts to reaffirm the importance of the bilateral security alliance, which formally began in the spring of 1996, came in the wake of the 1995 rape incident involving three American servicemen in Okinawa. This incident precipitated a crisis that literally sent thousands of Okinawans into the streets protesting the overbearing presence of U.S. troops and bases in their prefecture. Just weeks after this tragedy, as the survey data in chapter 5 shows, popular opposition to the U.S.–Japan security treaty soared to a post–Cold War high. Had the Okinawan opposition and heightened resistance to the security treaty been linked to the antinuclear movement in Japan, Tokyo and Washington would have had to contend with a crisis-like situation.

A recent heinous incident occurred in January 2001 when a U.S. marine lifted a high school girl's dress in Okinawa and snapped a picture.[60] Concerned that the community problems stemming from the presence of American troops in Okinawa had gone out of control, protests emerged within the prefecture, as well as elsewhere in Japan. Moreover, because of this incident, the Okinawan prefectural assembly drafted a resolution that explicitly called for the reduction of U.S. forces in Okinawa. This resolution prompted the U.S. commander in Okinawa, Lieutenant General Earl Hailston, to write in an e-mail message to several American military officers in the prefecture that stated that the political leaders there "are all nuts and a bunch of wimps." Upon learning of the lieutenant's comment, the Okinawan municipal assembly drafted a resolution calling for Hailston's firing.[61]

The issue of U.S. bases in Japan as a catalyst for change should not be minimized for two reasons. First, the Japanese antipathy toward the presence of U.S. bases and troops in Japan is a problem with deep historical roots.[62] Second, the bases issue visibly represents very serious problems that presently confront the Japanese people everyday. That a large percentage of the Japanese public wants to see a physical reduction of America's military presence in Japan notwithstanding, Washington and Tokyo continue to display what can easily be interpreted as a perfunctory attitude on this very important matter. The Status of Forces Agreement and Article VI of the Treaty of Mutual Cooperation and Security give the United States the legal right to use Japanese ports, as well as airports for military takeoffs and landings.[63] According to the Transport Ministry, during 1999 there was a 10 percent increase from 1998 in U.S. military use of civilian airports in Japan. In 1999, U.S. military aircraft used one-third of the eighty-seven civilian airports in Japan. Most often used was Nagasaki airport, which absorbed 35 percent of the 801 total takeoffs and landings by U.S. military aircraft in

1999. Adding to Okinawa's frustration with the huge American presence in the prefecture was that in February 2000 several U.S. military planes landed at Ishigaki airport, despite the official government request that they refrain from doing so.[64]

Spawned by the formation of strong popular opposition to the bilateral alliance, the movement of Japan to a new security trajectory should not be dismissed as simple idealism. Official Japanese security policy has been strongly associated for more than forty years with what some would too quickly categorize as idealism. The 1957 Basic Policy for National Defense remains an important component of Japan's security policy, a document in which there is an unambiguous directive that the United Nations would eventually replace the United States as the protector of Japan.[65] To dismiss the prospect of Japan moving onto a trajectory that categorically promotes UN-centered initiatives because of an American propensity to castigate idealism when it relates to security and to rely instead on so-called sober and realistic assessments that fundamentally depend on raw military power is an ideological appendage of *gaiatsu* politics.

Basic Elements of a Security Role That Reflect Japanese Interests

Although there are scholarly works that have pointed out the need for Japan to secure a significant post–Cold War international role, they encourage a Japanese position within the existing security paradigm.[66] However, there are several elemental reasons why Japan is currently in a position to design an alternative security paradigm. These reasons are as follows: the endurance of Article 9; continuing political interest in the realization of complete nuclear disarmament; a postwar culture that has revered and maintained antinuclear and antimilitarist norms; a perennial commitment to the United Nations, along with the professed desire to strengthen this institution; and the fact that Japan is an economic and technological superpower, making it both fitting and, arguably, obligatory that it take on leadership responsibilities in the areas of international and regional security.

In the early postwar years, there were commonly discussions, in one form or another, that emphasized that Japan's renunciation-of-war clause in its constitution was a reflection of the UN charter's concern for global peace and security. Similarly, there was discussion that Japan's pacifist constitution could serve as a model for other countries. Although these discussions ceased over time, the fact remains that Japan has retained Article 9,[67] despite some attempts to amend the constitution.

Not only has Japan remained staunchly opposed to the existence of nuclear weapons, it has also remained sensitive to problems that impede their reduction. In the wake of the refusal of the U.S. Congress to ratify the CTBT in fall 1999, Tokyo made the public commitment to heighten international interest in the accord.

Japan's continuing interest in bolstering the efficacy of the United Nations is noteworthy, especially given the actions of the United States over the past several years. Apart from its unenthusiastic economic commitment to the United Nations, the United States has not been providing this organization with the political support that is necessary to make it an effective multilateral institution. Despite this U.S. apathy toward the United Nations, Tokyo still considers it important to make this a stronger global institution.

As the second biggest economy in the world and as a leader in many key areas of science and technology Japan needs to find a way to contribute meaningfully to the international community. In doing this, Japan must rely not only on its own resources—including the skills and talents of its people—it must shape a security policy that echoes the interests and sentiments of its people, while remaining free of the influences of alliance politics. Moreover, Japan's contributions cannot be simply financial. Although Japan is aware that it cannot continue to postpone indefinitely its obligation to contribute to international dispute management and conflict resolution, it has yet to decide completely on how it is going to resolve this important matter.

Fashioning an Alternative Security Paradigm

There are basic reasons that make Japan uniquely qualified to construct a new security policy, but the immediate question that needs to be addressed is the components of a new security paradigm. If Tokyo truly wants an important international role for Japan, it must move off the sidelines and begin crafting policies that directly affect global security. Most important, it must be willing to shed Japan's "post–Occupation syndrome," which has caused it to be much too amenable to Washington's strategic policies.

It is true that Japan has not yet managed to recover completely from the problems related to its militarist past. As a result, significant mistrust and suspicion of Japan persists in the East Asian region. This is most evident in Japan's still troubled relationship with North Korea, which is now particularly worried that some in Tokyo are pushing hard to replace the country's "peace constitution" with a "war constitution" to permit unencumbered Japanese participation in overseas military adventures.[68] Moreover, despite the normalization of relations and the public display of amity between South Korea and Japan, Seoul still has reservations about Japanese intentions. Taiwan too remains latently suspicious of Japan, as does Russia. While recent improvements in Japanese-Russian relations since the October 1993 Tokyo Declaration publicly suggest the beginning of a new bilateral friendship, Moscow is nonetheless still somewhat wary of Japan's intentions. The Northern Territories/Kurile Islands dispute resurfaced in April 2000 when a Russian military ship fired on and captured a Japanese boat that was fishing near the islands.[69] The successful resolution of this dispute, which centers on islands taken from Japan by the Soviet Union after War World II, is the major condition for a comprehensive accord that will formally establish peace and completely normalize relations between Tokyo and Moscow.[70]

In short, several Asian countries are still very unsure of Japan's intentions in the twenty-first century and are predisposed to read remilitarization into much of what it does. This reading is not at all helped by Japan's enduring security alliance with the United States. Specifically, it is the result of Tokyo's complaisance with Washington or *taibei hairyo* (consideration toward the United States) on security issues, while too often ignoring the will and sentiments of the Japanese people. This work has stressed that a sizable part of the Japanese public remains antimilitarist, is uncertain at times about the bilateral security alliance, and clearly opposes Japan's possession of nuclear weapons. It is important to point out that ignoring public sentiment on national security is not new to Tokyo. It has ignored public opinion in the past when fashioning security policy. In January 1987, Tokyo broke through Japan's defense ceiling, which had been set at 1 percent of gross national product in 1976 and, according to survey data, was supported by much of the public. An *Asahi Shimbun* survey conducted in March 1987 showed that over 60 percent of the public was against government abandonment of the 1 percent ceiling. Subsequently, Tokyo was successful in getting public opinion to support this change in defense policy.[71]

Despite persistent efforts to make Japan a "normal country" since the Persian Gulf War,[72] the Japanese people stand behind Article 9 and continue to renounce war. What is therefore normal for Japan today is not some form of rearmament. Rather, what is normal is abiding by the norms that have sustained Japanese antimilitary and antinuclear sentiments.

Ending the Bilateral Security Alliance

Most important to the creation of a new Japanese security paradigm is that it must not include the present security alliance with the United States. Article X of the 1960 bilateral security treaty between the United States and Japan permits either party to end the accord after giving one year's notice.[73] Products of the Cold War, the security treaty and the more inclusive bilateral security alliance have been rationalized by the argument that the East Asia–Pacific region remains unsafe. Apart from the fact that perceptions of security threats are always subjective, relations in this part of the world have actually improved recently, compared to those in the early 1990s. Rapprochement is evident between China and Russia—some of which has resulted from the strengthened U.S.–Japan alliance—and North and South Korea have engaged in promising meetings that may lead to the reunification of the peninsula. Japan's bilateral relationships with China, South Korea, and Russia have improved. With Moscow, Tokyo is slowly moving closer to signing a formal and comprehensive peace agreement, including the resolution of problems relating to the small islands (the Kuriles, also known as the Northern Territories) north of Japan and south of Russia. By the beginning of 2000, even Japan's relationship with the DPRK had noticeably improved in comparison with the nadir reached only months before. Because of former prime minister Murayama's visit to North Korea in December 1999, Tokyo and Pyongyang began preliminary discussions intended ultimately to normalize bilateral relations between them. In the wake of the establishment of diplomatic ties between Italy and North Korea in January 2000, the DPRK has normalized relations with the Philippines, Australia, Canada, Spain, Belgium, Germany, Luxembourg, and Greece. DPRK has made it known that it wants to improve diplomatic relations with France, Ireland, the Netherlands, and Great Britain.[74] Further demonstrating North Korea's interest in removing the pejorative label of a rogue and recluse nation is that the DPRK also applied for membership in the ASEAN Regional Forum (ARF) in the first half of 2000 and was represented as a member at this organization's annual meeting held in Bangkok in July of that year.

However, finding sources of instability in East Asia has preoccupied officials in Washington and Tokyo. Too many officials in Washington and Tokyo go out of the way to taint relations by unjustifiably promoting suspicion, distrust, and ill will. An example of this is when President Bush claimed before Congress in January 2002 that North Korea is part of an "axis of evil." A remark like this unnecessarily raises tension and therefore intensifies the problem that Pyongyang is fully aware that both Washington and Tokyo perceive North Korea as the most obvious source of regional instability. Responding to Bush's comment, Pyongyang stressed that Washington was using the threat from North Korea as a "pretext" for the big increases in its military budget; moreover, it said that the proof that the United States is the "empire of devil" is that its military expenditures are growing quickly, despite the fact that "it has the largest number of weapons of mass destruction in the world." At the same time, Pyongyang stated that Tokyo's use of the "military threat" from North Korea is a result of "zealously following the U.S. policy of stifling the DPRK" so that Japan can falsely justify its increased "preparations for a war of overseas aggression."[75]

How officials in Washington and Tokyo frame international affairs does matter, since their views are quickly transmitted to the public. How the Japanese public can perceive a greater military threat to their country in the twenty-first century, compared to a few years ago, can be explained by the way policy makers frame security issues. According to recent poll data, the Japanese public's fear that there is a looming military threat that will affect their nation has *increased* during the last several years; 30.5 percent of the respondents to a January 2000 prime minister's survey believed that Japan will be involved in some international armed conflict, up from 21.1 percent in 1997. Reflecting the perceived threat attached to the August 1998 DPRK projectile launching, the survey data indicated that 56.7 percent of the respondents were most concerned about the potential danger that North Korea posed to Japan.[76] Besides the recent strengthening of the U.S.–Japan security alliance since 1996 and the decision by Tokyo to study a TMD system with Washington, Pyongyang has been upset with the continued presence of American troops in South Korea and the joint military exercises among the United States, Japan, and South Korea. Pyongyang attests that the last two problems have caused the DPRK to focus more attention on its national defense.[77] Most recently, Pyongyang has been struck by what it considers to be Tokyo's glaringly contradictory policy of "dialogue and deterrence" toward the DPRK—that is, continuing with discussions designed to establish formal diplomatic relations while retaining the U.S.–Japan security alliance. Pyongyang is very critical of the Japanese Ministry of Foreign Affairs' 2000 *Diplomatic Bluebook*, as it addresses both the potential DPRK missile threat and advocates a "balanced policy of dialogue and deterrence" in dealing with North Korea.[78]

But as this work has emphasized, Beijing and Moscow also perceive that there is still lingering distrust of China and Russia in Washington and Tokyo. One of the more recent initiatives of the U.S.–Japan security arrangement, joint TMD research, has greatly alarmed Beijing and Moscow[79] and therefore, like the problems perceived by Pyongyang because of the bilateral alliance, has added to regional instability. Russian opposition to the United States' proposal to build a limited, but still quite expensive,[80] National Missile Defense (NMD) system directly relates to the breach of the 1972 Antiballistic Missile Treaty that proscribes the deployment of this technology. Moscow reasons that NMD would severely compromise Russia's nuclear arsenal by leaving it completely vulnerable to American missiles, while the defensive shield would protect the United States. Because China has a small number of nuclear weapons, Beijing feels even more susceptible to the consequences of NMD, since its missiles could easily be rendered largely or completely ineffective by a functioning U.S. defensive shield. These manifest concerns of both Moscow and Beijing relating to the American NMD system, however, have overshadowed a more latent one associated with TMD and therefore the U.S.–Japan security alliance. The development and deployment of TMD would mean that America's line of defense would extend to the East Asia–Pacific region, thereby giving the United States a double layer of protection, in addition to early-warning notification. Not only is China terribly upset by the suggestion that Taiwan could be included in TMD, but when TMD is combined with NMD, Beijing, like Moscow, sees the United States as attempting to establish hegemonic global control with assistance from Japan. Because of the perceived threat posed by NMD to Russia and China, they have been discussing cooperative ways to counteract this system "to restore strategic stability."[81] Russia and China have also discussed how they can cooperate to counter TMD,[82] a defensive system that if deployed would add to regional tension.[83]

Rather than creating regional stability, the continuation of the Japan–U.S. security alliance is promoting instability. In the worse-case scenario, it would be the basis for a future regional arms race. Right now Russia, China, and North Korea cannot afford to become completely involved in an arms race with the United States and Japan. But this certainly does not mean that a quasi-regional arms race could not develop very soon and that in five or ten years from now a full-blown arms race could be under way. At present Russia, China, and North Korea have to consider counter strategies for any further advancement in the U.S.–Japan security alliance.[84]

The continuation of the security alliance between the United States and Japan, the world's top two economically, scientifically, and technologically advanced nations, *is* threatening to other countries. No matter how benign a military advancement may be between Japan and the United States, it will not be perceived in this way by other countries. A Cold War security alliance perpetuates Cold War anxieties. To reduce tension in East Asia, the Japan–U.S. security alliance must end. This is the first important step that Japan can take to create a new security trajectory.

Since the bilateral security alliance has been in place for nearly half a century, ending it will not be easy. Washington and Tokyo continue to promote a regional "fear factor." Moreover, because of the length of time the bilateral security alliance has existed, it has become a normative part of Japanese society. Still, authentic security and peace cannot continue to depend on a bilateral arrangement that engenders tension and distrust and is perceived as threatening by some countries. Tokyo's decision to study TMD with Washington—which in part is a good indication of how technology can drive a security alliance to a more sophisticated level—has created unnecessary problems in the East Asia–Pacific region. Deployment of TMD will cause tensions to grow exponentially and portends the eventual onset of a regional arms race, since it is unlikely that countries will sit idly by and accept being overshadowed by a progressively stronger and technologically improving U.S.–Japan security alliance. A bilateral security alliance that relies on threats of force and both nuclear and defensive shields is not in keeping with the desire for multilateral structures that are necessary to secure today's multipolar world.

By ending the bilateral security alliance, Japan will find it easier to build a strong security paradigm that befits the multilateral expectations that emerged during the past decade. As long as Japan remains commit-

ted to the security alliance with the United States, it will be very difficult for Tokyo to convince several skeptical governments that it is serious about nuclear disarmament. Ending the bilateral security alliance
would add to Tokyo's credibility in the area of nuclear disarmament.
The absence of the bilateral military alliance would also give Japan the
freedom to help the United Nations pursue a more dynamic international security role.

Preserving Article 9 and the Three Nonnuclear
Principles for Nuclear Disarmament

The Japanese government is currently discussing the possibility of constitutional change. To forsake the principle of forever renouncing war—
the gist of Article 9—suggests shallowness and political malleability,
since "forever" to the Japanese government would mean just a little over
a half century. Japan's antimilitarist norms are inseparable from Article
9. Constitutional change that would permit Japanese Self Defense Forces
to participate with the United States in military activities in the region
would be quickly perceived as remilitarization by some countries. Tokyo would be sending the signal that Japan is ready to engage in power
politics. While there is already serious criticism of the new guidelines
for defense cooperation between Japan and the United States, a constitutional change that would allow Japanese forces to participate with
American troops in regional disputes would be equivalent to the de jure
establishment of NATO in the East Asia–Pacific area.

Although there is some uncertainty among the Japanese public on the
issue of constitutional change, this is not true when the question turns
specifically to military activities. As shown in chapter 5, survey data demonstrate that the Japanese public still strongly supports Article 9. Any
attempt to change Article 9 therefore would at some point have to focus
on manipulating public opinion. Some Tokyo policy makers have already
been working to convince the public that a "normal country" status means
having defense forces that can actively participate without restriction in
military affairs. Despite the likelihood that the efforts of these policy
makers will continue, it does not seem that constitutional change involving significant revision of Article 9 will happen any time soon.

Japanese support for the three nonnuclear principles—which disal-
low the possession, manufacture, or introduction of nuclear weapons
into the country—remains quite strong. The resignation in October 1999

of parliamentary vice minister Shingo Nishimura of the Defense Agency because of his comments relating to the acquisition of nuclear weapons by Japan testifies to the enduring antinuclear sentiment in Japan. Nishimura created quite a stir in Japan and throughout the entire Asia–Pacific region when, during an interview with *Weekly Playboy*, he stated that the Japanese government "should consider the fact that Japan may be better off if it had armed itself with nuclear weapons."[85] Not only does the public overwhelmingly reject Japan's possession of nuclear weapons, there is an accompanying widespread sentiment in Japan that supports the complete elimination of nuclear weapons. The problem is that while both government and popular support for the nonnuclear principles remains very strong, Tokyo's official policy on nuclear weapons, in addition to being manifestly contradictory (proclaiming the need to abolish all nuclear weapons as Japan remains protected by America's nuclear shield), is not especially enthusiastic. As indicated above, the three nonnuclear principles remain policy rather than law. Tokyo has maintained an incrementalist policy on the abolition of nuclear weapons, wanting to see them *gradually* reduced over time. For example, at the 2000 review conference on the Nuclear Nonproliferation Treaty (NPT), Japanese ambassador for disarmament issues Seiichiro Noboru stated, "It is no use to appeal only to the idealism of nuclear abolition and make nuclear-weapon states isolated. Japan should take [a] gradual and realistic approach."[86] Tokyo maintains this incrementalist position not because it does not desire to isolate the nuclear weapons states but because it does not want to alienate Japan from them, especially the United States.

Putting itself on a new security trajectory will first necessitate that Japan make an unwavering commitment to the three nonnuclear principles. This would be best accomplished by establishing them as law and then linking this legal assurance to the nation's continuing popular enthusiasm for Article 9. Second, Tokyo will need to begin pressing for a planned and verifiable reduction of nuclear weapons, leading to their timely and scheduled elimination. The glaring omission of a time frame for the elimination of nuclear weapons is a major shortcoming of the final report issued in 1999 by the Tokyo Forum for Nuclear Nonproliferation and Disarmament.[87] Thus, it was not surprising that at the spring 2000 NPT review conference, which produced a statement that committed the nuclear powers to the ultimate elimination of nuclear weapons, Japan did not propose a time frame for the elimination of nuclear weapons. This omission again was evident in the fall of 2000 when Tokyo presented to the United Nations its most ambitious resolution to date entitled "A Path to the Total Elimination of Nuclear Weapons."[88] In addition to lacking a time frame, Japan's resolution did not include a substantive plan that would commit the nuclear states to a disarmament regime.

Without a specific time frame for the complete elimination of nuclear weapons, this inherently arduous process becomes illusory. Even with a time frame, nuclear powers are very likely to procrastinate, as the United States and Russia have demonstrated with START (Strategic Arms Reduction Treaty). Because of its visibility, the inclusion of a specific time frame, although surely providing no guarantee, can be the target of political and public condemnation if the process stalls or runs off track. The inclusion of a time frame for the abolition of all nuclear weapons also indicates the commitment of those countries possessing nuclear weapons to disarmament, while permitting the periodic monitoring of the process by multilateral institutions.

To be credibly involved in a leadership capacity in this process, Tokyo must discard its incrementalist position on the elimination of nuclear weapons and in its place design a timetable for disarmament that is realistic, achievable, and verifiable. This will be exceedingly difficult to do if Japan abandons the antimilitarism that is the essence of Article 9, reneges on its commitment to the three nonnuclear principles, or does not end the security alliance with the United States. As a leader in the nuclear disarmament process, Japan must therefore demonstrate neutrality, while forthrightly exuding the international significance and applicability of Article 9 and the three nonnuclear principles. In this way Japan can continue to make strong cases for the end to all nuclear testing, including subcritical nuclear testing, while pressing hard for all countries to sign and ratify the CTBT. Japan must be especially assertive with those countries that have not yet signed and ratified the treaty so that it can come into force.[89] Taking this neutralist and assertive approach to disarmament will also enable Japan to push for the realization of NPT's Article VI, which requires signatories "to take steps leading to nuclear disarmament."

Strengthening Institutions

Important to this new security paradigm is the manifestation of trust and unambiguous willingness to bolster multilateral institutions, such as the

United Nations and ARF. The end of the Cold War set the stage for the improvement of regional relations. Although the East Asia–Pacific and surrounding area have certainly not been problem free, regional relations definitely have the possibility to mature to the point where stability is the norm. In a leadership role, Japan must work to make this become reality. Developing a closer, more proactive security relationship with the United States will not enable Japan to do this. No matter how open the parties to a bilateral security alliance try to appear, such a relationship is inherently exclusive and somewhat secretive and could be perceived as potentially hostile by some countries. The stick and carrot approach, which is embodied in the U.S.–Japan security alliance, is an antiquated way of attempting to maintain regional stability. Under no circumstances can this alliance manufacture the requisite trust that an authentically stable security environment must have in the twenty-first century. To assume that Japan can establish genuine regional trust through confidence-building measures while retaining and strengthening the security alliance with the United States is much like pushing on a string: the effort soon becomes futile.[90]

As shown earlier in this work, public opinion in Japan largely endorses the country's becoming a permanent member of the UN Security Council. However, if this means assuming regular military obligations, public opinion also shows a discernible reluctance for Japan to become a permanent member of the Security Council. It is important to understand that there is nothing in Japan's constitution that expressly prevents it from becoming involved in UN security operations like other countries; the prohibitions against Japan's assumption of a military role are the result of the government's interpretation of the constitution, not the document itself.[91] Not only would Japan's active involvement in UN security operations be compatible with its constitution; this involvement would also demonstrate its interest in establishing a nonhegemonic and neutral international force focused on maintaining world peace and security.[92] By leaving Article 9 unchanged, Japan could also retain the constitutional parameters that prohibit it from waging an offensive war against another country. By allowing its military to participate in UN peacekeeping activities that have the single objective of conflict resolution, Japan would be helping to defend the international community's commitment to peace and security, while still, as a sovereign nation, renouncing war. Under complete UN auspices, Japan's participation in international peacekeeping would therefore not be prompted by issues relating to nationalism or sovereignty, but would be exclusively the result of the consensus of the global community.

Before it makes a commitment to participate fully in UN military activities, Japan needs to exert a much greater effort than it has up to the present to strengthen the United Nations. Although Japan has spoken frequently of the need to strengthen the United Nations, much more still has to be done to ensure that it becomes a viable multilateral institution that can effectively manage international security and promote global peace and disarmament. Long having a strong affinity with the United Nations, Japan recognized many years ago that this organization needs to broaden its responsibilities in the area of international security. But Japan's early post–Cold War enthusiasm for the United Nations, and especially for the emerging significance of multilateral security, has ebbed somewhat in recent years. This withering enthusiasm for multilateral security is the direct result of its moving to establish a symbolically stronger alliance with the United States since 1996.

To strengthen the United Nations, Japan will need to do several things. First, it must find ways to get a larger number of Japanese to work in high-level positions in the United Nations. Although Japan consistently makes significant financial contributions to the United Nations, persons of Japanese descent hold a relatively small number of top-level positions.[93] Second, Tokyo has to be persistent in its campaign to have Japan become a permanent member of the UN Security Council. It will be easier for Japan to start working on strengthening the international security mechanisms of the United Nations if it is a permanent member of the Security Council. Moreover, many Japanese feel that as a permanent member of the UN Security Council and as a nation that has made a sustained commitment not to become a nuclear power, Japan can make a very positive contribution to global disarmament. Third, Japan can strengthen the United Nations by working actively to promote ARF.[94] Article 52 of the UN charter encourages the use of regional arrangements and agencies to establish peace and security, "provided that such arrangements or agencies and their activities are consistent with the Purposes and Principles of the United Nations."[95] Encouraging the maturation of ARF, especially its role in the pacific settlement of disputes through multilateral diplomacy, would therefore strengthen the United Nations. By assuring its consistency with the objectives of the United Nations, a stronger ARF that is seen as a legitimate regional institution would provide another effective layer to international security. Finally, by working much harder than it is presently doing to build sound, trust-based bilateral relationships, particularly with Russia, North Korea, and China, Japan will be demonstrating that it sincerely wants to promote peace and real security in the East Asia–Pacific region and throughout the world, thereby making its efforts to strengthen the United Nations somewhat easier.

Strengthening Bilateral Relationships

While a security paradigm that has global peace and disarmament as its objectives requires strong multilateral institutions, the nation that is assuming a leading role in this activity must work hard at establishing solid bilateral relationships with as many countries as possible, most especially those with which it has experienced problems. For Japan, this means that it must work extra hard to ameliorate bilateral relations with China, North Korea, and Russia. Tokyo's improved relationship with Moscow during the past few years promises to get better with the signing of a bilateral peace accord. But Tokyo must be very careful not to let the prospect of completely normalized relations be undermined because of an ongoing territorial dispute. Beyond this, Japan can continue to provide assistance to Russia's efforts to disarm and dispose of its nuclear weapons. Since 1993, Japan has contributed ¥11.7 billion ($100 million) to the former Soviet countries for the disposal of nuclear weapons and wastes, about 70 percent ($70 million) of which has gone to Russia.[96] Although Japan's economy is still struggling to recover, financial and technological assistance to beleaguered Russia will demonstrate Tokyo's determination to improve and solidify the bilateral relationship.

Japan's bilateral relationship with China has also improved during the past few years, though not to the extent that it has with Russia. Still, there is clear evidence of some acrimony and distrust in the Sino-Japanese relationship. Unless these are eliminated, Tokyo will have a difficult time convincing Beijing to participate without strong reservations in a security agenda that seeks to abolish nuclear weapons and improve global security. Japan must demonstrate that it is fully committed to a "one China policy" and must leave no doubt that it does not intend to support Taiwan and the United States in a military dispute with the mainland. Japanese initiatives to further develop the common ground that appears in the 1998 joint statement signed in Japan by Chinese president Jiang Zemin and Prime Minister Keizo Obuchi, most especially the mutual agreement for the need to eliminate nuclear weapons,[97] would signal a genuine willingness by Tokyo to design an alternative security agenda. A major step in the direction of building a stronger Sino-Japanese relationship would be Tokyo's public approbation of China's pledges not to be the first country to use nuclear weapons and never to use them against a nonnuclear nation.[98] Tokyo can win big political points from Beijing by calling international attention to these pledges and by working hard to convince other countries that the Chinese example is an especially good one to follow. Demonstrating to Beijing that it is firmly committed to multilateral security solutions to regional problems would be another positive step that Japan could take in building a stronger Sino-Japanese relationship.

Japan's toughest bilateral challenge is North Korea. Both Japan and the DPRK have remained skeptical of each other's intentions, even as normalization discussions have been in progress. While Beijing has had a difficult time dealing with the "history" issue, this is even more the case with Pyongyang. Japanese concerns center on the purported missile and nuclear threats coming from North Korea. Certainly, Japan needs to work as hard as it can to resolve the history problem in a way that is mutually satisfactory. Japan must remain openly committed to the Korean Economic Development Organization (KEDO) and encourage Pyongyang to focus its emergent technological strength away from military development and toward efforts that will precipitate growth in the North Korean economy. This will be markedly easier for Tokyo to do if Pyongyang does not feel threatened by Japan and its security alliance with the United States. Japan must take advantage of North Korea's recent "reaching out" campaign—specifically, Pyongyang's new diplomatic initiatives. Japan must approach normalization talks with North Korea carefully and with an open mind. This does not mean that Japan must comply with unreasonable demands from Pyongyang. What it does mean is that Japan should show that it is willing to be flexible and prepared to be empathic during the normalization discussions. The Japanese public has already indicated its support for improving their country's relationship with North Korea. Recent survey data show that 73 percent of the Japanese respondents supported providing aid to North Korea, as long as it demonstrates that it can be trusted and that the assistance is not used for military purposes. Moreover, 52 percent of the Japanese respondents favored normalizing relations with the DPRK.[99] During normalization talks, Tokyo must make it perfectly clear that Japan does not harbor a retrogressive desire to use military power in Korea or elsewhere in Asia. Foreign aid will need to be added to Japan's bilateral agenda with the DPRK, as will technological assistance. This support will be especially important, because by providing financial and technological aid for civilian purposes, the DPRK will begin to see Japan in a favorable light—that of a country willing to help a neighbor improve the quality of life. The upshot will be a diminution of threat and suspicion and a marked increase in bilateral trust, which together may lead Pyongyang to give up on its demand that Japan provide reparation monies to North Korea.

Taking the Lead in Establishing a Nuclear Disarmament Regime

A major security problem that Japan is facing today is that it is juxtaposing the appearance of renouncing war (the constitutional ban on warmaking activities) with a high level of military preparedness. This has been a paramount concern of Beijing, Pyongyang, and Moscow.[100] This serious problem, of course, rests on top of Japan's contradiction relating to nuclear weapons: the popular opposition to their existence while remaining under America's nuclear shield. The widespread Japanese interest in the complete abolition of nuclear weapons cannot be developed into a viable international policy until Tokyo begins to approach this issue with the political resolve needed to achieve this important objective. Tokyo must shed Japan's nascent image of working toward establishing an "offensive defense"[101] and in its place demonstrate commitment to the establishment of a viable nuclear disarmament regime. To do this successfully, Tokyo must take politically visible steps in the direction of nuclear disarmament independent of the United States.

In addition to strengthening the security mechanisms of the United Nations and ARF and working to ameliorate its bilateral relationships, Japan needs to structure its domestic policies so that there is no ambiguity of intention or objective pertaining to nuclear disarmament. To accomplish this objective it is critical that the Japanese public and interested groups that make up civil society constantly monitor and if necessary react to the commitment of Tokyo to the three nonnuclear principles. Some officials in Tokyo have catered to popular sentiment on the issue of nuclear arms by formulating and supporting the three nonnuclear principles, the third being that Japan will not permit the introduction of these weapons into the country. However, they have not been firmly committed to the execution of all of these principles. Good evidence exists today that shows that in the past Tokyo permitted U.S. nuclear weapons to enter Japan.[102] As we have seen, Tokyo recently has had to contend with the heightened concerns of many local port communities relating to whether U.S. war ships are carrying nuclear weapons, since the new guidelines permit American vessels access to Japanese ports during emergencies.[103]

An unwavering commitment to campaign assertively for NPT and CTBT is an important and requisite move that Japan must make to establish an international disarmament regime. Already in place in Japan is an Official Development Assistance (ODA) program designed to minimize military activities among recipient countries. Japan has previously used ODA as a policy stick for purposes somewhat analogous to disarmament after China conducted nuclear testing in 1995 and subsequent to both India and Pakistan's nuclear tests in the spring of 1998. There is no reason why Tokyo could not make the restrictions coming from the use of the ODA stick more punitive while it provides additional incentives for compliance with global nuclear disarmament. The Japanese public strongly supports using tougher economic sanctions than currently exist to achieve compliance with evolving norms that discourage nuclear testing. A 1998 *Yomiuri Shimbun* survey indicates that 59 percent of the respondents believed that the Japanese government should more strictly use its economic assistance programs to gain the compliance of countries that perform nuclear tests.[104]

As the only nation that has ever experienced the devastating effects of atomic warfare, Japan is well positioned to push hard for the countries required to sign and ratify the CTBT to do so. For this same reason, Japan can make a credible case to get NPT to come into force, but not without sustained and strong diplomatic efforts on its part. If it really wants to be seen as a bona fide proponent of nuclear disarmament, Japan will need to extend its desire to see the complete ban on nuclear testing to include subcritical nuclear tests. Because of Tokyo's security alliance with Washington, ignoring the U.S. capability to perform subcritical nuclear testing while supporting CTBT, which seeks to establish an international norm prohibiting actual nuclear testing, promotes the appearance of a double standard or, at the very least, pays no heed to a gaping loophole in current disarmament efforts.

Assertively promoting verifiable and steady movement on START is still another project that Japan can add to its disarmament portfolio. In doing this, Japan will definitely need to authenticate its international appearance by genuinely projecting the image of neutrality. Getting involved in the START process while still aligned with the United States has a spurious appearance, since this creates the suspicion in Moscow of disproportionate disarmament. By assuming a neutralist position, Japan can work more effectively than it can now to promote START, linking Japanese efforts in this project with the CTBT and NPT.

Finally, Japan's staunch leadership activities in a global disarmament process will substantially elevate its credibility in the world community—and in a much different way from Tokyo's current efforts to bolster the security alliance with the United States. These activities will demonstrate that Japan is serious about constitutional diffusion (*fuken-shugi*) as it relates to Article 9, that is, spreading the principle of the renunciation of war to other countries, and that it genuinely wants to promote and establish world peace.[105] To some countries, however, Japan's commitment to a nuclear disarmament process will appear genuine only if it also ends the security alliance with the United States. By taking these steps, Japan can have its Self Defense Forces participate in the peacekeeping operations of a strengthened United Nations without violating Article 9 and without creating too much anxiety in the East Asia–Pacific region. Since involvement in authentic peacekeeping missions *completely sanctioned and managed by the United Nations* would not be Japanese aggression that would benefit Japan as a sovereign nation, Article 9 would not be violated. Ending the security alliance with the United States would substantially reduce the perception of threat in the East Asia–Pacific region, since the intention to diffuse Article 9 and promote nuclear disarmament would at the very least minimize the suspicion that Japan harbors ulterior motives.[106] Taking on leadership responsibilities in a global disarmament process would confirm that Japan is determined to establish international peace and security.

Conclusion

Japan's two major security options leave little ambiguity about directions for policy development in the twenty-first century. Staying the present course, that is, maintaining the existing alliance with the United States, means that Japan has selected to sustain a regional environment that perpetuates distrust and tension. There is little chance to avoid this, as it is easy to see that the combined military power of the United States and Japan represents a formidable challenge to any potential adversary. Moreover, two serious problems accompany the decision to remain on the present security trajectory. First, the inevitably of an incrementally stronger military posture assumed by Japan could lead to the definitive formation of an "offensive defense"; second, and even worse for the region, is the possibility that sometime in the future Tokyo will become less dependent on the United States, eventually disconnect Japan from the bilateral security relationship, and independently remilitarize. Revising Article 9 could more easily induce this potential regional crisis.

But Japan does have a second security option. At the very least, the Japanese public is very sensitive to the issues that constitute this option. A strong United Nations supported by a regional security structure provides the multilateral institutional support that is acceptable to the public. Abolishing all nuclear weapons through the realization of a global disarmament policy—the only surefire way to prevent a nuclear catastrophe—has also remained a prominent interest of the Japanese public. It is important that deliberate, sustained, and coordinated action by Tokyo and the Japanese public will need to occur before these conceptualized standards materialize into international norms and policy. For this option to take shape, Japan must end its current security relationship with the United States and retain the nation's commitment to renouncing war. Furthermore, it must be understood that this option offers an alternative to the existing security structure of trying to maintain regional and international stability through the existence of threatening military repercussions delivered by alliance politics.

Notes

Chapter 1

1. See, for example, "Japan–U.S. Security Pact Still Vital" (editorial), *Daily Yomiuri On-line*, June 21, 2000.

2. "Clinton Tells Marines to Be Neighborly," *Daily Yomiuri*, July 24, 2000, p. 3.

3. The 1997 defense guidelines between the United States and Japan clearly indicate that: "Both Governments will conduct bilateral work, including bilateral defense planning in case of an armed attack against Japan, and mutual cooperation planning in situations in areas surrounding Japan." (See chapter 2 for more details on the new bilateral defense guidelines.)

4. Yoichi Kato, "Japan–U.S. Alliance Has Taken a Step Backward," *Asahi Shimbun*, March 14, 2001; "Sub Accident Shakes Japan's Security Ties with the United States," *New York Times*, February 23, 2001.

5. "Clinton Scraps Plan to Address Okinawans," *Daily Yomiuri*, July 19, 2000; "Clinton Reaffirms the Importance of Japan–U.S. Security Alliance," *Daily Yomiuri*, July 22, 2000.

6. Leon Sigal, "Rogue Concepts," *Harvard International Review* 22, no. 2 (summer 2000): 62–66.

7. See "Withdrawal of U.S. Forces from S. Korea Urged," Korean Central News Agency, April 28, 2001; "Withdrawal of U.S. Troops from South Korea, Prerequisite for Disarmament," Korean Central News Agency, April 29, 2001. The Korean Central News Agency is the official news agency of the Democratic People's Republic of Korea.

8. See "New Round of Diplomatic Bargaining: Bush and DPRK Relationship," *People's Korea*, February 21, 2001.

9. Zhou Bian, "The Trend in the Bush Administration's China Policy," *Beijing Review* (February 22, 2001).

10. People's Republic of China, Information Office of State Council, *China's National Defense in 2000*, white paper (Beijing, 2000). Document accessed at http://www.china.org.cn/english/2791.htm on January 12, 2001.

11. Zhang Tuosheng, "Seven Issues in East Asian Security," *Beijing Review*, no. 9 (March 1, 2001).

12. "The Korean Peninsula: What If?" *Far Eastern Economic Review* (June 29, 2000).

13. Department of Defense, *Annual Report on the Military Power of the People's Republic of China, Report to the Congress* (Washington, DC: June 2000). Accessed on the Worldwide Web June 26, 2000 at http://www.defenselink.mil/news/Jun2000/china06222000.htm.

14. Office of the Secretary of Defense, *Proliferation: Threat and Response* (Washington, DC: U.S. Department of Defense, January 2001).

15. Contrary to the claims of some observers who see TMD and NMD as different defensive systems, the former for regional defense against mid-range missiles and the latter to protect against intercontinental missiles, TMD and NMD have a number of things in common, including problems. See Yoichi Funabashi, "Tokyo's Temperance," *Washington Quarterly* 23, no. 3 (summer 2000): 135–144; insert by Daniel Dupont in George Lewis, Theodore Postol, and John Pike, "Why National Missile Defense Won't Work," *Scientific American* (August 1999): 36–41.

16. "TMD Study Worries Russian Official," *Japan Times Online* (December 19, 2000).

17. "Japan's Defense Plan Creates Anxiety," *Beijing Review*, no. 2 (January 11, 2001).

18. Concerning the important matter that countries respond to perceived threats see Stephen Walt, *The Origins of Alliance* (Ithaca, NY: Cornell University Press, 1987).

19. Office of the Assistant Secretary of Defense for International Security Affairs, East Asia Pacific Region, *A Strategic Framework for the Asian Pacific Rim* (Washington, DC: Department of Defense, 1992), p. 10.

20. "North Korea Extends Missile Moratorium," *New York Times*, May 3, 2001; "Kim's Vow Aimed at Keeping U.S. on Track," *Asahi Shimbun*, May 4, 2001.

21. See the Cox Report. Document accessed on the Worldwide Web at http://www.conservativenews.org/SpecialReports/cox/index.html.

22. Officially, Beijing posted a 121.29 billion yuan ($14.6 billion) defense budget for 2000, increasing from 107.67 billion yuan in 1999. In 1998, China's official defense budget was 93.47 billion yuan. Beijing maintains that China's 2000 defense expenditures amounted to 5 percent of the U.S. and 30 percent of the Japanese military budgets. See People's Republic of China, Information Office of State Council, *China's National Defense in 2000*. For further information on Chinese military spending see People's Republic of China, Information Office of State Council, *China's National Defense in 1998*, white paper (Beijing, July 1998); Center for Defense Information, "Chinese Defense Spending: A Great Increase, But to Where?" *Weekly Defense Monitor* 2, no. 17 (April 30, 1998); June Teufel Dryer, "State of the Field Report: Research on the Chinese Military," *AccessAsia Review* 1, no. 1 (August 1997).

23. See Wang Hucheng "Rising Military Budgets and International Security," *Beijing Review*, no. 14 (April 5, 2001); "Arms Race Gains Speed, Headed by US," *China Daily*, July 3, 2000.

24. See China–Russia Joint Declaration on Defense; "China, Russia Blast U.S. Shield Plans," *Asahi Evening News*, July 19, 2000, "Russia, China Denounce U.S.

Missile Shield," *Daily Yomiuri*, July 19, 2000; "Putin: N. Korea May Be Ready to Abandon Missile Program," *Daily Yomiuri*, July 20, 2000.

25. Quoted in "TMD: Safety Net or Threat?" *Far Eastern Economic Review* (February 4, 1999).

26. Quoted in "Time to Rethink the Japan–U.S. Security Treaty," *Asahi Shimbun*, June 24, 2000.

27. See Anthony DiFilippo, "*Hikaku sekai ni muketa Nihon no koken*" (The Japanese contribution to an anti-nuclear world), *Asahi Shimbun*, Op-ed, September 25, 1998, p. 4.

28. Toshio Saito, "Japan's Security Policy," Washington, DC: National Defense University, Strategic Forum, Institute for National Strategic Studies, May 1999.

29. Advisory Group on Defense Issues, *The Modality of the Security and Defense Capability of Japan: The Outlook for the Twenty-first Century*, Tokyo, August 12, 1994.

30. Matake Kamiya, "The U.S.–Japan Alliance and Regional Security Cooperation: Toward a Double-Layered Security System," in *Restructuring the U.S.–Japan Alliance: Toward a More Equal Partnership*, ed. Ralph Cossa (Washington, DC: Center for Strategic and International Studies, 1997), pp. 19–28.

31. An *Asahi Shimbun* poll conducted in March 1987 showed that while 15 percent of the public supported the cabinet's abandonment of the 1 percent ceiling, 61 percent of the public expressed disapproval. See Ronald Dolan, "National Security," in *Japan: A Country Study*, ed. Ronald Dolan and Robert Worden (Washington, DC: U.S. Government Printing Office, 1992), p. 432.

32. Some recent disparities between Tokyo's security policies and Japanese public opinion are discussed in Anthony DiFilippo, "Japan's National Security Policy Ignores Public Sentiment," *Japan Times*, Op-ed, May 25, 2000.

33. Professor Kenji Urata at Waseda University School of Law first made this suggestion to me.

Chapter 2

1. See Department of Defense, *Report of the Quadrennial Defense Review* (Washington, DC: Department of Defense, May 1997).

2. Despite the end of the Cold War, U.S. military spending declined only by about $50 billion between 1990 and 1997.

3. Japan is often said to have the second largest economy in the world. According to an estimate by the Organization for Economic Cooperation and Development, China's gross domestic production was second only to that of the United States in 1997. See United States General Accounting Office, *China Trade: WTO Membership and Most-Favored-Nation Status* (Washington, DC: U.S. General Accounting Office, June 17, 1998), p. 3.

4. See Anthony DiFilippo, *Cracks in the Alliance: Science, Technology, and the Evolution of U.S.–Japan Relations* (Aldershot, England, and Brookfield, VT: Ashgate, 1997, chapter 4).

5. President Clinton's trip to China in July 1998 established (1) that China was both a regional and global military power; (2) that its economic relations with the United States were important; and (3) that America's tolerance of China's differences had limits. For U.S. concerns about the threats posed by North Korea and China, see Office of the Secretary of Defense, *Proliferation: Threat and Response*

(Washington, DC: Department of Defense, January 2001), pp. 7–18.

6. Office of the Assistant Secretary of Defense for International Security Affairs (East and Pacific Region), *A Strategic Framework for the Asian Pacific Rim* (Washington, DC: Department of Defense, 1992), p. 2.

7. Including U.S. military personnel stationed in Hawaii (32,708) and Guam (3,621), the total number of American military personnel in the region totals 134,435. See Department of Defense, Washington Headquarters Services, Directorate for Information Operations and Reports, *Selected Manpower Statistics, Active Duty Military Personnel Strengths by Regional Area and by Country* (Washington, DC, Fiscal Year 1999); United States General Accounting Office, *Overseas Presence: Issues Involved in Reducing the Impact of the U.S. Military Presence in Okinawa* (Washington, DC: U.S. General Accounting Office, March 1998), p. 14.

8. See George Packard, *Protest in Tokyo: The Security Treaty Crisis of 1960* (Princeton, NJ: Princeton University Press, 1966).

9. See Ministry of Foreign Affairs (MOF), *Diplomatic Bluebook 1992* (Tokyo: MOF, 1993), pp. 49, 59; MOF, *Diplomatic Bluebook 1993* (Tokyo: MOF, 1994), p. 49; and MOF, *Diplomatic Bluebook 1994* (Tokyo: MOF, 1994).

10. The Higuchi Report was the work of a special advisory group established by former prime minister Morihiro Hosokawa to study Japanese defense issues. Translated into English, the report bears the title *Modality of the Security and Defense Capability of Japan: Outlook for the Twenty-first Century* (August 12, 1994).

11. Japan, however, did support the U.S. effort to use military force against Iraq.

12. Japan responded quickly to India and Pakistan's nuclear testing by canceling grant and loan assistance to both countries; exempted were funds directed strictly for humanitarian assistance.

13. Japanese economic assistance (grants and loans) to both India and Pakistan is substantial. In 1996 India was the fourth largest recipient of Japanese loans, which amounted to more than $522 million, and received over $35 million in grants, making it the twenty-third largest recipient of grant aid from Japan. In 1996 Pakistan was the seventh largest recipient of grant aid from Japan, which exceeded $68 million, and was the sixth biggest recipient of loans from Japan, which totaled more than $192 million. See MOF, *ODA Summary, 1997* (accessed on the Worldwide Web).

14. See essays in *Restructuring the U.S.–Japan Alliance: Toward a More Equal Partnership*, ed. Ralph Cossa (Washington, DC: Center for Strategic and International Studies, 1997).

15. See DiFilippo, *Cracks in the Alliance*.

16. Office of the Assistant Secretary of Defense, *A Strategic Framework for the Asian Pacific Rim* (1992).

17. Seung-Ho Joo, "Russia–North Korea Rapprochement and Its Implication for Korean Peace Regime" (Paper presented at the International Studies Association Conference, Los Angeles, CA, March 14–18, 2000).

18. U.S. Department of State, *Background Notes: North Korea, June 1996* (Washington, DC: U.S. Department of State, 1996).

19. "'93 Rodong May Have Flown over Japan, Agency Admits," *Japan Times Online*, October 23, 1998.

20. United States General Accounting Office, *Nuclear Nonproliferation: Difficulties in Accomplishing IAEA's Activities in North Korea* (Washington, DC: United States General Accounting Office, July 1998), p. 5.

21. South Korea and Japan pledged the most of the $4.6 billion for the construc-

tion of the light water reactors, the former $3.2 billion and the latter $1 billion. See Howard Diamond, "KEDO Resolves Cost-Sharing for North Korean Reactor Project," *Arms Control Today* 28, no. 5 (June/July 1998). Later, the European Atomic Energy Community joined KEDO, as well as Canada, Poland, New Zealand, Argentina, Australia, Chile, Indonesia, Finland, and the Czech Republic.

22. Joo, "Russia–North Korea Rapprochement and Its Implication for Korean Peace Regime."

23. The United States Information Agency commissioned Central Research Services, Inc., to survey the Japanese public on the question of whether or not North Korea possessed nuclear weapons. Interviews were conducted between January 19 and January 26, 1994. Survey data were obtained from the Roper Center for Public Opinion Research, University of Connecticut.

24. United States General Accounting Office, *Nuclear Nonproliferation: Difficulties in Accomplishing IAEA's Activities in North Korea,* July 1998, pp. 19–20.

25. "North Korea Site an A-Bomb Plant, U.S. Agencies Say," *New York Times,* August 17, 1998.

26. Office of the Assistant Secretary of Defense for International Security Affairs (East Asia and Pacific Region), *United States Security Strategy for the East Asia–Pacific Region* (Washington, DC: Department of Defense, February 1995), p. 18.

27. Ibid., p. 10.

28. Ministry of Foreign Affairs, *Joint Announcement, Japan–U.S. Security Consultative Committee,* September 1995. Document accessed on the Worldwide Web at www.mofa.go.jp/region/n-america/security/index.html.

29. U.S. Department of State, *Dispatch Magazine* 7, no. 39 (September 23, 1996).

30. U.S.–Japan Subcommittee for Defense Cooperation, *Interim Report on the Review of the Guidelines for U.S.–Japan Defense Cooperation,* June 1997.

31. See U.S.–Japan Security Consultative Committee, *Completion of the Review of the Guidelines for U.S.–Japan Defense Cooperation,* New York, September 23, 1997; Jianwei Wang and Xinbo Wu, "Against Us or with Us? The Chinese Perspective of America's Alliances with Japan and Korea," Asia/Pacific Research Center, Stanford University, May 1998; Chu Shulong, "China and the U.S.–Japan and U.S.–Korea Alliances in a Changing Northeast Asia," Asia/Pacific Research Center, Stanford University, June 1999.

32. See Richard Montaperto and Hans Binnendijk, "PLA Views on Asia Pacific Security in the Twenty-first Century" (Washington, DC: National Defense University, Strategic Forum, Institute for National Strategic Studies, June 1997); "China's Position on Current International Issues, *Beijing Review* 42, no. 41 (October 11, 1999); "Crazy for Hegemony," *Beijing Review,* no. 21 (May 24, 2001).

33. Beijing's foreign policy explicitly states that "China opposes hegemonism." See People's Republic of China, Foreign Ministry, *Foreign Policy,* accessed on the Worldwide Web at http://www.fmprc.gov.cn/e/c/ec.htm; David Shambaugh, "China's Military Views the World: Ambivalent Security," *International Security* 24, no. 3 (winter 1999/2000): 52–79.

34. See "Defense Bills Fan Instability," *China Daily,* June 8, 1999; Xu Zhixian and Yang Bojiang, "New Acts of Historical Retrogression," *Beijing Review* 42, no. 24 (June 14, 1999).

35. "U.S.–Japan Alliance Shifts Cloud Peace in Asia," *People's Korea,* October 8, 1997.

36. Ibid.

37. "Residents, Experts Worried by Review," *Japan Times Online*, September 18, 1997.

38. "Constitutional Scholars Oppose Japan–U.S. Guidelines," *Asahi Evening News*, November 3, 1997 (accessed on the Worldwide Web at http://www.asahi.com/english/english.html/).

39. *U.S.–Japan Joint Declaration on Security—Alliance for the Twenty-first Century*, April 17, 1996, Tokyo, Japan.

40. *Joint Statement, U.S.–Japan Security Consultative Committee, Completion of the Review of the Guidelines for U.S.–Japan Defense Cooperation*, New York, September 23, 1997.

41. "Japan Doesn't Know Whether It Supports U.S. Missile Attacks," *Japan Times Online*, August 21, 1998.

42. "Albright Voices Appreciation of Japan Stance on Attacks," *Kyodo News*, August 24, 1998, accessed on the Worldwide Web at http://www.home.kyodo.co.jp.

43. This same survey reported that 69 percent of the respondents thought that the mutual security treaty currently helps to maintain Japan's security. See Takubo Tadae, "The Okinawan Threat to the Security Treaty," *Japan Echo* (autumn 1996): 46–52. Concerning the concept of "unarmed neutrality," see J.A.A. Stockwin, *The Japan Socialist Party and Neutralism* (London: Melbourne University Press, 1968).

44. Special Action Committee on Okinawa (SACO), *The SACO Final Report*, Tokyo, December 2, 1996.

45. *Joint Announcement: U.S.–Japan Security Consultative Committee*, Tokyo, December 2, 1996.

46. *The SACO Final Report*.

47. SACO, *The SACO Final Report on the Futenma Air Station*, Tokyo, December 2, 1996.

48. "Okinawa/Tokyo Divided; Base/Economy Not," *Okinawa Times* (Weekly Times), August 22, 1998.

49. "Central Govt. Welcomes Ota Comment," *Daily Yomiuri On-line*, August 28, 1998.

50. Total number of active U.S. military personnel in Japan and South Korea as of September 30, 1999. See Department of Defense, *Selected Manpower Statistics* (Fiscal Year 1999).

51. Victor Cha, *Alignment despite Antagonism: The United States–Korea–Japan Security Triangle* (Stanford, CA: Sanford University Press, 1999).

52. "Expert: Fading Hopes Leave Okinawans Accepting Bases," *Mainichi Daily News*, May 20, 2001. Additional data from this survey can be found in "Pro-U.S. Base Residents in Okinawa Top Foes," *Daily Yomiuri On-line*, May 20, 2001.

53. Joseph Nye, "Strategy for East Asia and the U.S.–Japan Security Alliance," *Defense Issues* 10, no. 35 (1995), (comments by Assistant Secretary of Defense for International Security Affairs Nye at the Pacific Forum Center for Strategic and International Studies/Japanese Institute of International Affairs Conference held in San Francisco, March 29, 1995.)

54. For example, see Thomas Berger, *Cultures of Antimilitarism: National Security in Germany and Japan* (Baltimore, MD: Johns Hopkins University Press, 1998).

55. Ted Carpenter, "Pacific Fraud: The New U.S.–Japan Defense Guidelines," (Washington, DC: Cato Institute, October 16, 1997).

56. See the article by former Japanese prime minister Morihiro Hosokawa, "Are

U.S. Troops Needed in Japan? Reforming the Alliance" *Foreign Affairs* 77, no. 4 (July/August 1998): 2–5; Mike Mochizuki and Michael O'Hanlon, "The Marines Should Come Home: Adapting the U.S.–Japan Alliance to a New Security Era," *Brookings Review* 14, no. 2 (spring 1996).

57. United States General Accounting Office, *Overseas Presence: Issues Involved in Reducing the Impact of the U.S. Military Presence on Okinawa*, March 1998.

58. See Chalmers Johnson and E.B. Keehn, "The Pentagon's Ossified Strategy," *Foreign Affairs* 74, no. 4 (July/August 1995): 103–114; Ted Carpenter, "Paternalism and Dependence: The U.S.–Japan Security Relationship," policy analysis (Washington, DC: Cato Institute), November 1995.

59. The most common argument is that North Korea continued to "play the nuclear card" to get concessions from the United States, Japan, and South Korea. See, for example, Christopher Hughes, *Japan's Economic Power and Security: Japan and North Korea* (London: Routledge, 1999).

60. U.S. Department of State, Office of the Spokesman, Press Statement, "Report on the U.S. Visit to the Site at Kumchang-Ni, Democratic People's Republic of Korea," Washington, DC, June 25, 1999.

61. William J. Perry, U.S. North Korea policy coordinator and special advisor to the president and secretary of state, *Review of United States Policy toward North Korea: Findings and Recommendations*, unclassified report (Washington, DC: October 12, 1999).

62. Department of Defense, *2000 Report to the Congress, Military Situation on the Korean Peninsula* (Washington, DC: Department of Defense, September 12, 2000).

63. Ibid.

64. Quoted in "Pentagon Says North Korea Is Still a Dangerous Military Threat," *New York Times*, September 22, 2000.

65. Quoted in "Cohen Urges North Korea on Peace," *New York Times*, September 22, 2000.

66. The Report of the Tokyo Forum for Nuclear Non-proliferation and Disarmament, *Facing Nuclear Dangers: An Action Plan for the Twenty-first Century*, Tokyo, July 25, 1999.

67. Secretary of State Madeleine K. Albright, Japanese Foreign Minister Kono, Japanese Defense Minister Torashima, and U.S. Secretary of Defense William Cohen, press conference by the U.S.–Japan Security Consultative Committee, New York, September 11, 2000.

68. "Japan, U.S. Flayed for Tampering with Situation of Korean Peninsula," Korean Central News Agency, September 26, 2000.

69. Ministry of Foreign Affairs, *Announcement by the Chief Cabinet Secretary on Japan's Immediate Response to North Korea's Missile Launch*, Tokyo, September 1, 1998. Obtained on the Worldwide Web at the following address: www.mofa.go.jp/announce/anounce/1998/9/901-2.html.

70. "That Was No Satellite: Defense Agency," *Japan Times*, October 30, 1998. Former prime minister Keizo Obuchi stated before the United Nations: "The recent missile launch by North Korea, even if it was an attempt to launch a satellite into orbit, poses a serious problem, which directly concerns both Japan's national security and peace and stability in Northeast Asia." See Ministry of Foreign Affairs, *Statement by Mr. Keizo Obuchi Prime Minister of Japan at the Fifty-third Session of*

the General Assembly of the United Nations, New York, September 21, 1998.

71. "Spy Satellites Planned," *Asahi Shimbun,* October 31, 1998.

72. Japan first considered the theater missile defense project in 1993 after North Korea launched a Rodong 1 missile in the Sea of Japan. See "Tokyo Opts Out of TMD: New York Times," *Japan Times Weekly International Edition,* February 24–March 2, 1998, pp. 1, 6.

73. "Successful Launch of First Satellite in DPRK," Korean Central News Agency, September 4, 1998.

74. *Nikkei Weekly,* September 1998; "Japan, US to Jointly Research Missile Defense Initiative," *Nikkei Net (Nihon Keizai Shimbun)* , September 4, 1998; "N. Korea: Missile Was a Satellite," *Asahi Shimbun;* "N. Korea May Have Launched a Satellite," *Washington Post,* September 5, 1998; "A North Korean Satellite? U.S. Is Searching," *New York Times,* September 6, 1998; "Hard Target," *Far Eastern Economic Review* (September 24, 1998).

75. "North Korean Rocket Intended for Satellite Launch: U.S.," *Kyodo News,* September 12, 1998; "N. Korea Missile a Satellite Launch, U.S. Officials Say," *Asahi Shimbun,* September 12, 1998; "N. Korea Missile Likely Had Satellite," *Daily Yomiuri On-line,* September 15, 1998.

76. "North Korea Warns U.S. It Can Launch Another Missile, *New York Times,* December 26, 1998.

77. Emphasis added. "U.S. Warned not to Try to Test DPRK," Korean Central News Agency, December 25, 1998.

78. See "N. Korea Exports Missile Parts to Pakistan: Report," *Kyodo News,* September 15, 1998.

79. See "Normalization of DPRK-Japan Relations Urged," Korean Central News Agency, September 2, 1999.

80. "Militarism Brewing in Japan," *China Daily,* September 25, 2000.

81. *Security Treaty between the United States of America and Japan,* San Francisco, September 8, 1951 (signed), April 28, 1952 (effective).

82. *Treaty of Mutual Cooperation and Security between Japan and the United States of America,* Washington, DC, January 19, 1960.

83. Defense Agency, *Basic Policy for National Defense,* Tokyo, May 20, 1957, accessed on the Worldwide Web at http://www.jda.go.jp/e/index_.htm.

84. See, for example, Ministry of Foreign Affairs, *Diplomatic Bluebook 1992* (Tokyo: Ministry of Foreign Affairs, 1993), pp. 49, 59.

85. In February 1998, U.S. arrears to the United Nations came to nearly $1.3 billion. At that time, the U.S. State Department contended that because of America's unpaid dues, "the atmosphere in the United Nations toward the U.S. delegation has certainly made it very difficult for us to negotiate." See United States General Accounting Office, *United Nations: Financial Issues and U.S. Arrears* (Washington, DC: U.S. General Accounting Office, June 1998).

86. ARF was established in 1994 as a potentially viable Asian security organization. It currently has twenty-three members, which include the United States, Japan, Russia, China, South Korea, and, most recently, North Korea. The DPRK became a member of ARF in summer 2000.

87. Ministry of Foreign Affairs, *Japan's Policy toward the United Nations in the Post-Cold War World.* This document can be accessed on the Worldwide Web at the following address: http://www.mofa.go.jp/policy/un/pamph96/japan.html.

88. See *The Guidelines for U.S.–Japan Defense Cooperation*.

89. See the report of the Tokyo Forum for Nuclear Non-proliferation and Disarmament, *Facing Nuclear Dangers: An Action Plan for the Twenty-first Century*, Tokyo, July 25, 1999.

90. Other examples of Japan's recent efforts in the area of disarmament can be found in Anthony DiFilippo, "Creating Global Security: Japan as a Potential Catalyst," in *Economics of Conflict and Peace*, ed. Jurgen Brauer and William Gissy (Aldershot, England, and Brookfield, VT: Ashgate, 1997), pp. 376–396.

91. Ministry of Foreign Affairs, *Statement by Mr. Keizo Obuchi Prime Minister of Japan at the Fifty-third Session of the General Assembly of the United Nations*.

92. *Statement by State Secretary for Foreign Affairs Masahiko Koumura to the United Nations Conference on Disarmament Issues in Sapporo*, July 22, 1997. Information accessed on the Worldwide Web at www.mofa.go.jp/press/c_s/disarmament.

93. International Court of Justice, *Advisory Opinion: Legality of the Threat or Use of Nuclear Weapons*, July 8, 1996.

94. *Verbatim Excerpts of Oral Statements to the International Court of Justice on the Legality of the Threat or Use of Nuclear Weapons*, October 30–November 15, 1995.

95. Ibid.

96. However, the statements by Takashi Hiraoka, Mayor of Hiroshima, and Iccho Itoh, Mayor of Nagasaki, both given on November 7, 1995, to the World Court, clearly emphasize the illegality of the use of nuclear weapons in international law. See note 93.

97. Department of Defense, *Annual Report to the President and Congress, 2000* (Washington, DC: Department of Defense, 2000).

98. Department of Defense, Report to Congress, *Annual Report on the Military Power of the People's Republic of China* (Washington, DC: Department of Defense, June. 2000).

99. The National Institute for Defense Studies, *East Asian Strategic Review 2000* (summary), Tokyo, March 2000.

100. "Defense Agency Cautious over Korean Developments," *Japan Times*, July 29, 2000.

Chapter 3

1. "Tanaka Hits Japan–U.S. Pact," *Asahi Shimbun*, June 6, 2001; "Tanaka's Reported Faux Pas Concern for U.S., Yanai Says," *Japan Times Online*, June 7, 2001.

2. See Hideo Sato, "Prospects for Global Leadership Sharing: The Economic Dimension," School of Public Affairs, Center for International and Security Studies, University of Maryland at College Park, Maryland/Tsukuba Papers on U.S.–Japan Relations, October 1996; C. Fred Bergsten and Marcus Nolan, *Reconcilable Differences? United States–Japan Economic Conflict* (Washington, DC: Institute for International Economics, 1993), pp. 233–242; *Framework for a New Economic Partnership between Japan and the United States*, July 1993; U.S.–Japan *Common Agenda for Cooperation in Global Perspective*, July 1993; Koji Tsuruoka, "The Common Agenda in the Twenty-first Century" (Tokyo: Ministry of Foreign Affairs, March 1997).

3. Department of Defense, Office of International Security Affairs (East Asia and Pacific Region), *United States Security Strategy for the East Asia-Pacific Region* (Washington, DC: Department of Defense, February 1995), p. 2.

4. For a recent example, see "U.S. Again Urges Japan to Lower Trade Barriers," *Japan Times Online*, April 1, 2001.

5. These issues are discussed fully in Anthony DiFilippo, *Cracks in the Alliance: Science, Technology and the Evolution of U.S.–Japan Relations* (Aldershot, England and Brookfield, VT: Ashgate, 1997).

6. Trade data from the U.S. Census Bureau, Foreign Trade Division, Data Dissemination Branch, Washington, DC.

7. Growing from $6.4 billion in 1982, U.S. direct investments in Japan—mainly in the manufacturing, finance, and banking sectors—amounted to $39.2 billion dollars in 1995. See U.S. Department of State, Bureau of East Asian and Pacific Affairs, *Background Notes: Japan, April 1998* (Washington, DC: U.S. Department of State, 1998).

8. NEC was slapped with antidumping charges amounting to 454 percent on the price of its products, Fujitsu's totaled 173.08 percent; all others came to 313.54 percent. See U.S. International Trade Commission, *Vector Supercomputers from Japan* (Washington, DC: U.S. International Trade Commission, October 1997); "Japanese Firms Face Penalties: Trade Panel Approves Anti-dumping Duties," *Washington Post*, September 27, 1997; "U.S. Antidumping Law Routs Japanese Supercomputers," *Daily Yomiuri On-line*, September 28, 1997.

9. "U.S. Supercomputer Maker Wins Ruling," *Associated Press*, September 26, 1997, accessed on the Worldwide Web from the *Washington Post*'s site at http://search.washingtonpost.com/wp-srv/wapo/19970926/v000916–902697–idx.html.

10. "NEC to Bring Supercomputer Dumping Case to US Supreme Court," *Nikkei Net* (*Nihon Keizai Shimbun*), November 5, 1998.

11. *The Government of Japan's Comments on the 1997 National Trade Estimates (NTE) Report*, April 15, 1997; Subcommittee on Unfair Trade Policies and Measures, Industrial Structure Council, *1998 Report on the WTO Consistency of Trade Policies by Major Trading Partners* (Tokyo: Ministry of International Trade and Industry, Industrial Structure Council, 1998).

12. Japanese Subcommittee on Unfair Trade Policies and Measures, *1998 Report on the WTO Consistency of Trade Policies by Major Trading Partners*.

13. "U.S. Court Backs Japan in Supercomputer Feud," *Daily Yomiuri On-Line*, December 19, 1998.

14. See Michael Green, "Interests, Asymmetries, and Strategic Choices," in *The U.S.–Japan Security Alliance for the Twenty-first Century* (New York: Council on Foreign Relations, 1997); Susumu Awanohara, "Scenarios that Divide: An Abiding Need for Diplomacy" (New York: Council on Foreign Relations, December 4, 1996); Yoshihide Soeya, *Japan's Dual Identity and the U.S.–Japan Alliance*, Stanford University, Asia/Pacific Research Center, May 1998; Ivo Daalder, "Prospects for Global Leadership Sharing: The Security Dimension," Maryland/Tsukuba papers on U.S.–Japan Relations, Center for International and Security Studies at Maryland, School of Public Affairs, University of Maryland at College Park, July 1996.

15. Two examples of incremental adjustments to the security alliance are the 1960 *Treaty of Mutual Cooperation and Security between Japan and the United States of America*, and the (Special Action Committee on Okinawa) *SACO Final Report*, 1996. Today there are those who support and oppose the incremental ap-

proach. Those who support incremental changes feel that the endurance of the bilateral security alliance depends upon an asymmetrical alliance. See, for example, Michael Green, "State of the Field Report: Research on Japanese Security Policy," *AccessAsia Review* 2, no. 1 (September 1998): 21–22. For some, however, the incremental approach makes instability an inherent component of the bilateral security relationship, since it leaves in place Japanese dependency; this, in turn, makes Japan reluctant to become more active in security matters, including those involving regional security. See Mike Mochizuki "A New Bargain for a Stronger Alliance," in *Toward a True Alliance: Restructuring U.S.–Japan Security Relations*, ed. Mike Mochizuki (Washington, DC: Brookings Institution, 1997), pp. 17–23.

16. *Japan–U.S. Joint Declaration on Security—Alliance for the Twenty-first Century*, Tokyo, April 17, 1996; Speech by Prime Minister Ryutaro Hashimoto at Columbia University, "Japan–U.S. Relations: A Partnership for the Twenty-first Century," New York, June 23, 1997.

17. See, for example, Curt Campbell, "Energizing the U.S.–Japan Security Partnership," *Washington Quarterly* (autumn 2000): 125–134; "The United States and Japan: Advancing toward a Mature Partnership," National Defense University, Institute for National Strategic Studies, special report, October 11, 2000.

18. See Yoshihide Soeya, "Japan's Dual Identity and the U.S.–Japan Alliance," p. 17; Kenneth Pyle, *The Making of Modern Japan* (Lexington, MA: D.C. Heath, 1996), pp. 232–240, 271–277; Sun-Ki Chai, "Entrenching the Yoshida Doctrine: Three Techniques for Institutionalization," *International Organization* 51, no. 3 (summer 1997): 389–423. The Yoshida Doctrine takes its name from the early postwar prime minister Shigeru Yoshida. This doctrine mainly advocated growing Japan's economy while shunning involvement in international affairs.

19. Ronald Dolan, "National Security," in *Japan: A Country Study*, ed. Ronald Dolan and Robert Worden (Washington, DC: U.S. Government Printing Office, 1992).

20. "Japan, U.S. Agree on SDI Participation," *Aviation Week and Space Technology* (July 27, 1987): 23.

21. See Office of the Assistant Secretary of Defense for International Security Affairs, East Asia Pacific Region, *A Strategic Framework for the Asian Pacific Rim* (Washington, DC: Department of Defense, 1992).

22. Department of Defense, Office of International Security Affairs, *United States Security Strategy for the East Asia-Pacific Region* (February 1995).

23. Approved by the Japanese National Defense Council and the cabinet on May 20, 1957, Japan's *Basic Policy for National Defense* is still a major element in the foundation of the nation's defense policy. The third principle of this document is as follows: "To develop incrementally the effective defense capabilities necessary for self-defense, with regard to the nation's resources and the prevailing domestic situation."

24. For a favorable discussion of the incremental position see Green, "State of the Field Report: Research on Japanese Security Policy."

25. Policy recommendations supporting the reduction or removal of U.S. troops can be found in Mike Mochizuki and Michael O'Hanlon, "The Marines Should Come Home: Adapting the U.S.–Japan Alliance to a New Security Era," *Brookings Review* 14, no. 2 (spring 1996): 10–13; and Morihiro Hosokawa, "Are U.S. Troops Needed in Japan? Reforming the Alliance," *Foreign Affairs* 77, no. 4 (July/August 1998): 2–5. For a view opposing the removal of U.S. troops from Okinawa, see Noboru Yamaguchi, "Why the U.S. Marines Should Remain in Okinawa: A Mili-

tary Perspective," in *Restructuring the U.S.–Japan Alliance*, ed. Ralph Cossa (Washington, DC: Center for Strategic and International Studies, 1997), pp. 98–110.

26. For a "liberal position" that argues for an expansion of the Japanese military role beyond that set out in the 1997 guidelines for defense cooperation, see Mike Mochizuki and Michael O'Hanlon, "A Liberal Vision for the U.S.–Japanese Alliance," *Survival* 40, no. 2 (summer 1998): 127–134.

27. See Chalmers Johnson and E. B. Keehn, "The Pentagon's Ossified Strategy," *Foreign Affairs* 74, no. 4 (July/August 1995): 103–114; Ted Carpenter, "Paternalism and Dependence: The U.S.–Japanese Security Relationship" (Washington, DC: Cato Institute, November 1, 1995); Ted Carpenter, "Pacific Fraud: The New U.S.–Japan Defense Guidelines" (Washington, DC: Cato Institute, October 16, 1997), http://www.cato.org/dailys/id-16–97.html.

28. The National Institute for Defense Studies, *East Asian Strategic Review: 1997–1998*, Tokyo (January 1998): 31.

29. "Poll: Voters Want Bases Removed," *Asahi Shimbun*, November 11, 1998.

30. "Problems at U.S. Bases in Okinawa Fuel Public Ire over Military Presence," *Japan Economic Almanac 1997* (Tokyo: Nihon Keizai Shimbun, 1997), pp. 30–31.

31. United States General Accounting Office, *Overseas Presence: Issues Involved in Reducing the Impact of the U.S. Military Presence in Okinawa* (Washington, DC: U.S. General Accounting Office, March 1998), pp. 2, 14.

32. See Okinawa Homepage at www.pref.okinawa.jp ("U.S. Military Bases in Okinawa"); Masahide Ota (former Governor of Okinawa), "Letter to President Clinton," September 27, 1995.

33. See for example, The Center for Strategic and International Studies, *Alliance for the Twenty-first Century: The Final Report of the U.S.–Japan Twenty-first Century Committee*, ed. Eri Hirano and William Piez (Washington, DC: The Center for Strategic and International Studies [CSIS], August 1998), p. 46. This CSIS report goes so far as to claim that the alliance "has been responsible for much of the good that has taken place in East Asia and has facilitated constructive engagement in undertakings elsewhere."

34. For example, Okamoto Yukio in his article, "Why We Still Need the Security Treaty," *Japan Echo* (winter 1995): 11, writes that it is not the Japanese Self Defense Forces, but rather "[t]he cornerstone of Japan's defense is instead the Japan–U.S. Security Treaty"; Ralph Cossa concludes in his article, "U.S.–Japan Security Relations: Separating Fact from Fiction," in *Restructuring the U.S.–Japan Alliance*, ed. Ralph Cossa, p. 46, that: "The U.S.–Japan alliance has played a vital role in promoting regional stability and prosperity in the past and promises to continue serving the national security interests of both nations and the region as a whole in the future, provided both nations continue to nurture the relationship and deal seriously with the challenges that most certainly lie ahead."

35. Ralph Cossa, "Korea: The Achilles' Heel of the U.S.–Japan Alliance," Stanford University, Asia/Pacific Research Center, May 1997, p. 6.

36. Department of Defense, Office of International Security Affairs, *The United States Security Strategy for the East Asia-Pacific Region* (Washington, DC: Department of Defense, November 1998), p. 30.

37. The difference between engagement and containment is not clear. Engagement sounds more amicable, while containment suggests a lack of tolerance and

therefore it is politically acerbic. It would be enormously unwise for the United States to openly maintain a containment policy toward China today. Unlike during the Cold War, when rival superpowers contended for hegemony, the United States today is unquestionably the world's only military superpower. Announcing a containment policy toward China would thus unequivocally expose the effort by the United States to establish unchallenged hegemony in the Asia–Pacific area. By claiming to have an engagement policy toward China, however, the United States can create the impression of political benignity, that is, playing its part to maintain regional stability.

38. See, for example, "Crazy for Hegemony," *Beijing Review*, no. 21 (May 24, 2001).

39. Nakanishi Hiroshi, "Redefining Comprehensive Security in Japan," in *Challenges for China–Japan–U.S. Cooperation*, ed. Kokubun Ryosei (Tokyo and New York: Japan Center for International Exchange, 1998), pp. 44–69.

40. Having the United States, the world's most advanced military power, and Japan, which, although it maintains a defensive security system, nonetheless has one of the largest military budgets in the world, retain a Cold War security alliance has to make China feel uncomfortable. For a comparison of the countries with the largest military expenditures see, U.S. Arms Control and Disarmament Agency, *World Military Expenditures and Arms Transfers 1996* (Washington, DC: U.S. Arms Control and Disarmament Agency, 1997); also see Foreign Press Center, *Facts and Figures of Japan* (Tokyo: Foreign Press Center, 1998), pp. 21–22.

41. Joseph Nye, "China's Re-emergence and the Future of the Asia-Pacific," *Survival* 39, no. 4 (winter 1997–1998): 65–79. That the United States cannot predict Chinese development is hardly a justification for a continued American presence in the Asia–Pacific region. To argue that this is a "better" course to follow than alternative strategies is nothing short of fusing cultural semantics with a political position.

42. Department of Defense, Office of International Security Affairs, *The United States Security Strategy for the East Asia-Pacific Region*, November 1998, p. 31.

43. Secretary of State Madeleine Albright on occasion facetiously commented that the objective of U.S. foreign policy is to establish hegemony in East Asia. For example, she did this before the 2000 ARF meeting.

44. Wang Jisi, "The Role of the United States as a Global and Pacific Power: A View from China," *Pacific Review* 10, no. 1 (1997): 1–18.

45. Japan's Defense Agency is concerned about the Senkaku Islands dispute. The Defense Agency states very clearly that these islands "constitute the proper territory of Japan." The agency also draws attention to China's statements, which indicate that it is important to defend Chinese interests in these islands. See Defense Agency, *Defense of Japan 1997* (Tokyo: Japan Times, 1997), p. 51.

46. Charles Morrison, ed., *Asia Pacific Security Outlook 1998* (Tokyo and New York: Japan Center for International Exchange, 1998), p. 44.

47. Quotes from the July 1998 Chinese white paper on defense in this paragraph are from "Guarded Efforts on Defense Ties," *Asahi Evening News*, November 25, 1998.

48. On May 24, 1999, one year and eight months after the United States and Japan signed the new guidelines, the Japanese government officially approved them.

49. Xiao Li, "Japan's 'New Acts' Arouse Objections," *Beijing Review* 42, no. 20 (May 17, 1999).

50. "Guidelines May Push Japan into China's Anti-U.S. Storm," *Kyodo News*, May 24, 1999.

51. A very large number of Chinese, including some top officials in the communist party and in the military, believe that the U.S. bombing of the Chinese embassy in Belgrade was intentional. See "Double-Edged Fury," *Far Eastern Economic Review* (May 20, 1999); Wang Jie, "Trampling on International Laws Deserves Punishment," *Beijing Review* 42, no. 22 (May 31, 1999); Luo Tongsong, "Who Whips Up Anti-American Feeling?" *Beijing Review* 42, no. 23 (June 7, 1999).

52. "U.S. Trying to Divert Attention from Bombing," *China Daily*, May 21, 1999.

53. Morrison, *Asia Pacific Security Outlook 1998*, p. 43.

54. "Building a Friendly and Cooperative Sino-Japanese Relationship," *Beijing Review* 41, no. 44 (November 2–8, 1998); Ministry of Foreign Affairs, *Japan–China Relations*, 1997 (accessed from the Ministry of Foreign Affairs' Web page); and Yong Deng, "Chinese Relations with Japan: Implications for Asia-Pacific Regionalism," *Pacific Affairs* 70, no. 3 (fall 1997): 374.

55. See Anthony DiFilippo, "China's Side of the History Equation," *Japan Times*, December 10, 1998, p. 21.

56. Quoted in "Jiang Hails New Era in Japan–China Ties, Three Hecklers Held for Interrupting Waseda Speech," *Daily Yomiuri On-Line*, November 29, 1998.

57. Jianwei Wang and Xinbo Wu, "Against Us or with Us? The Chinese Perspective of America's Alliances with Japan and Korea," Stanford University, Asia/Pacific Research Center, May 1998.

58. Morrison, ed., *Asia Pacific Security Outlook 1998*, p. 44.

59. "Southeast Asia: China Steps in Where U.S. Fails," *Far Eastern Economic Review* (November 23, 2000).

60. For an attempt to justify the development of a U.S.–Japan TMD system that presents no threat to China see Michael Green, "Theater Missile Defense and Strategic Relations with the People's Republic of China," in *Restructuring the U.S.–Japan Alliance*, ed. Ralph Cossa, pp. 111–118.

61. See "U.S. Mulls Scrapping Asia Missile Defense Plan," *Japan Times Weekly International Edition*, March 30–April 5, 1998, p. 3.

62. Several months after the Ministry of Foreign Affairs gave its immediate response to the North Korean launch, Tokyo and Washington formally agreed to undertake missile defense research. See Ministry of Foreign Affairs, *Exchange of Notes Concerning a Program for Cooperative Research on Ballistic Missile Technologies Based on the Mutual Defense Assistance Agreement between Japan and the United States of America*, Tokyo, August 16, 1999; Barber Wanner, "United States, Japan Ink Accord on TMD Research," *JEI Report*, no. 33 (August 27, 1999).

63. See David Shambaugh, "China's Military Views the World: Ambivalent Security," *International Security* 24, no. 3 (winter 1999/2000): 52–79. However, it is misleading (analogous to hitting only half the target) to suggest, as this author does, that Washington, and therefore Tokyo, must be on the alert for any sign of an attempt by Beijing to destabilize East Asia and threaten U.S. security interests. As Beijing sees it, Washington and Tokyo together present a far more formidable challenge to Chinese regional security interests than China does to those of the United States and Japan.

64. Ministry of Foreign Affairs, *Japan–China Relations* (see n. 54).

65. See "China's Foreign Trade," *Beijing Review* 43, no. 14 (April 3, 2000).

66. Ministry of Foreign Affairs, *Japan's Official Development Assistance, Annual Report 1999* (Tokyo: Ministry of Foreign Affairs, 1999). Accessed on the World-

wide Web at the following address: http://www.mofa.go.jp/policy/oda/summary/1999/index.html.

67. Japan verbally expressed its "deep remorse" for Japanese military aggression against China in the 1998 Joint Declaration. In October 2000, Chinese premier Zhu suggested that China would no longer pursue an official apology from Japan.

68. Ministry of Foreign Affairs, *Japan–China Joint Declaration on Building a Partnership of Friendship and Cooperation for Peace and Development*, Tokyo, November 26, 1998.

69. Some feel that in a military conflict between Washington and Beijing over Taiwan, Tokyo would at first respond slowly and minimally, but in the end, provide support to the U.S. effort. See Aurelia George Mulgan, "The US–Japan Security Relationship," in *The New Security Agenda in the Asia-Pacific Region*, ed. Denny Roy (New York: St. Martin's, 1997), pp. 156–157.

70. *Joint Declaration*, November 26, 1998.

71. In mid-December 1998, when the United States decided to bomb Iraq, assisted by Great Britain, Tokyo quickly approved of America's decision. China, however, vehemently opposed it, as did Russia. The fifth permanent member of the United Nations security council, France, while not as critical as China or Russia of the U.S. response, maintained that it deplored the use of military force to deal with the Iraqi crisis.

72. Japan canceled grant assistance to China because of its nuclear testing, which began in 1995. See Anthony DiFilippo, "Creating Global Security: Japan as a Potential Catalyst," in *Economics of Conflict and Peace*, ed. Jurgen Brauer and William Gissy (Aldershot, England and Brookfield, VT: Ashgate, 1997), pp. 376–396. China announced in July 1996 that it would not conduct any more nuclear tests. Japan resumed Chinese grant assistant in March 1997 when its foreign minister, Yukihiko Ikeda, visited China. See Ministry of Foreign Affairs, *Diplomatic Bluebook 1998* (Tokyo: Ministry of Foreign Affairs, 1998).

73. Subcritical nuclear testing, which can be performed only by nations with sufficient science and technology competency in the nuclear-weapons area, is an experimental procedure that stops short of the actual production of a nuclear chain reaction. For this reason, some maintain that this test procedure does not violate the Comprehensive Test Ban Treaty (CTBT). However, some also argue that subcritical nuclear testing violates the "spirit" of the CTBT, which was overwhelmingly approved (158 to 3) by the United Nations General Assembly on September 10, 1996. The U.S. Department of Energy, which is responsible for conducting subcritical nuclear testing at its underground Nevada site, maintains that such experimentation is needed to safeguard the stockpile of America's nuclear weapons. Over the next several years, the United States will spend at least $40 billion on the Stockpile Stewardship and Management Plan to maintain its nuclear weapons. For information on subcritical nuclear testing and the CTBT, see the web site maintained by the NGO (nongovernmental organization) Committee on Disarmament at the following address: http://www.igc.apc.org/disarm/index.html.

74. Ministry of Foreign Affairs, *Press Conference by the Press Secretary*, October 2, 1998 (accessed on the Worldwide Web).

75. Joint Declaration, November 26, 1998 (emphasis added).

76. Ministry of Foreign Affairs, *Press Conference by the Press Secretary*, Tokyo, October 2, 1998.

77. Russia conducted its first subcritical nuclear test in November 1997. More

recently, Russia performed three subcritical nuclear tests between August 28 and September 3, 2000. For information on subcritical nuclear tests conducted by the United States and Russia, including protest letters from the city of Hiroshima see the Hiroshima City Homepage at the following address: http://www.city.hiroshima.jp/indexe.html.

78. See Department of Defense, Office of International Security Affairs, *The United States Security Strategy for the East Asia–Pacific Region*, November 1998; and Defense Agency, *Defense of Japan 1997*, pp. 35–39.

79. "Paper Raises Fear of North Korean Nuclear Weapon," *Nikkei Weekly*, June 8, 1998, p. 4.

80. Pyongyang has continually stressed that the projectile, Kwangmyongsong No. 1, was an artificial satellite and that Japan is the only country to contend that the launch was a ballistic missile. See "Japanese Crimes since DPRK Satellite Launch," Korean Central News Agency, December 10, 1998.

81. Other countries, including the United States and South Korea, have acknowledged that a civilian satellite was attached to the projectile that flew over Japan. However, Tokyo has painted a different picture. The Japanese Defense Agency stresses that the projectile more than likely was a ballistic missile, and even if it was a satellite, it was just an attempt to cover up Pyongyang's real intention, which was to demonstrate North Korea's technological capabilities. See "That Was No Satellite: Defense Agency," *Japan Times On-line*, October 30, 1998; and "N. Korea Sanctions to Stay," *Asahi Evening News*, October 31, 1998.

82. See "Japan Hesitant about U.S. Antimissile Project," *New York Times*, February 15, 1997, p. 3; "Tokyo Opts Out of TMD: N.Y. Times," *Japan Times Weekly International Edition*, February 24–March 2, 1997.

83. See Ministry of Foreign Affairs, *Announcement by the Chief Cabinet Secretary on Japan's Immediate Response to North Korea's Missile Launch*, Tokyo, September 1, 1998; also see "Japan, U.S. Agree on Missile System," *Asahi Shimbun*, September 21, 1998. The Japanese government formally approved the study of the TMD system late in December 1998. See "Japan Approves Theater Missile Defense Study with U.S." *Japan Times Online*, December 25, 1998.

84. "Japanese Crimes since DPRK Satellite Launch," Korean Central News Agency, December 10, 1998.

85. See "Spy Satellites Planned," *Asahi Evening News*, October 31, 1998; and "Pyongyang Launch Puts Satellite Plan in Motion," *Japan Times Online*, November 6, 1998.

86. "DPRK Foreign Ministry Spokesman on Japan's Military Challenge," Korean Central News Agency, November 18, 1998; "Minju Joson on Japan's Scheme to Possess Satellite," Korean Central News Agency, November 13, 1998.

87. "News and Information Topics," *North Korea Quarterly* (spring/summer 1995): 23.

88. See Ministry of Foreign Affairs, *Diplomatic Bluebook 1998*.

89. See, for example, "Sophistry Unacceptable to Anyone," Korean Central News Agency, December 10, 1998.

90. "North Koreans May Be Preparing Another Missile Test," *New York Times*, September 4, 1998; also see "N. Korea Expanding Missile Programs," *Washington Post*, November 20, 1998.

91. "Provocative Remarks of Warmongers: KCNA Commentary," Korean Central News Agency, December 14, 1998.

92. See "DPRK's Military Warns of 'Annihilating Blow' to U.S.," Korean Central News Agency, December 2, 1998.

93. Department of Defense, Office of International Security Affairs, *The United States Security Strategy for the East Asia-Pacific Region*, November 1998.

94. President William Clinton and South Korean president Kim Young Sam proposed calling together a "four party meeting" on April 16, 1996. See U.S. Department of State, *Background Notes: North Korea, June 1996* (Washington, DC: U.S. Department of State, 1996). Also see Daniel Okimoto, "The Japan-American Security Alliance: Prospects for the Twenty-first Century," Stanford University, Asia/Pacific Research Center, January 1998, pp. 41–42 for a discussion of the four-party talks.

95. "DPRK Foreign Ministry Spokesman on U.S. Argument about Maintenance of Its Troops in East Asia," Korean Central News Agency, December 3, 1998.

96. Ibid.; "Rodong Sinmun on 'Operation Plan 5027,'" Korean Central News Agency, December 14, 1998; "'Operation Plan 5027' Carried into Practice," Korean Central News Agency, December 20, 1998.

97. "DPRK's Ministry Warns of 'Annihilating Blow' to U.S.," Korean Central News Agency, December 2, 1998.

98. Ibid.

99. "DPRK Foreign Minister Sends Letter to Yugoslav Counterpart," Korean Central News Agency," April 8, 1999.

100. Quoted in "U.S./North Korean Confrontation Causing Rifts in Tokyo and Seoul," in *Asia Intelligence Update: Red Alert* (Austin, TX: Stratfor, December 9, 1998). Stratfor, Inc. is a private intelligence-gathering company.

101. The White House, Office of the Press Secretary, press briefing, Washington, DC, December 7, 1998.

102. The United States government maintains an embargo on most economic dealings with North Korea for American citizens and businesses. According to the U.S. Department of State, because of the Agreed Framework, the United States began easing some of the economic restrictions on North Korea in January 1995. See U.S. Department of State, *Background Notes: North Korea, June 1996*.

103. See C. Kenneth Quinones, "North Korea's 'New' Nuclear Site—Fact or Fiction?" The Nautilus Institute, October 5, 1998. Accessed on the Worldwide Web at http://www.nautilus.ors. Quinones had been involved in U.S.-North Korean relations from 1992 to 1997. Between 1992 and 1994, he was the U.S. Department of State's desk officer on North Korean affairs. Between 1995 and 1997, he participated in U.S. government (Energy, State, and Defense) delegations sent to North Korea. See also the interview with Quinones in "The Tension Is Much Higher," *Nikkei Weekly*, December 28, 1998, p. 9 and January 4, 1999, p. 19.

104. This policy paper was authored by former assistance secretary of defense Richard Armitage and later deputy secretary of state in the administration of George W. Bush and entitled "A Comprehensive Approach to North Korea," Washington, DC: National Defense University, Strategic Forum, Institute for National Strategic Studies, March 1999 (emphasis added). Note that the use of the word "discovery," which appears twice in this report to relate the same message, explicitly conveys confirmation and is incongruent with the phrase "at least one suspect site."

105. "North Korea Said to Drop Demand on Atom Inspection," *New York Times*, December 15, 1998.

106. "State Department Noon Briefing December 22, 1998," from the *Daily Report*, The Nautilus Institute, December 23, 1998; also see "Three Allies See No Sign of N. Korean Missile Firing," Kyodo News, December 23, 1998.

107. "Japan Left Behind in Rush to Cozy Up to North Korea," *Daily Yomiuri Online*, October 22, 2000.

108. The joint statement was issued on October 12, 2000. See "Joint Communiqué between DPRK and USA," Korean Central News Agency, October 12, 2000.

109. For an idea of the suspicion directed at North Korea in the late 1990s, see Department of Defense, Office of International Security Affairs, *The United States Security Strategy for the East Asia-Pacific Region*, November 1998; and "Foreign Ministry Focuses on North Korea," *Nikkei Weekly*, December 28, 1998, and January 4, 1999. Many analysts also view North Korea as a flash point in the East Asia–Pacific area. See, for example, Institute for National Strategic Studies, *1997 Strategic Assessment: Flashpoints and Force Structure* (Washington, DC: National Defense University, 1997); also see Mike Mochizuki, "Security and Economic Interdependence in Northeast Asia," Asia/Pacific Research Center, Stanford University, May 1998; pp. 21–25.

110. "Japan's Dangerous Moves," Korean Central News Agency, November 10, 2000.

111. *Statement of Secretary of State–Designate Colin L. Powell, Prepared for the Confirmation Hearing of the U.S. Senate Committee on Foreign Relations, Scheduled for 10:30 am January 17, 2001.*

112. "N. Korea Cancels Talks with S. Korea," *New York Times*, March 13, 2001.

113. "DPRK Gives Warning to Provokers," Korean Central News Agency, March 17, 2001: "U.S. Warned against Its Hardline Policy toward DPRK," Korean Central News Agency, March 18, 2001.

114. Quoted in "Bush Tells Seoul Talks with North Won't Resume Now," *New York Times*, March 8, 2001.

115. "Spokesman for DPRK Foreign Ministry on New U.S. Administration's Policy towards DPRK," Korean Central News Agency, February 22, 2001; "Report on Delay in Construction of Light-Water Reactor Project Issued," Korean Central News Agency, May 16, 2001.

116. "Dangerous Moves on the Part of Japan," Korean Central News Agency, January 2, 1999. Also reported was the following: "If the Japanese reactionaries encroach upon the sovereignty of the DPRK in league with the U.S., it will soon result in the ruin of Japan."

117. Ralph Cossa, "Korea: The Achilles' Heel of the U.S.–Japan Alliance," Stanford University, Asia/Pacific Research Center, May 1997.

118. "TMD Study Worries Russian Official," *Japan Times Online*, December 19, 2000; "China, Russia and India Take Aim at US Missile Shield," *Space Daily*, July 27, 2000.

119. "Russia's Possible Measures to Counteract US Missile Defense," *Itar/Tass News Agency*, April 5, 2001.

120. "Chinese, Russian PMs Sign Joint Communiqué," *China Daily*, November 3, 2000.

121. See Monterey Institute of International Studies, Center for Nonproliferation Studies at the following address: http://cns.miis.edu. This joint declaration can be viewed in its entirety in "DPRK-Russia Joint Declaration," Korean Central News Agency, July 20, 2000.

Chapter 4

1. Office of the Assistant Secretary of Defense for International Security Affairs (East Asia and Pacific Region), *A Strategic Framework for the Asian Pacific Rim* (Washington, DC: Department of Defense, 1992), pp. 10–12.

2. Mike Mochizuki, "The Future of the U.S.–Japan Alliance," *Sekai Shuho*, February 6, 1996.

3. Advisory Group on Defense Issues, *The Modality of the Security and Defense Capability of Japan: The Outlook for the Twenty-first Century*, Tokyo, August 12, 1994.

4. See Tsuneo Akaha, "Beyond Self-Defense: Japan's Elusive Security Role under the New Defense Guidelines for U.S.-Japan Defense Cooperation," *Pacific Review* 11, no. 4 (1998), pp. 461–483; Tsunea Akaha, "U.S.–Japan Security Alliance Adrift?" Prepared for presentation at the Annual Meeting of Asian Studies on the Pacific Coast, June 26–29, 1997.

5. Takubo Tadae, "The Okinawan Threat to the Security Treaty," *Japan Echo* (autumn 1996), pp. 46–52; Chalmers Johnson, "The Okinawan Rape Incident and the End of the Cold War," Working Paper #16, Japan Policy Research Institute, February 1996.

6. "Japan Hesitant about U.S. Antimissile Project," *New York Times*, February 15, 1997, p. 3; "Tokyo Opts Out of TMD: N.Y. Times," *Japan Times Weekly International Edition*, February 25–March 22, 1997, pp. 1, 6.

7. "U.S. Mulls Scrapping Asia Missile Defense Plan," *Japan Times Weekly International Edition*, March 30–April 5, 1998, p. 3.

8. See, for example, the interview with former prime minister and director-general of the Defense Agency Yasuhiro Nakasone in "Japan Needs an Independent Defense Policy," *Asahi Shimbun*, September 22, 2000.

9. Department of Defense, Office of International Security Affairs (East Asia and Pacific Region), *United States Security Strategy for the East Asia-Pacific Region* (Washington, DC: U.S. Department of Defense, February 1995).

10. *National Defense Program Outline in and after FY 1996*, Tokyo, November 28, 1995, accessed on the Worldwide Web, Japanese Defense Agency at http://www.jda.go.jp/index_.htm.

11. In addition to the alliances with Japan, South Korea, and Australia, Washington has security arrangements with Thailand, Singapore, and the Philippines in the Asia–Pacific region, as well as with the Republic of the Marshall Islands, the Republic of Palau, and the Federated States of Micronesia.

12. Akihiko Tanaka, " Japan's Security Policy in the 1990s," in *Japan's International Agenda*, ed. Yoichi Funabashi (New York: New York University Press, 1994), p. 32.

13. Ministry of Foreign Affairs, *Security* at http://www.mofa.go.jp/region/n-america/us/index.html.

14. Joseph Nye, "The Case for Deep Engagement," *Foreign Affairs* (July/August 1995): 90–102; Patrick Cronin, "The Japan–U.S. Alliance Redefined," Washington, DC: National Defense University, Strategic Forum, Institute for National Strategic Studies, May 1996; Patrick Cronin and Ezra Vogel, "Unifying U.S. Policy on Japan," Washington, DC: National Defense University, Strategic Forum, Institute for National Strategic Studies, November 1995, Japan Forum on International Rela-

tions, *The Policy Recommendations on the Perspective of Security Regimes in Asia-Pacific Region* (Tokyo: Japan Forum on International Relations, 1996); Inoguchi Takashi, "The New Security Treaty Setup and Japan's Options," *Japan Echo* (autumn 1996): 36–39; Okamoto Yukio, "Why We Still Need the Security Treaty," *Japan Echo* (winter 1995): 10–13; Toshio Saito, "Japan's Security Policy," Washington, DC: National Defense University, Strategic Forum, Institute for National Strategic Studies, May 1999.

15. Michael Green, "Interests, Asymmetries, and Strategic Choices," in *The U.S.–Japan Security Alliance in the Twenty-first Century* (New York: Council on Foreign Relations, 1998), pp. 1–24; Michael Green, "State of the Field Report: Research on Japanese Security Policy," *AccessAsia Review* 2, no. 1, September 1998.

16. The notion of benign hegemony can be found in Thomas Christensen, "China, the U.S.–Japan Alliance, and the Security Dilemma in East Asia," *International Security* 23, no. 4 (spring 1999): 49–80. This argument ignores a key point: Beijing opposes bilateral security alliances.

17. See the essays in Mike Mochizuki, ed. *Toward a True Alliance: Restructuring U.S.–Japan Security Relations* (Washington, DC: Brookings Institution, 1997); Ralph Cossa, ed., *Restructuring the U.S.–Japan Alliance: Toward a More Equal Partnership* (Washington, DC: Center for Strategic International Studies, 1997); Mike Mochizuki and Michael O'Hanlon, "A Liberal Vision for the US-Japanese Alliance," *Survival* 40, no. 2 (summer 1998): 127–134.

18. Morihiro Hosokawa, "Are U.S. Troops in Japan Needed? Reforming the Alliance," *Foreign Affairs* 77, no. 4 (July/August 1998): 2–5; Mike Mochizuki and Michael O'Hanlon, "The Marines Should Come Home: Adapting the U.S.–Japan Alliance to a New Security Era," *Brookings Review* 14, no. 2 (spring 1996): 10–13.

19. See, for example, Takashi Inoguichi, "Adjusting America's Two Alliances in East Asia: A Japanese View," Asia/Pacific Research Center, Stanford University, July 1999, p. 6.

20. Sharif Shuja, "Japan' Asia Policy," *Contemporary Review* 274, no. 1600 (May 1999): 236–241.

21. Jianwei Wang and Xinbo Wu, "Against Us or with Us? The Chinese Perspective on America's Alliances with Japan and Korea," Asia/Pacific Research Center, Stanford University, May 1998, pp. 29–34; Xu Zhixian and Yang Bojiang, "New Acts—A Historical Retrogression," *Beijing Review* 42, no. 24 (June 14, 1999).

22. The five countries that are parties to the Shanghai and Moscow Agreements are China, Russia, Kyrgyzstan, Kazakhstan, and Tajikistan.

23. Chu Shulong, "China and the U.S.–Japan and U.S.–Korea Alliances in a Changing Northeast Asia," Asia/Pacific Research Center, Stanford University, June 1999, pp. 8, 11–12; Charles Morrison, ed. *Asia Pacific Security Outlook 1998* (Tokyo and New York: Japan Center for International Exchange, 1998), pp. 43, 47.

24. "Summit: Regional Security Vital," *China Daily*, August 26, 1999.

25. Andrew Kuchins and Alexei Zagorsky, "When Realism and Liberalism Coincide: Russian Views of U.S. Alliances in Asia," Asia/Pacific Research Center, Stanford University, July 1999, pp. 9–10.

26. "Papers Call for Averting Danger of War and Defending Peace," Korean Central News Agency, June 25, 1999. According to Pyongyang, the United States originally launched operation plan 5027 in 1993.

27. "Japan, Dangerous Entity for Aggression," *Korean Central News Agency*, June 12, 1999.

28. Ted Galen Carpenter, "Breaking Allies' Dependency on American Military Power," *USA Today Magazine*, July 1999, p. 19.

29. Alan Tonelson, "Time for a New U.S.–Japan Security Relationship," *Comparative Strategy* 16, no. 1 (January–March 1997): 1–11.

30. Chalmers Johnson and E.B. Keehn, "The Pentagon's Ossified Strategy," *Foreign Affairs* 74, no.4 (July/August 1995): 103–114; Ted Galen Carpenter, "Paternalism and Dependence: The U.S.–Japanese Security Relationship" (Washington, DC: Cato Institute, November 1, 1995).

31. Barbara Conry, "U.S. 'Global Leadership': A Euphemism for World Policeman" (Washington, DC: Cato Institute, February 5, 1997); Ted Galen Carpenter, "Pacific Fraud: The New U.S.–Japan Defense Guidelines" (Washington, DC: Cato Institute, October 16, 1997).

32. Ministry of Foreign Affairs, "Is Japan Getting a Free Ride on Defense?" *Japanese Viewpoints* (Tokyo: Overseas Public Relations Office, Ministry of Foreign Affairs, September 1995). Accessed on the Worldwide Web at http://www.mofa.go.jp.

33. Survey conducted between February and March 1999 by the Gallup Organization of U.S. opinion leaders (including some in government positions) and of the public. Japan's Ministry of Foreign Affairs commissioned the survey entitled, *1999 Survey in the United States of Opinions toward Japan*, May 1999.

34. This argument is made in Cato Institute, *Cato Handbook for Congress: Toward a New Relationship with Japan* (Washington, DC: Cato Institute, 1997).

35. Department of Defense, Office of International Security Affairs, *United States Security Strategy for the East Asia-Pacific Region*, February 1995.

36. Johnson and Keehn, "The Pentagon's Ossified Strategy," p. 112.

37. "Japan, U.S. to Cooperate on Satellites," *Daily Yomiuri On-line*, September 23, 1999.

38. Anthony DiFilippo, *Science, Technology, and the Evolution of U.S.–Japan Relations* (Aldershot, England, and Brookfield, VT: Ashgate, 1997).

39. Eric Heginbotham and Richard Samuels, "Mercantile Realism and Japanese Foreign Policy," *International Security* 22, no. 4 (spring 1998): 171–204.

40. Tim Larimer and Hiroko Tashiro, "National Colors," *Time South Pacific*, August 30, 1999.

41. "Ishihara Takes 'Ugly, Illegitimate' Constitution to Task," *Mainichi Daily News*, December 2, 2000.

42. Shintaro Ishihara and Akio Morita, *No to ieru Nihon* (The Japan that can say no) (Tokyo: Kobunsha, 1989). A version of this book with Shintaro Ishihara named as the only author was translated into English by Frank Baldwin, *The Japan That Can Say No* (New York: Simon and Schuster, 1991).

43. See "Ishihara Now Wants All Base Land Back," *Japan Times Online*, June 28, 1999; "Base Not Ishihara's Only Target," *Japan Times Online*, June 28, 1999.

44. Ishihara and Morita, The *Japan That Can Say No*.

45. Ishihara's comments are from an interview, "Japan, Wake Up!" in *By the Way* 8, no. 4 (June/July 1998): 8–12.

46. "Flying the Flag," *Far Eastern Economic Review*, August 12, 1999.

47. Located in Tokyo, the *Yasukuni Jinja* (*jinja* is a Shinto shrine) is the burial place of many Japanese who died in military conflicts, including a number from the

Pacific War. Asians generally view the shrine as a symbol of Japan's militarist history and many who are buried there as war criminals. For a North Korean reaction to a recent visit to the shrine see "Japanese Militarists Visit to Yasukuni Shrine," Korean Central News Agency, August 20, 1999.

48. Quoted in "Japanese Mark War Anniversary with Less Reticence," *New York Times*, August 16, 1999.

49. "Japan: Extending Tokyo's Reach," *Far Eastern Economic Review* (January 18, 2001). Also see "Japan's Wild Design for Overseas Aggression under Fire," Korean Central News Agency (January 6, 2001).

50. See "Storm Clouds Gather over Satellite Project," *Daily Yomiuri On-line*, August 3, 1999.

51. "No National Consensus on National Symbols," *Japan Times Online*, July 22, 1999.

52. "Flying the Flag," *Far Eastern Economic Review*"; "Japan's Move for Resurgence of Militarism Assailed," Korean Central News Agency, July 4, 1999; "Japan's Approval of Criminal Bill," Korean Central News Agency, July 29, 1999; "KCNA on Japanese Diet's Endorsement of Bill on *Hinomaru* and *Kimigayo*," Korean Central News Agency, August 11, 1999; "Symbol of Revised Japanese Militarism," Korean Central News Agency, August 20, 1999.

53. Tang Tianri, "Japan's Stubborn 'History Syndrome' Requires Treatment," *Beijing Review* 12 (March 22, 2001). For North Korean objections to the textbook issue that also incorporate criticism from South Korea, see "Japan's Distortion of History Textbook Condemned in South Korea," Korean Central News Agency, March 28, 2001; "Japan's Moves to Distort History under Fire," Korean Central News Agency, March 30, 2001.

54. In late March 2001, South Korean civic groups organized an Internet protest against Tokyo's approval of a history textbook that significantly minimized Japan's military exploits in Korea. By urging computer users to access concurrently the homepage of the Japanese Ministry of Education, civic groups hoped to cause the site to crash. See "Koreans Take History Book Protest to the Net," *Japan Times Online*, April 1, 2001.

55. "Seoul Wants Envoy Back for Briefing," *Asahi Shimbun*, April 10, 2001.

56. For the Chinese reaction to Tokyo's approval of the new history book, which will be used in 2002, see "China Slams Japan over History Textbook," *China Daily*, April 3, 2001.

57. For Pyongyang's reaction to the controversial textbook issue, see "KCNA on Japan's Approval of History Textbooks," Korean Central News Agency, April 6, 2001.

58. Gavan McCormack, "Nationalism and Identity in Post-Cold War Japan, *Pacifica Review: Peace, Security and Global Change* 12, no. 3 (October 2000): 249–254; "Japan's Resurgent Far Right Tinkers with History," *New York Times*, March 25, 2001.

59. "Japan, Wake Up!" *By the Way*, 8, no. 4 (June/July 1998).

60. Article V of the 1960 *Treaty of Mutual Cooperation and Security between Japan and the United States of America* specifies that: "Each Party recognizes than an armed attack against either Party in the territories under the administration of Japan would be dangerous to its own peace and safety and declares that it would act to meet the common danger in accordance with its constitutional provisions and processes."

61. U.S.–Japan Consultative Committee, *Guidelines for Defense Cooperation*, November 27, 1978, accessed at http://www.jda.go.jp/e/index_.htm. See also U.S.–Japan Consultative Committee, *Completion of the Review of the Guidelines for U.S. Japan Defense Cooperation*, New York, September 23, 1997.

62. See Toshimaru Ogura and Ingyu Oh, "Nuclear Clouds over the Korean Peninsula and Japan," *Monthly Review* 48, no. 11 (April 1997): 18–31, quoted in Ishihara Shintaro, Watanabe Shoichi, and Ogawa Kazuhisa, *Soredemo no to ireu Nippon* (Japan which can still say no) (Tokyo: Kobunsha, 1990).

63. "Japan OK'd No-Notice Entry of US Nukes," *Mainichi Daily News*, April 14, 2000; "Secret Nuke Pact," *Mainichi Daily News*, August 31, 2000.

64. See "Sato Mulled Nuclear Weapons Option in '65," *Japan Times Weekly International Edition*, June 8–14, 1998. However, an American observer has alleged that Prime Minister Sato was bluffing subsequent to China's successful test of its first atomic weapon in October 1964 so that the United States would extend its nuclear shield to protect Japan. See "Former PM Bluffing on Japanese Nukes," *Mainichi Shimbun*, August 6, 1999.

65. "Peace Prize Winner Sato Called Nonnuclear Policy 'Nonsense,'" *Japan Times Online*, June 11, 2000.

66. "Japan Needs an Independent Defense Policy," *Asahi Shimbun*, September 22, 2000.

67. "Nakasone OK'd Nukes for Japan," *Asahi Shimbun*, December 20, 2000.

68. Ibid.

69. Nakasone Yasuhiro, "Japan's Firm Nonnuclear Resolve," *Japan Echo* 25, no. 5 (October 1998).

70. Anthony DiFilippo, "Can Japan Craft an International Nuclear Disarmament Policy?" *Asian Survey* 40, no. 4 (July/August 2000): 574–575.

71. Although Japan does not have weapons-grade plutonium, it does possess a large quantity of reactor-grade plutonium. Since nuclear weapons are not made from the latter, there is a debate over whether Japan's stockpile of plutonium could be used to make nuclear weapons. See Andrew Mack, "Japan and the Bomb: A Cause for Concern?" *Asia-Pacific Magazine*, no. 3 (June 1996): 5–9; Matake Kamiya, "Japan, Nuclear Weapons, and the U.S.–Japan Alliance," paper presented at the conference on U.S.–Japan Security Relations, Washington, DC, May 2, 1996; Eiichi Katahara, "Japan's Plutonium Policy: Consequences for Nonproliferation," *Nonproliferation Review* 5, no. 1 (fall 1997): 53–61.

72. "Asian Instability May Force Japan's Nuclear Hand," *Japan Times Online*, July 30, 1999.

73. "Obuchi Rallies His Troops," *The Economist* (January 9, 1999); "Constitutional Talk," *The Economist* (February 22, 1999); "Japan's Shift to the Right Reminds Many of War," *Christian Science Monitor*, August 16, 1999.

74. "Political Pulse/Times Change, and So Do Positions on Constitution," *Daily Yomiuri On-line*, September 22, 1999. For a historical discussion of constitutional change in Japan, see Donald Seekins, "The Political System," *Japan: A Country Study*, ed. Ronald Dolan and Robert Worden (Washington, DC: U.S. Government Printing Office, 1992), p. 308.

75. Anthony DiFilippo, "China's Side of the History Equation," *Japan Times*, December 10, 1998, p. 21.

76. "History Cannot Be Distorted," *China Daily*, November 29, 2000.

77. "Japan's Moves to Draw up War Constitution under Fire," Korean Central News Agency, December 28, 2000. Also see "High Vigilance against Japan Called For," Korean Central News Agency, January 5, 2001.

78. See *Political Parties in Japan.* Document accessed at http://www.kanzaki.com/jinfo/PoliticalParties.html#SDP on March 7, 2001, excerpted from *Japan: A Pocket Guide* (Tokyo: Foreign Press Center, 1996).

79. Japan Communist Party, *JCP's View on Relationship between Constitution's Article 9 and the Self Defense Forces*, accessed on March 7, 2001 at http://www.jcp.or.jp/english/jps_weekly/e000930_03.html.

80. Thomas Berger, *Cultures of Assimilation: National Security in Germany and Japan* (Baltimore, MD: Johns Hopkins University Press, 1980); Peter Katzenstein, *Cultural Norms and National Security* (Ithaca, NY: Cornell University Press, 1996).

81. George Packard, *Protest in Tokyo: The Security Treaty Crisis of 1960* (Princeton, NJ: Princeton University Press, 1966).

82. See Ministry of Foreign Affairs, *Diplomatic Bluebook 1992* (Tokyo: Ministry of Foreign Affairs, 1993), pp. 48–49; Ministry of Foreign Affairs, *Diplomatic Bluebook 1993* (Tokyo: Ministry of Foreign Affairs, 1994), pp. 49–50.

83. "Survey Shows Big Decline in Sino-Japanese Relations," *Daily Yomiuri On-line*, September 29, 1999; "Distrust Heightens between Japanese, Chinese," *Daily Yomiuri On-line*, October 1, 1999.

84. "Japan has, ever since its accession to the U.N. [in 1956], attached great importance to the U.N. activities and has made a commitment to the U.N. one of the main pillars of its foreign policy. Japan intends to further enhance its cooperation with the U.N. and to play a more active role for world peace and prosperity in the years to come." Ministry of Foreign Affairs, *Japan and the United Nations*, accessed on the Worldwide Web at http://www.mofa.go.jp.

85. Information on Japan's defense policy can be found on the Defense Agency's Worldwide Web page at http://www/jda.go.jp/index_.htm.

86. Beijing claims that China's military spending is considerably less than Japan's. Chinese premier Zhu has emphasized that Japanese conservatives who claim that China's military spending is a threat to Japan are misrepresenting the facts. Zhu states that Chinese military spending is only about one-third of that of Japan's. See "China's Military Spending Just a Third of Japan's," *China Daily*, October 16, 2000.

87. Dollar amounts on military spending for China, Japan, and the United States come from the International Institute for Strategic Studies, *The Military Balance 1999/2000*, London. These data can be accessed on the Japanese website at http://jin.jcic.or.jp/stat/stats/04DPL22.html. The figure for North Korea is from the U.S. Department of State, Bureau of Verification and Compliance, *World Military Expenditures and Arms Transfers, 1998* (Washington, DC: U.S. Government Printing Office, April 2000). U.S. government figures differ noticeably from those reported here. According to the U.S. State Department, Chinese military spending was $75 billion in 1997, while Japan's defense expenditures are listed at about $41 billion.

Chapter 5

1. See, for example, Japanese Defense Agency, *Basic Policy for National Defense*, Tokyo.

2. Interviews conducted by *Asahi Shimbun* on October 4 and October 5, 1998.

Survey data acquired from the Roper Center for Public Opinion Research, University of Connecticut [hereafter the Roper Center].

3. Ministry of Foreign Affairs, *The United Nations and Japan 1995* (Tokyo: Ministry of Foreign Affairs, 1995), accessed on the Worldwide Web at www.mofa.go.jp/region/europe/russia/assistance/other.html. Recently, the Russian Defense Ministry expressed an interest in establishing military cooperation with Japan. See "Russian for Military-tech Cooperation with Japan, DPRK," Itar/Tass News Agency, December 5, 2000.

4. "Asia Divided over Passage of U.S.–Japan Defense Cooperation Guidelines," *Kyodo News*, April 28, 1999; "Defense Bills Evoke Worry and Comfort," *Japan Times*, April 27, 1999.

5. Ministry of Foreign Affairs, *Japan-China Joint Declaration on Building a Partnership of Friendship and Cooperation for Peace and Development*, Tokyo, November 26, 1998.

6. People's Republic of China, Foreign Ministry, *Foreign Policy*. Accessed on the Worldwide Web at the following address: http://www.fmprc.gov.cn/e/c/ec.htm.

7. "China's Stand on Non-proliferation," *Beijing Review* 6, no. 2 (February 8–14, 1999).

8. The rest of the respondents gave another answer or none at all. *Asahi Shimbun* conducted interviews on May 17 and 18, 1998. Data obtained from the Roper Center.

9. *Yomiuri Shimbun* conducted interviews on October 26 and 27, 1997. Data obtained from the Roper Center. Since respondents were permitted to select multiple answers for this question, percentages exceed 100 percent.

10. The United States Information Agency sponsored three surveys (November 6, 1991; May 25, 1993; and October 18, 1993) that asked the following question: "How much danger would you say there is of North Korea developing its own nuclear weapons in the next three years or so . . . a great deal, a fair amount, not very much, or none at all?" In the last survey, 78 percent of the respondents said that there was either a great deal (37 percent) or that there was a fair amount (41 percent). Data acquired from the Roper Center.

11. United States Information Agency, January 1, 1994. In this survey, 1,051 Japanese adults were asked three questions. (1) "How much of a threat, if any, do you think North Korea poses to the national security of Japan . . . a great deal, a fair amount, not very much, or none at all?" The responses to this question were that 18 percent felt that the DPRK (Democratic People's Republic of Korea) was "a great threat" to Japan and 42 percent believed that North Korea represented "a fair amount" of threat. (2) "Do you think North Korea has nuclear weapons now?" Only 6 percent of the respondents answered no to this question. (3) "If North Korea has nuclear weapons, would you favor or oppose Japan's developing its own nuclear weapons? Is that favor/oppose strongly or only somewhat?" Sixty-four percent of the respondents replied that they "strongly oppose" Japan's developing nuclear weapons, while 14 percent said that they "somewhat oppose" this. Data acquired from the Roper Center.

12. The rest of the respondents answered as follows: 9 percent somewhat disagreed, 3 percent strongly disagreed, and 7 percent said that they did not know. The Shin Joho Center conducted this survey for the United States Information Agency, interviewing respondents between June 6 and June 12, 1991. Data obtained from the Roper Center.

13. Only 14 percent thought that Japan would eventually possess nuclear weap-

ons; 7 percent gave no response. *Yomiuri Shimbun* conducted interviews on January 28 and January 29, 1995. Data acquired from the Roper Center.

14. Only 18 percent of the respondents indicated that they feel that it is acceptable for a nation to possess nuclear weapons as a means of self-defense; 4 percent provided another answer or did not respond. *Asahi Shimbun* conducted interviews on October 4 and 5, 1998. Data acquired from the Roper Center.

15. Subsequent to the passage of the bills related to the Guidelines for Japan–U.S. Defense Cooperation by the Lower House in late April 1999, which virtually guaranteed approval by the Upper House, Pyongyang announced that the phrase "areas surrounding Japan" effectively means problems arising on the Korean Peninsula. According to Pyongyang, Japan can now justify military responses beyond the defense of the homeland. See "Reinvasion Will Lead to Self-Destruction," Korean Central News Agency, May 1, 1999.

16. "U.S. Will Take Responsibility for Consequences of Nuclear Confrontation," Korean Central News Agency, January 21, 1999.

17. According to Pyongyang, the Hyonmu missile has a range of 300 kilometers, well above the 180-kilometer limit for South Korean missiles stipulated in the 1979 U.S.–South Korea memorandum of understanding on missile control. See "U.S. Double Standard as Regards 'Missile Issue' Flailed," Korean Central News Agency, April 26, 1999.

18. Hyung Kook Kim, "Japan, Korea, and Northeast Asia: A Korean View," in *Japan's Quest: The Search for International Role, Recognition, and Respect*, ed. Warren Hunsberger (Armonk, NY: M.E. Sharpe, 1997), pp. 170–172.

19. "World Community Urged to Denounce Nuclear Power's Attempt," Korean Central News Agency, March 2, 1999.

20. Wolf Mendl, *Japan's Asia Policy: Regional Security and Global Interests* (London: Routledge, 1995), pp. 63–64.

21. Central Research Services, Inc. performed this survey for the United States Information Agency, conducting interviews between May 16 and 23, 1990. Data obtained from the Roper Center.

22. The Shin Joho Center conducted interviews for the United States Information Agency between June 6 and 12, 1991. Data acquired from the Roper Center.

23. Central Research Services, Inc. performed interviews for the United States Information Agency between October 12 and 18, 1993. Data acquired from the Roper Center.

24. *Asahi Shimbun* performed interviews between March 14 and 17, 1999. Data acquired from the Roper Center.

25. Office of the Assistant Security of Defense for International Security Affairs, *A Strategic Framework for the Asia Pacific Rim* (Washington, DC: Department of Defense, 1992).

26. Department of Defense, Office of International Security Affairs (East Asia and Pacific Region), *United States Security Strategy for the East Asia–Pacific Region* (Washington, DC: Department of Defense, February 1995); Department of Defense, Office of International Security Affairs, *The United States Security Strategy for the East Asia-Pacific Region* (Washington, DC: Department of Defense, November 1998).

27. Twelve percent either gave another answer or did not respond. *Asahi Shimbun* conducted interviews between March 14 and March 17, 1999. Data acquired from the Roper Center.

28. Less than 40 percent of the respondents saw the treaty as important to the security of Japan, 27 percent felt that the accord prevented resurgence of Japanese militarism, 22 percent thought that it kept bilateral economic conflicts from becoming more severe, and 14 percent indicated that it permitted Japan to spend less on the military. *Yomiuri Shimbun* conducted interviews on October 28 and 29, 1995. Data obtained from the Roper Center.

29. Denny Roy, "Hegemon on the Horizon? China's Threat to East Asian Security," *International Security* 19, no. 1 (summer 1994): 149–168; Gerald Segal, "East Asia and the 'Constrainment' of China," *International Security* 20, no. 4 (spring 1996): 159–187; both articles were reprinted in *East Asian Security*, ed. Michael Brown, Sean Lynn-Jones, and Steven Miller (Cambridge, MA: MIT Press, 1996); Joseph Nye, "China's Re-emergence and the Future of the Asia-Pacific," *Survival* 39, no. 4 (winter 1997–98): 65–79; and David Shambaugh, "China's Military Views the World: Ambivalent Security," *International Security* 24, no. 3 (winter 1999/2000): 52–79.

30. Institute for National Strategic Studies, National Defense University, *1997 Strategic Assessment: Flash Points and Force Structure* (Washington, DC: National Defense University, 1997).

31. "President Seeks an End of Obstacles to Friendship," *China Daily*, May 5, 1999.

32. Prime Minister's Office, Public Relations Office, *Opinion Survey on Foreign Affairs* (Tokyo: Prime Minister's Office, January 1998).

33. Arguments that claim the U.S.–Japan security alliance brings stability to what would be in its absence an unstable Asia–Pacific area, or analogously those that maintain that should the United States withdraw from this region, instability would quickly emerge, typically fall far short of being convincing. These arguments assume, without providing substantive details, that an American military presence, via alliance politics, acts as a deterrent to potential political problems in the Asia–Pacific region. See, for example, Susan Shirk, "Asia-Pacific Regional Security: Balance of Power or Concert of Powers?" in *Regional Orders: Building Security in a New World Order*, ed. David Lake and Patrick Morgan (University Park: Pennsylvania State University Press, 1997), p. 257. See also, Aurelia George Mulgan, "Beyond Self-Defense? Evaluating Japan's Regional Security Role under the New Defense Cooperation Guidelines," *Pacifica Review: Peace Security and Global Change* 12, no. 3 (October 2000): 221–246.

34. The remaining 5 percent provided other responses or did not answer. See "Wide Gap between Japan, U.S. on Base Issue," *Asahi Evening News* (*Asahi Shimbun*), April 13, 1999.

35. G. William Domhoff made this argument on foreign policy some time ago in his *Higher Circles: The Governing Class in America* (New York: Vintage Books, 1970), pp. 111–155.

36. Koseki Soichi, *The Birth of Japan's Postwar Constitution*, ed. and trans. Ray Moore (Boulder, CO: Westview, 1997), pp. 82–86.

37. Koichi Hamada, "The Pacifist Constitution in Post-war Japan—Economic Dividends or Political Burdens?" *Disarmament: A Periodic Review by the United Nations* 19, no. 3 (1996): 46–62; Donald Seekins, "The Political System, in *Japan: A Country Study*, ed. Ronald Dolan and Robert Worden (Washington, DC: U.S. Government Printing Office, 1992), p. 308.

38. George Packard, *Protest in Tokyo* (Princeton, NJ: Princeton University Press, 1964).

39. While not technically part of the *Treaty of Mutual Cooperation and Security between Japan and the United States*, the "Guidelines" are intimately connected to it. The guidelines relate directly to Articles 5 and 6 of the treaty. Included in the revised bills to the new guidelines is the phrase: "The purpose of the bill contributes to the effective use of the Japan–U.S. Security Treaty." See also Satoshi Morimoto, "A Tighter Japan–U.S. Alliance Based on Greater Trust," in *Toward a True Alliance: Restructuring U.S.–Japan Security Relations*, ed. Mike Mochizuki (Washington, DC: Brookings Institution, 1997), pp. 143–146.

40. Interview dates in this NHK sponsored survey conducted March 4 and 5, 1995; data accessed from Roper Center.

41. Ibid. Only 8 percent of the respondents believed that the power of the Self Defense Forces should increase; the rest indicated that it was too difficult to say (4 percent) or they did not know or did not respond (7 percent).

42. *Yomiuri Shimbun* poll conducted January 18 and 19, 1997; data accessed from Roper Center.

43. NHK survey conducted between June 27 and June 29, 1997; data accessed from the Roper Center.

44. *Yomiuri Shimbun* poll conducted between August 30 and 31, 1997; data accessed from the Roper Center.

45. It is not likely that this phrase became biased because of the translation from Japanese to English. According to the Roper Center, which is responsible for the translation: "We have made great pains to reproduce the spirit of the question as it was asked in the original Japanese survey. Although we tried to choose English wording closest to the Japanese wording, we were more sensitive to replicating the actual meaning of the question."

46. A nonbiased question would have certainly omitted the phrase "on the assumption that a war or conflict could threaten Japan's security." For a discussion of biased or leading questions see Earl Babbie, *The Practice of Social Research* (Belmont, CA: Wadsworth, 1998), pp. 152–153; Royce Singleton et al., *Approaches to Social Research* (New York: Oxford University Press 1988), p. 280.

47. See "43 Percent Oppose Guideline Bills," *Asahi Evening*, March 19, 1999.

48. See Douglas Mendel, *The Japanese People and Foreign Policy: A Study of Public Opinion in Post-treaty Japan* (Berkeley: University of California Press, 1961), pp. 84–86.

49. *Yomiuri Shimbun* survey conducted between October 28 and 29, 1995; data accessed from the Roper Center.

50. Five percent of the respondents did not provide an answer. *Yomiuri Shimbun* interviewed respondents on July 17 and 18, 1999. Data acquired from the Roper Center.

51. Seven percent of the respondents gave another answer or did not respond. *Asahi Shimbun* interview conducted between March 14 and 17, 1999. Data obtained from the Roper Center.

52. Ibid. Fourteen percent gave another answer or did not respond.

53. The remaining 12 percent answered either that they did not know or provided another response. NHK interviewed respondents on March 6 and 7, 1993. Data acquired from the Roper Center.

54. *Nihon Keizai Shimbun* interviewed respondents between April 25 and April 27, 1997. Data acquired from the Roper Center.

55. *Yomiuri Shimbun* interviewed respondents on March 15 and 16, 1997. *Asahi*

Shimbun conducted interviews on April 20 and 21, 1997. Data for both surveys obtained from the Roper Center.

56. *Yomiuri Shimbun* conducted interviews on March 21 and 22, 1998. Data obtained from the Roper Center.

57. "Poll: 54 Percent Back Changes to Constitution," *Daily Yomiuri Online*, April 4, 2001. *Yomiuri Shimbun* conducted interviews on March 24 and 25, 2001.

58. In this survey, 11 percent of the respondents did not give an answer. *Yomiuri Shimbun* conducted interviews on March 21 and 22, 1998. Data obtained from the Roper Center.

59. Seven percent of the respondents said that they were unsure about this issue. *Nihon Keizai Shimbun* conducted interviews between October 8 and 10, 1999. Data acquired from the Roper Center.

60. Concerning the questions of how and why to amend the constitution, the *Yomiuri Shimbun* queried only those respondents who supported revision.

61. The rest of the respondents to the question on how the constitution should be revised either believed there should be a new constitution (13 percent) or did not provide an answer (4 percent). Five percent of the respondents to the question of why the constitution should be amended gave another answer, said that they did not know, or they did not reply. *Yomiuri Shimbun* conducted interviews on March 21 and 22, 1998. Data acquired from the Roper Center.

62. Nine percent thought that Japan should not cooperate in any way with U.S. military forces, and 17 percent either provided another answer or did not respond. *Yomiuri Shimbun* conducted interviews on October 25 and 26, 1997. Data obtained from the Roper Center.

63. Ibid.

64. Nine percent provided another answer or did not respond. *Asahi Shimbun* conducted interviews between March 14 and 17, 1999. Data acquired from the Roper Center.

65. Five percent of the respondents said that they did not know or did not provide a response. NHK interviewed respondents on March 6 and 7, 1993. Data obtained from the Roper Center.

66. Armitage and Wolfowitz were two among several authors of the report issued by the Institute for National Strategic Studies at the National Defense University. This report stresses that "Japan's prohibition against collective self-defense [that is, Article 9] is a constraint on its alliance cooperation. Lifting this constraint would allow for closer and more efficient security cooperation. This is a decision that only the Japanese people can make. The United States has respected decisions that form the character of Japanese security policies and should continue to do so. But Washington must make clear that it welcomes a Japan that is willing to make a greater contribution and to become a more equal alliance partner." See Institute for National Strategic Studies, "The United States and Japan: Advancing toward a Mature Partnership" (Washington, DC: National Defense University, October 11, 2000).

67. Quoted in "KCNA Ridicules Remarks of U.S. Ambassador to Japan," Korean Central News Agency, July 20, 2001. The ambassador made similar comments during an interview with the *Asahi Shimbun* in "Baker Urges More Missile Involvement," July 26, 2001.

68. Eight percent of the respondents to this question gave another answer or none

at all. *Asahi Shimbun* conducted interviews on April 20 and 21, 1997. Data obtained from the Roper Center.

69. NHK conducted interviews between October 31 and November 3, 1997. Data acquired from the Roper Center.

70. Eight percent provided another answer or gave no response. *Yomiuri Shimbun* interviewed respondents on October 25 and October 26, 1997. Data obtained from the Roper Center.

71. *Asahi Shimbun* conducted interviews on April 20 and 21, 1997. Data obtained from the Roper Center.

72. Ibid. Eleven percent of the respondents provided another answer or gave none at all.

73. See "Poll: More Support Article 9," *Asahi Shimbun*, May 2, 2000. *Asahi Shimbun* interviewed respondents on April 8 and 9, 2001.

74. "The Second *Yomiuri Shimbun* Proposal for Revision of the Constitution," *Daily Yomiuri On-line*, May 3, 2000.

75. Ibid.

76. Respondents from eight countries, including Japan, South Korea, China, India, and the United States were interviewed between August and September 1999. Strengthening the United Nations so that it can use dialogue to resolve conflicts and maintain peace and security in Asia was the first or second choice for most respondents in the eight countries included in the survey, except South Korea and India. See "U.N. Seen as Key to Security in Asia," *Asahi Shimbun*, October 28, 1999.

77. Reinhard Drifte, *Japan's Quest for a Permanent Security Council Seat: A Matter of Pride or Justice?* (London: Macmillan, 2000).

78. NHK interviewed respondents for the first survey between March 10 and 17, 1993. Interviews for the second survey took place between September 4 and 5, 1993. Data for both surveys acquired from the Roper Center.

79. In the first 1994 survey NHK interviewed respondents on June 25 and 26, 1994, and in the second on September 24 and 25, 1994. Data for both surveys obtained from the Roper Center.

80. *Yomiuri Shimbun* interviewed respondents on January 28 and 29, 1995. Data obtained from the Roper Center.

81. *Nihon Keizai Shimbun* interviewed respondents between August 4 and 6, 1995. Data acquired from the Roper Center.

82. Shin Joho Center conducted interviews between October 12 and 22, 1995. Data obtained from the Roper Center.

83. Shin Joho Center interviewed respondents for the prime minister's office between October 3 and 13, 1996. Data acquired from the Roper Center. This position goes back to 1970 at least. In his 1970 speech to the United Nations foreign minister Kiichi Aichi stated the following: "Thus nuclear military capability should not become a decisive factor in any consideration of qualification for permanent membership, although most of the present permanent members are nuclear powers. Attention should rather be paid to such a pertinent factor as a positive attitude towards universal prohibition of nuclear weapons." Quoted in Drifte, *Japan's Quest for a Permanent Security Council Seat*, pp. 28–29.

84. Respondents were interviewed between September 25 and October 5, 1997. See Prime Minister's Office, Public Relations Office, *Opinion Survey on Foreign Affairs* (Tokyo: Prime Minister's Office, January 1998).

85. Interviews for this survey took place between November 19 and 29, 1998. See Prime Minister's Office, Public Relations Office, *Opinion Survey on Foreign Affairs* (Tokyo: Prime Minister's Office, 1999).

86. Interviewers were conducted between October 19 and 29, 2000. See Prime Minister's Office, Public Relations Office, *Opinion Survey on Foreign Affairs* (Tokyo: Prime Minister's Office, January 22, 2001).

87. *Asahi Shimbun* conducted interviews on September 18 and 19, 1994. Data acquired from the Roper Center.

88. NHK interviewed respondents on September 24 and 25, 1994. Data obtained from the Roper Center.

89. *Yomiuri Shimbun* conducted interviews on July 18 and 19, 1999. Data acquired from the Roper Center.

90. See, for example, Thomas Berger, *Cultures of Antimilitarism: National Security in Germany and Japan* (Baltimore, MD: Johns Hopkins University Press, 1998).

91. All 1998 Japanese census data are from Management and Coordination Agency, Statistics Bureau, *Estimates on All Japan Population by Age Group and Sex* (Tokyo: Management and Coordination Agency, March 1998).

92. "Hiroshima and Nagasaki Seek Security without U.S. Nuclear Umbrella," *Asahi Evening News*, August 16, 1998.

93. "Poll: Voters Want Bases Removed," *Asahi Shimbun*, November 11, 1998.

94. Nine percent of those surveyed gave another answer or did not respond to the question. *Asahi Shimbun* interviewed respondents between March 14 and 17, 1999. Data acquired from the Roper Center.

95. "Jiang: Use Science to Construct Modern Army," *China Daily*, June 28, 1999.

96. During a Diet session on the constitution held in late November 2000, Tokyo governor Shintaro Ishihara, responding to a comment by a member of the Japanese Communist Party who pointed out that the world can still learn from the war-renouncing meaning of Article 9, stated the following: "Which country would renounce war potentials by following the example of Japan? There are none." Quoted in "Ishihara Takes 'Ugly, Illegitimate' Constitution to Task," *Mainichi Daily News*, December 2, 2000.

97. "Japan Urged to Drop Its Bid to Sit on UNSC," Korean Central News Agency, December 17, 2000; Drifte, *Japan's Quest for a Permanent Security Council Seat*, pp. 150–152.

98. I am indebted to Kazumi Mizumoto of the Hiroshima Peace Institute for making this point to me.

Chapter 6

1. Regarding the alliance with the United States, Japanese defense policy emphasizes the "significance of the Japan–U.S. Security Arrangements." In addition to the constitution, specifically Article 9, the war-renouncing clause, the *Basic Policy for National Defense* remains fundamental to Japan's defense policy. However, as it did in the past, Tokyo continues to be selective in determining what is important in the *Basic Policy for National Defense*, prioritizing Japan's security alliance with the United States, and the need to grow the nation's defense while ignoring the contri-

bution of the United Nations. See the Japanese Defense Agency's web site at http:/
/www/jda.go.jp/policy. For a discussion of incrementalism, see Michael Green, "State
of the Field Report: Research on Japanese Security Policy," *AccessAsia Review* 2,
no. 1 (September 1998). For a critical discussion of incrementalism, see Mike
Mochizuki, "A New Bargain for a Stronger Alliance," in *Toward a True Alliance:
Restructuring U.S.–Japan Security Relations*, ed. Mike Mochizuki (Washington,
DC: Brookings Institution, 1997), pp. 17–23.

2. Because its economy has been lethargic for the past several years, Japan has
recently been attempting to convince Washington that it must reduce the *omoiyari
yosan* (sympathy budget)—the expenditures annually provided since the 1970s to
help defray the costs of the U.S. military presence in Japan. See "Cost Cuts for U.S.
Military Pushed," *Asahi Shimbun*, January 6, 2000.

3. According to the Department of Defense, in 1999 Japan had the largest
military budget among American allies, though still well below that of the United
States. See U.S. Department of Defense, *Report on Allied Contributions to the
Common Defense* (Washington, DC: U.S. Department of Defense, March 2000).
International data for 1999 shows that Japan's military budget was the third largest
in the world—behind only those of the United States and Russia, and slightly ahead
of China's. Data from the International Institute of Strategic Studies, *The Military Balance*, 2000/2001 edition, London, October 2000. Accessed on the Japan Information Network's website at http://www.jin.jcic.or.jp/stat/stats/
04dpl22.html.

4. While Beijing and Pyongyang's objections to the recent efforts by Washington and Tokyo to strengthen the bilateral security alliance are generally known,
less publicized are Moscow's apprehensions, which have become more evident
since the Japanese government approved the nation's involvement in TMD research
with the United States. For an analysis of the Russian perspective on the U.S.–
Japan security arrangement see, Andrew Kuchins and Alexei Zagorsky, "When
Realism and Liberalism Coincide: Russian Views of U.S. Alliances in Asia," Asia/
Pacific Research Center, Stanford University, July 1999.

5. See "U.S. Missile Shield Will Set Off a New Arms Race, China Warns," *New
York Times*, November 25, 1999; "China Condemns US–Japan Pact," *Financial Times*,
June 7, 1999; "DPRK Foreign Ministry Spokesman on Danger of U.S. 'TMD' Plan,"
Korean Central News Agency, August 30, 1999; "Russia Chides US, Japan over
Planned ABM System," *China Daily*, February 26, 2000.

6. Sponsored by the U.S. Information Agency and conducted by the Shin Joho
Center, this survey reported that 63 percent of the respondents strongly agreed with
the three nonnuclear principles, 18 percent somewhat agreed with them, 9 percent
said that they somewhat disagreed, 3 percent strongly disagreed, and 7 percent indicated that they did not know. Interviews were conducted between June 6 and June
12, 1991. Survey data obtained from the Roper Center for Public Opinion Research,
University of Connecticut.

7. "Koizumi: Eliminate Nukes," *Asahi Shimbun*, August 7, 2001, p. 20.

8. "Poll: Only 19 Percent Support Cabinet," *Asahi Shimbun*, January 22, 2001.

9. Interviews conducted by *Yomiuri Shimbun* on July 17 and July 18, 1999;
survey data obtained from the Roper Center for Public Opinion Research, University of Connecticut.

10. Twenty percent of the respondents to this question either answered that they

did not know or gave no reply. NHK conducted interviews between May 14 and May 16, 1999. Data acquired from the Roper Center for Public Opinion Research, University of Connecticut.

11. Thirty-two percent of the respondents said that they support the relocation plan. A further problem that Tokyo must deal with in the Futenma issue is that Okinawa's governor has proposed that there be a fifteen-year limit to the use of the base by the United States, a suggestion that is supported by 52 percent of Okinawan respondents. Survey conducted by *Asahi Shimbun* and the *Okinawan Times*; interviews conducted December 4 and 5, 1999. More that 60 percent of the respondents believed that Tokyo had not done all that it could to decrease the U.S. military's impact on Okinawa. See "Poll: 45 Percent Oppose Futenma Plan," *Asahi Shimbun*, December 7, 1999.

12. See, for example, Office of the Secretary of Defense, *Proliferation: Threat and Response* (Washington, DC: Department of Defense, January 2001), p. 8. At a December 2000 press conference, Japanese Defense Agency chief Saito indicated that Japan had to improve its military readiness, since "North Korea is maintaining and strengthening its military muscle." Quoted in "Remark of Director General of Defense Agency," Korean Central News Agency, December 15, 2000. On Tokyo's claim that China is an emergent military threat to Japan, see "White Paper Targets China," *Asahi Shimbun*, July 10, 2001.

13. Anthony DiFilippo, "Can Japan Craft an International Nuclear Disarmament Policy? *Asian Survey* 40, no. 4 (July/August 2000): 571–598.

14. For a recent example of a statement by Tokyo at the United Nations in which it calls for nuclear disarmament see *Statement by Mr. Masahiko Koumura Minister for Foreign Affairs of Japan at the Fifty-fourth Session of the General Assembly of the United Nations*, September 1999. Accessed on the Worldwide Web at http://www.mofa.go.jp/announce/fm/koumura/index.html.

15. The Report of the Tokyo Forum for Nuclear Non-proliferation and Disarmament, *Facing Nuclear Dangers: An Action Plan for the Twenty-first Century*, Tokyo, July 25, 1999.

16. "Japan Accused of Frantic Anti-DPRK Campaign," Korean Central News Agency, August 30, 1999. Pyongyang does not appear to be at all convinced that Tokyo is sincere about completely and expeditiously eliminating all nuclear weapons.

17. The suggestion that Japan come out from under America's nuclear umbrella is not new. See Kumao Kaneko, "Japan Needs No Umbrella," *Bulletin of the Atomic Scientists* 52, no. 2 (March/April 1996): 46–51; "Hiroshima and Nagasaki Seek Security without U.S. Nuclear Umbrella," *Asahi Evening News*, August 16, 1998.

18. *Statement by State Secretary for Foreign Affairs Masahiko Koumura to the United Nations Conference on Disarmament Issues in Sapporo*, July 22, 1997. Accessed on the Worldwide Web at http://www.mofa.go.jp/press/c_s/disarament.

19. Andrew Mack, "Japan and the Bomb: A Cause for Concern?" *Asia-Pacific Magazine*, no. 3 (June 1996), pp. 5–9; Eiichi Katahara, "Japan's Plutonium Policy: Consequences for Nonproliferation," *Nonproliferation Review* 5, no. 1 (fall 1997).

20. Nakasone Yasuhiro, "Japan's Firm Nonnuclear Resolve, *Japan Echo* 25, no. 5 (October 1998).

21. See, for example, "Whither US-Russian Relations," *Beijing Review* 43, no. 9 (February 28, 2000).

22. Seung-Ho Joo, "Russia–North Korea Rapprochement and Its Implications for Korean Peace Regime." Paper delivered at the forty-first annual meeting of the International Studies Association, Los Angeles, CA, March 14–18, 2000. Also see "Russia Demands Development of Good-Neighborly Relations with DPRK," Korean Central News Agency, February 11, 2000; "Spokesman of FM on Korea Visit of Russian FM," Korean Central News Agency, February 28, 2000.

23. Along with Belarus, Russia and China submitted a resolution to the U.N. General Assembly on December 1, 1999, that emphasized the need to maintain the ABM Treaty; the resolution was passed by the General Assembly. See "Wither US-Russian Relations," *Beijing Review* 43, no. 9 (February 28, 2000).

24. See "Sino-Russia Joint Statement," *Beijing Review* 42, no. 51 (December 20, 1999); "China, Russia Advance Strategic Partnership," *Beijing Review* 42, no. 51 (December 20, 1999).

25. The Report of the Tokyo Forum, *Facing Nuclear Dangers*.

26. "Japan Hit over Weak Antinuclear Stance," *Japan Times Online*, November 12, 1999.

27. "China's Security Environment in the Early 2000s," *Beijing Review* 43, no. 2 (January 10, 2000).

28. The following is the Chinese official position on nuclear weapons: "China consistently stands for the comprehensive prohibition and thorough destruction of nuclear weapons." People's Republic of China, Foreign Ministry, *Foreign Policy*. Accessed on the Worldwide Web at www.fmprc.gov.cn/e/c/ec.htm. Accessed on February 13, 1999. The Japanese official position on nuclear weapons is as follows: "Japan, the only country to have suffered atomic bombings, firmly maintains the three nonnuclear principles that prohibit the nation from possessing, producing, or introducing onto its territory any nuclear weapons." Ministry of Foreign Affairs, *Japanese Viewpoints* (Tokyo: Overseas Public Relations Office, Ministry of Foreign Affairs, September 1995).

29. In a joint policy statement Tokyo and Beijing have indicated that: "Both sides stress the importance of the ultimate elimination of nuclear weapons and oppose the proliferation of nuclear weapons in any form whatsoever, and furthermore, strongly call upon the nations concerned to cease all nuclear testing and nuclear arms race, in order to contribute to the peace and stability of the Asian region and the world." The Ministry of Foreign Affairs, *Japan–China Joint Declaration on Building a Partnership of Friendship and Cooperation for Peace and Development*, Tokyo, Japan, November 26, 1998.

30. See Ministry of Foreign Affairs, *In Quest of a New Role: United Nations and Japan*, Tokyo, 2000. Document accessed at http://www.mofa.go.jp/policy/un/pamph2000/index.html.

31. Ministry of Foreign Affairs, *Diplomatic Bluebook 1993* (Tokyo: Ministry of Foreign Affairs, 1994), p. 49.

32. Advisory Group on Defense Issues, *The Modality of the Security and Defense Capability of Japan: The Outlook for the Twenty-first Century*, Tokyo, August 12, 1994.

33. See Kuchins and Zagorsky, "When Realism and Liberalism Coincide: Russian Views of U.S. Alliances in Asia."

34. See People's Republic of China, Foreign Ministry, *Foreign Policy*, accessed on the Worldwide Web at http://www.fmprc.gov.cn/e/c/ec.htm; "China's Position on Current International Issues," *Beijing Review* 42, no. 41 (October 11, 1999).

35. "China, Russia Advance Strategic Partnership," *Beijing Review* 42, no. 51 (December 20, 1999).

36. See National Institute for Defense Studies, *East Asian Strategic Review, 1998– 1999, Summary*, Tokyo, 1999.

37. Sheldon Simon, "Is There a U.S. Strategy for East Asia?" *Contemporary Southeast Asia: A Journal of International and Strategic Affairs* 21, no. 3 (December 1999): 325–343.

38. National Institute for Defense Studies, *East Asian Strategic Review, 1998– 1999* (Summary).

39. "KCNA [Korean Central News Agency] Slams U.S. Ambition for Hegemony in Asia and Pacific," Korean Central News Agency, March 21, 2000.

40. Chuck Downs, *Over the Line: North Korea's Negotiating Strategy* (Washington, DC: American Enterprise Institute, 1999); Christopher Hughes, *Japan's Economic Power and Security: Japan and North Korea* (London: Routledge, 1999).

41. A recent example of Pyongyang's continuing concern about Tokyo's plans to invade Korea appear in "Japan's Plan to Create Commando Force Blasted," Korean Central News Agency, January 27, 2000.

42. See, for example, "Japan's Militarist Aggression to Lead to Its Self-Destruction," Korean Central News Agency, March 21, 2000.

43. "Japan's Bid for UNSC Permanent Membership Rejected," Korean Central News Agency, February 2, 2001.

44. Thomas Christensen, "China, the U.S.–Japan Alliance, and the Security Dilemma in East Asia," *International Security* 23, no. 4 (spring 1999): 49–80; Yong Deng, "The Asianization of East Asian Security and the United States' Role," *East Asia: An International Quarterly* 16, nos. 3–4 (autumn/winter 1998): 87–110; Rajan Menon, "The Once and Future Superpower," *Bulletin of Atomic Scientists* 53, no.1 (January/February 1997): 29–34. The libertarian perspective is that the United States maintains the bilateral security alliance, because it still does not trust Japan. See Ted Galen Carpenter, "Paternalism and Dependence: The U.S.–Japan Security Relationship" (Washington, DC: Cato Institute, November 1, 1995).

45. Thomas Berger, "From Sword to Chrysanthemum: Japan's Culture of Antimilitarism," *International Security* 17, no. 4 (spring 1993). Reprinted in *East Asian Security*, ed. Michael Brown, Sean Lynn-Jones, and Steven Miller (Cambridge, MA: MIT Press, 1996), pp. 300–331.

46. Ministry of Foreign Affairs, *2000 Survey in the United States of Opinions toward Japan* (Tokyo: Overseas Relations Office, Ministry of Foreign Affairs, May 2000). Accessed at http://www.mofa.go.jp/region/n-america/us/survey/survey2000.html.

47. Simon, "Is There a U.S. Strategy for East Asia?"; Mack, "Japan and the Bomb: A Cause for Concern"; Matake Kamiya, "Japan, Nuclear Weapons, and the U.S.–Japan Alliance," paper presented at the conference on U.S.–Japan Security Relations, Washington, DC, May 2, 1996.

48. See *Appeal from Hiroshima and Nagasaki for a Total Ban and Elimination of Nuclear Weapons*, nd. Available at http://www.ask.ne.jp/~hankaku/english/appeal.html; "Hiroshima, Nagasaki Protest U.S. Subcritical Test," *Kyodo News*, February 4, 2000; and the "Letter of Protest" sent by Tadatoshi Akiba, mayor of Hiroshima, to President Clinton on February 4, 2000, remonstrating America's ninth subcritical nuclear test. This letter can be found at the following address on the

Worldwide Web: http://www.pcf.city.hiroshima.jp/peacesite/English/Stage0/info/ protest000204E.html.

49. See the editorial "U.S., Russia Must Stop Conducting Subcritical Tests," in *Asahi Shimbun*, February 5, 2000.

50. See DiFilippo, "Can Japan Craft an International Nuclear Disarmament Policy?" pp. 574–575.

51. Herman Kahn, *The Emerging Japanese Superstate* (Englewood Cliffs, NJ: Prentice Hall, 1970).

52. "U.N. Seen as Key to Security in Asia," *Asahi Shimbun*, October 28, 1999. Interviews were conducted in August and September 1999.

53. See, for example, "Hiroshima and Nagasaki Seek Security without U.S. Nuclear Umbrella," *Asahi Evening News*, August 16, 1998.

54. The resolution is as follows: "We, Kobe City Council, reject the visit of all nuclear-armed warships into Kobe port. See *Nuclear Free Kobe*, accessed on the Worldwide Web at the following address: http://www.prop1.org/prop1/jkobef.htm

55. See "Kochi Submits Nuke Bill Revision," *Asahi Shimbun*, February 24, 1999; "With Familiar Name and Reform Plans, This Hashimoto Manages to Carry the Day," *Nikkei Weekly*, February 22, 1999, pp. 1, 23.

56. "Kobe Declaration a Thorn in the Side of Diplomacy," *Japan Times Online*, March 22, 2001.

57. "City Refuses to Let U.S. Warship Pay Call," *Japan Times Online*, January 21, 2001.

58. "Mayor Drops Opposition to Warship's Visit," *Japan Times Online*, February 2, 2001.

59. Aurelia George Mulgan, "Beyond Self-Defense? Evaluating Japan's Regional Security Role under the New Defense Cooperation Guidelines," *Pacifica Review: Peace, Security and Global Change* 12, no. 3 (October 2000): 239; "Defense Dilemma: Central, Local Governments at Odds, U.S. Warships Not Welcome in Hokkaido," *Japan Times Online*, March 21, 2001.

60. See "U.S. Marine Held for Lifting Girl's Skirt and Taking Photo," *Japan Times Online*, January 11, 2001.

61. "Marine Fined for Lifting Girl's Skirt," *Japan Times Online*, January 27, 2001; "Okinawa Demands Hailston Be Fired," *Japan Times Online*, February 8, 2001; "U.S. Commander Contrite over Okinawa Remarks," *Japan Times Online*, February 9, 2001.

62. Douglas Mendel, *Japanese People and Foreign Policy* (Berkeley: University of California Press, 1961), pp. 94–121.

63. The relevant words in Article VI of the Treaty of Mutual Cooperation and Security are as follows: "[T]he United States of America is granted the use by its land, air and naval forces of facilities and areas in Japan." The Status of Forces Agreement affirms that: "United States and foreign vessels and aircraft operated by, for, or under the control of the United States for official purposes shall be accorded access to any port or airport of Japan free from toll or landing charges." See *Agreement under Article VI of the Treaty of Mutual Cooperation and Security between Japan and the United States of America, Regarding Facilities and Areas and the Status of United States Armed Forces in Japan*, Washington, DC, January 19, 1960.

64. The Transport Ministry also reported the increased use in 1999 of aircraft

belonging to Japan's Self Defense Forces at civilian airports. See "More U.S. Craft Use Civil Airports," *Asahi Shimbun*, April 7, 2000.

65. The *Basic Policy for National Defense* states: "To deal with external aggression on the basis of the Japan–U.S. security arrangements, pending the effective functioning of the United Nations in the future in deterring and repelling such aggression."

66. For example, see Akihiko Tanaka, "Japan's Security Policy in the 1990s," in *Japan's International Agenda*, ed. Yoichi Funabashi (New York: New York University Press, 1994), pp. 28–56; Masaru Tamamoto, "Japan's Search for Recognition and Status," in *Japan's Quest: The Search for International Role, Recognition, and Respect*, ed. Warren Hunsberger (Armonk, NY: M.E. Sharpe, 1997), pp. 3–14; Richard Finn, "Japan's Search for a Global Role: Politics and Security," in Humsberger, *Japan's Quest*, pp. 113–132.

67. Okubo Shiro, "Japan's Constitutional Pacifism and United Nations Peacekeeping," in Hunsberger, *Japan's Quest*, pp. 96–112.

68. See, for example, "High Vigilance against Japan Called For," Korean Central News Agency, December 30, 2000; "Japan's Moves to Justify Overseas Aggression Assailed," Korean Central News Agency, January 24, 2001.

69. "Russian Navy Fires on Japan Fishing Boat," *China Daily*, April 21, 2000; "Russia Seizes Japanese Vessel in Maritime Boundary Dispute," *New York Times*, April 22, 2000.

70. Ministry of Foreign Affairs, *Japan's Northern Territories*, 1999; Ministry of Foreign Affairs, accessed at http://infojapan.org/region/europe/russia/territory/index.html; *Japan's Policy on the Russian Federation*, nd., accessed at http://www.mofa.go.jp/index.html.

71. However, a survey sponsored by the prime minister's office ten months later, in January 1988, indicated that 58 percent of the public had by then endorsed the defense spending to gross national product ratio of 1.004. See Ronald Dolan, "National Security," in *Japan: A Country Study*, ed. Ronald Dolan and Robert Worden (Washington, DC: U.S. Government Printing Office, 1992), pp. 431–432.

72. Ozawa uses this term. Discussion of the "normal country" issue can be found in Chalmers Johnson, "In Search of a 'Normal' Role," Institute on Global Conflict and Cooperation, University of California, July 1992.

73. *Treaty of Mutual Cooperation and Security between Japan and the United States of America*, Washington, DC, January 19, 1960.

74. "Achievements in DPRK Diplomacy," Korean Central News Agency, December 8, 2000.

75. Quoted from "KCNA on U.S. National Defense Budget," Korean Central News Agency, February 8, 2002; "Japan Urged to Drop Hostile Policy toward DPRK," Korean Central News Agency, February 8, 2002.

76. See "30 Percent Fear Japan May Be Involved in War: Poll." *Japan Times Online*, May 14, 2000; "More Concerned about Conflicts Involving Japan," *Asahi Evening News*, May 14, 2000.

77. "U.S. Warmongers' Sheer Sophism," Korean Central News Agency, May 7, 2000.

78. See "Report Focuses on NGO's, Missile Threat," *Japan Times Online*, May 10, 2000; "KCNA Advises Japan to Fulfill Its Responsibility," Korean Central News Agency, May 12, 2000.

79. Early Russian uneasiness with the U.S.–Japan plan to develop TMD is ex-

pressed in "Russian Concerned with Wider Military Union of Japan, USA," Itar/ Tass, February 21, 1999.

80. The Congressional Budget Office estimates that the U.S. limited NMD system would ultimately cost nearly $60 billion. See "Missile Defense May Have Price of $60 Billion, *New York Times*, April 26, 2000.

81. "China Says U.S. Missile Shield Could Force an Arms Buildup," *New York Times*, May 11, 2000; "U.S. Missile Shield May Force China Arms Buildup," *People's Daily Online*, May 12, 2000.

82. Kuchins and Zagorsky, "When Realism and Liberalism Coincide: Russian Views of U.S. Alliances in Asia," p. 10; "Power of U.S. Draws China and Russia to Amity Pact," *New York Times*, January 14, 2001.

83. For critical comments on TMD by a Japanese military analyst, see "Missile-Defense Plan Blasted," *Mainichi Daily News*, January 14, 2000.

84. There are still persistent calls to strengthen the U.S.–Japan security alliance. See Kurt Campbell, "Energizing the U.S.–Japan Security Partnership," *Washington Quarterly* 23, no. 4 (autumn 2000): 125–134; Institute for National Strategic Studies, "The United States and Japan: Advancing toward a Mature Partnership" (Washington, DC: National Defense University, Special Report, October 11, 2000).

85. "Nishimura Resigns over Nuclear Remarks," *Japan Times*, October 20, 1999.

86. "Japan Caught in the Middle of Dispute over NPT: Confrontations Intensify at Conference for Nuclear Disarmament," *Asahi Shimbun*, May 10, 2000. For a detailed analysis of Japan's national policy on nuclear weapons, see DiFilippo, "Can Japan Craft an International Nuclear Disarmament Policy?"

87. The Report of the Tokyo Forum for Nuclear Nonproliferation and Disarmament, *Facing Nuclear Dangers*.

88. See the General Assembly, United Nations, *A Path to the Total Elimination of Nuclear Weapons*, New York, November 2000. Several other times in the past Japan has presented resolutions to the United Nations on the abolition of nuclear weapons.

89. For the CTBT to come into force, forty-four countries must sign and ratify it. To date, forty-one of these countries have signed the CTBT (North Korea, India, and Pakistan are not yet signatories), and thirty-one nations have signed and ratified it. As noted in this chapter, Japan was the first nation to both sign and ratify the CTBT of the forty-four states that must do so before the accord can take effect. See the website of the Comprehensive Nuclear Test Ban Treaty at http://pws.ctbto.org.

90. This assumption pervades the paper by Benjamin Self, "Confidence-Building Measures and Japanese Security" (Washington, DC: The Henry Stimson Center, 2000).

91. Anthony DiFilippo, *Kempo kyu jyo ni kanau chi kyu teki anzenhosyo* (Global security according to the constitution, Article 9), *Asahi Shimbun*, February 13, 1997. Reprinted as "The Future Is Now: Japan's Place in UN Politics," *Asahi Evening News*, March 2, 1997.

92. This is much different from the "unarmed neutrality" espoused by the socialists during the early part of the Cold War. In the post–Cold War period, if Japan's neutrality were linked directly to an actively pursued disarmament agenda it would lend great credibility to its efforts. Note too that this would be active neutrality, in contrast to the passivity characterizing Japan's Cold War international behavior.

93. Japan's contribution makes up more than 15 percent of the UN's annual budget, which is far more than any other country, except the United States. However,

there are only a little over 100 Japanese holding top-level positions at the UN Secretariat, well below the number of Germans and Russians (both about 130). See "Japanese Lament How Few of Them Hold Top UN Jobs," *Nikkei Weekly*, February 16, 1998; Ministry of Foreign Affairs, *Diplomatic Bluebook 2000* (Tokyo: Ministry of Foreign Affairs, 2000).

94. Anthony DiFilippo, "Why Japan Should Redirect Its Security Policy," *Japan Quarterly* 45, no. 2 (April–June 1998): 29–31.

95. United Nations Charter, San Francisco, June 26, 1945. Document accessed at http://www/un.org/aboutun/charter/index.html on February 6, 2001.

96. See Ministry of Foreign Affairs, *Japan's Assistance Programs for Russia*, Tokyo, May 1997, accessed at http://www.mofa.go.jp/region/europe/russia/assistance/index.html. Also see Ministry of Foreign Affairs, *Japan-Russian Federation Joint Efforts for Disarmament and Environmental Protection: New Initiatives by the Government of Japan in the Areas of Assistance for Denuclearization, Disarmament and Non-proliferation*, Tokyo, May 1999, accessed at http://www.mofa.go.jp/region/europe/russia/fmv9905/joint.html.

97. Ministry of Foreign Affairs, *Japan-China Joint Declaration on Building a Partnership of Friendship and Cooperation for Peace and Development*, Tokyo, November 26, 1998. Document accessed at http://www.mofa.go.jp/region/asia-paci/china/visit98/joint.html.

98. Dingli Shen, "China's Negative Security Assurances" (Washington, DC: The Henry Stimson Center, 1998); Liu Huaqiu, "No-First-Use and China's Security" (Washington, DC: The Henry Stimson Center, 1998). Both of these papers are made available by The Henry Stimson Center at the following address: http://www.stimson.org.

99. "Strong Support for Aid to North Korea," *Asahi Shimbun*, October 20, 1999. Data from a joint *Asahi Shimbun/Dong-a Ilbo* (South Korea) survey conducted in September 1999.

100. Zhou Xinhua, "Too Hasty to Become a Military-Political Power," *Beijing Review* 43, no. 21 (May 22, 2000); "KCNA Assails Japan's Arms Buildup," Korean Central News Agency, June 6, 2000.

101. See "Japan: Extending Tokyo's Reach," *Far Eastern Economic Review* 164, no. 2 (January 18, 2001); "Japan's Defense Plan Creates Anxiety," *Beijing Review*, no. 2 (January 11, 2001).

102. See Hans Kristensen, "Japan under the U.S. Nuclear Umbrella," Berkeley, CA, Nautilus Institute, July 21, 1999, p. 1. Paper can be accessed on Worldwide Web at http://www.nautilus.org.

103. "Kobe Declaration a Thorn in the Side of Diplomacy," *Japan Times Online*, March 22, 2001; "Kochi Tests Nation's Nuclear Principles," *Japan Times Online*, March 11, 1999.

104. Another 31 percent of the respondents felt that the sanctions that the government employed against countries that performed nuclear testing were fine; only 3 percent thought that the measures used were too strict, and 7 percent said that they did not know or did not answer. *Yomiuri Shimbun* conducted interviews for this survey on June 13 and June 14, 1998. Data acquired from the Roper Center for Public Opinion Research.

105. Tadakazu Fukase, "Proposals for Everlasting World Peace from the Constitution of Japan," in *In Quest of World Peace for All Time—Proposals Based on the*

Constitution of Japan, ed. Tadakazu Fukase, Yasuo Sugihara, Yoichi Higuchi, and Kenji Urata (Tokyo: Keiso Shobo, May 1998), pp. 6–8.

106. For a discussion of revising Article 9 that reviews the proposal of three leading Japanese politicians, Yasuhiro Nakasone, Ichiro Ozawa, and Yukio Hatoyama, all of whom leave unanswered the serious problems of retaining the Japan–U.S. Security Treaty, see Mayumi Itoh, "Japanese Constitutional Revision," *Asian Survey* 41, no. 2 (March/April 2001): 310–327.

Bibliography

Newspapers/News Agencies

Asahi Evening News (Asahi Shimbun)
Asahi Shimbun
Associated Press
China Daily
Christian Science Monitor
Daily Yomiuri (Yomiuri Shimbun)
Daily Yomiuri On-line (Yomiuri Shimbun)
Financial Times
Itar/Tass
Japan Times
Japan Times Online
Japan Times Weekly International Edition
Korean Central News Agency
Kyodo News Service
Mainichi Daily News
New York Times
Nikkei Net (Nihon Keizai Shimbun)
Nikkei Weekly
Okinawan Times
People's Daily Online
People's Korea
Space Daily
Washington Post

Books and Articles

Akaha, Tsuneo. "U.S.–Japan Security Alliance Adrift?" Paper prepared for the annual meeting of Asian Studies on the Pacific Coast, June 26–29, 1997.
———. "Beyond Self-Defense: Japan's Elusive Security Role under the New Defense Guidelines for U.S.–Japan Defense Cooperation." *Pacific Review* 11, no. 4 (1998): 461–483.
Asia Intelligence Update: Red Alert. Austin, TX: Stratfor, December 9, 1998.
Awanohara, Susumu. "Scenarios that Divide: An Abiding Need for Diplomacy." New York: Council on Foreign Relations, December 4, 1996.
Babbie, Earl. *The Practice of Social Research.* Belmont, CA: Wadsworth, 1998.
Berger, Thomas. *Cultures of Antimilitarism: National Security in Germany and Japan.* Baltimore: Johns Hopkins University Press, 1998.
———. "From Sword to Chrysanthemum: Japan's Culture of Anti-militarism." *International Security* 17, no. 4 (spring 1993).
Bergsten, C. Fred, and Nolan Marcus. "Reconcilable Differences? United States-Japan Economic Conflict." Washington, DC: Institute for International Economics, 1993.
Brown, Michael, Sean Lynn-Jones, and Steven Miller, eds. *East Asian Security.* Cambridge, MA: MIT Press, 1996.
"Building a Friendly and Cooperative Sino-Japanese Relationship." *Beijing Review* 41, no. 44 (November 2–8, 1998).
Campbell, Curt. "Energizing the U.S.–Japan Security Partnership." *Washington Quarterly* (autumn 2000), pp. 125–134.
Carpenter, Ted. "Breaking Allies' Dependency on American Military Power." *USA Today Magazine,* July 1999.
———. "Pacific Fraud: The New U.S.–Japan Defense Guidelines." Washington, DC: Cato Institute, October 16, 1997. http://www.cato.org/dailys/10–16–97.html.
———. "Paternalism and Dependence: The U.S.–Japan Security Relationship." Washington, DC: Cato Institute, November 1995.
Cato Institute. *Cato Handbook for Congress: Toward a New Relationship with Japan.* Washington, DC: Cato Institute, 1997.
Center for Defense Information. "Chinese Defense Spending: A Great Increase, But to Where?" *Weekly Defense Monitor* 2, no. 17 (April 30, 1998).
Cha, Victor. *Alignment despite Antagonism: The United States-Korea-Japan Security Triangle.* Stanford, CA: Stanford University Press, 1999.
Chai, Sun-Ki. "Entrenching the Yoshida Doctrine: Three Techniques for Institutionalization." *International Organization* 51, no. 3 (summer 1997): 389–423.
"China, Russia Advance Strategic Partnership." *Beijing Review* 42, no. 51 (December 20, 1999).
"China's Foreign Trade." *Beijing Review* 43, no. 14 (April 3, 2000).
"China's Position on Current International Issues." *Beijing Review,* vol. 42, no. 41, October 11, 1999.
"China's Security Environment in the Early 2000s." *Beijing Review* 43, no. 2 (January 10, 2000).
"China's Stand on Non-proliferation," *Beijing Review* 6, no. 2 (February 8–14, 1999).
Christensen, Thomas. "China, the U.S.–Japan Alliance, and the Security Dilemma in East Asia." *International Security* 23, no. 4 (spring 1999): 49–80.

Chu Shulong. "China and the U.S-Japan and the U.S.-Korean Alliances in a Changing Northeast Asia." Asia/Pacific Research Center, Stanford University, June 1999.

Committee of Disarmament Homepage accessed on the Worldwide Web at http://www.igc.apc.org/disarm/index.htlm.

Conry, Barbara. "U.S. 'Global Leadership': A Euphemism for World Policeman." Policy analysis. Washington, DC: Cato Institute, February 5, 1997.

"Constitutional Talk." *The Economist*, January 9, 1999.

Cossa, Ralph. "Korea: The Achilles Heel of the U.S.–Japan Alliance." Asia/Pacific Research Center, Stanford University, May 1997.

———. "U.S.–Japan Security Relations: Separating Fact from Fiction." In *Restructuring the U.S.–Japan Security Alliance: Toward a More Equal Partnership*, ed. Ralph Cossa, 31–49. Washington, DC: Center for Strategic and International Studies, 1997.

"Crazy for Hegemony." *Beijing Review*, no. 21 (May 24, 2001).

Daalder, Ivo. "Prospects for Global Leadership Sharing: The Security Dimension." School of Public Affairs, Center for International and Security Studies, University of Maryland at College Park, July 1996.

Deng, Yong. "The Asianization of East Asian Security and the United States' Role." *East Asia: An International Quarterly* 16, nos. 3–4 (autumn/winter 1998): 87–110.

———. "Chinese Relations with Japan: Implications for Asia-Pacific Regionalism," *Pacific Affairs* 70, no. 3 (fall 1997): 373–391.

Diamond, Howard. "KEDO Resolves Cost-Sharing for North Korean Reactor Project." *Arms Control Today* 28, no. 5 (June/July 1998).

DiFilippo, Anthony. "Can Japan Craft an International Nuclear Disarmament Policy?" *Asian Survey* 40, no. 4 (July/August 2000): 571–598.

———. "China's Side of the History Equation." *Japan Times*, Op-ed, December 10, 1998, p. 21.

———. *Cracks in the Alliance: Science, Technology, and the Evolution of U.S.–Japan Relations*. Aldershot, England, and Brookfield, VT: Ashgate, 1997.

———. "Creating Global Security: Japan as a Potential Catalyst." In *Economics of Conflict and Peace*, ed. Jurgen Brauer and William Gissy. Aldershot, England, and Brookfield, VT: Ashgate, 1997.

———. "*Hikaku sekai ni muketa Nihon no koken*" (The Japanese contribution to an anti-nuclear world). *Asahi Shimbun*, Op-ed, September 25, 1998, p. 4.

———. "*Kempo kyu jyo ni kanau chi kyu teki anzenhosyo*" (Global security according to the constitution, Article 9). *Asahi Shimbun*, Op-ed, February 13, 1997. Reprinted as "The Future Is Now: Japan's Place in UN Politics," *Asahi Evening News*, March 2, 1997.

———. "Japan's National Security Policy Ignores Public Sentiment." *Japan Times*, Op-ed, May 25, 2000.

———. "Why Japan Should Redirect Its Security Policy." *Japan Quarterly* 45, no. 2 (April–June 1998): 24–31.

Domhoff, G. William. *Higher Circles: The Governing Class in America*. New York: Vintage, 1970.

"Double-Edged Fury." *Far Eastern Economic Review* (May 20, 1999).

Downs, Chuck. *Over the Line: North Korea's Negotiating Strategy*. Washington, DC: American Enterprise Institute, 1999.

Drifte, Douglas. *Japan's Quest for a Permanent Security Council Seat: A Matter of Pride or Justice?* London: Macmillan, 2000.

Dupont, Daniel. Insert in George Lewis, Theodore Postol, and John Pike, "Why National Missile Defense Won't Work." *Scientific American*, August 1999, pp. 36–41.

Finn, Richard. "Japan's Search for a Global Role: Politics and Security." In *Japan's Quest: The Search for International Role, Recognition, and Respect*, ed. Warren Hunsberger, 113–132. Armonk, NY: M.E. Sharpe, 1997.

"Flying the Flag." *Far Eastern Economic Review* (August 12, 1999).

Foreign Press Center. *Facts and Figures of Japan*. Tokyo: Foreign Press Center, 1998.

Fukase, Tadakazu. "Proposals for Everlasting World Peace from the Constitution of Japan." In *In Quest of World Peace for All Time—Proposals Based on the Constitution of Japan*, ed. Tadakazu Fukase, Yasuo Sugihara, Yoichi Higuchi and Kenji Urata, 6–8. Tokyo: Keiso Shobo, May 1998.

Funabashi, Yoichi. "Tokyo's Temperance." *Washington Quarterly* 23, no. 3 (summer 2000): 135–144.

Green, Michael. "Interests, Asymmetries, and Strategic Choices." In *The U.S.–Japan Security Alliance for the 21st Century*. Study group on the U.S.–Japan Security Alliance, Bruce Stokes, project director. New York: Council on Foreign Relations, 1997.

———. "State of the Field Report: Research on Japanese Security Policy." *AccessAsia Review* 2, no.1 (September 1998).

———. "Theater Missile Defense and Strategic Relations with the People's Republic of China." In *Restructuring the U.S.–Japan Alliance: Toward a More Equal Partnership*, ed. Ralph Cossa, 111–118. Washington, DC: Center for Strategic and International Studies, 1997.

Hamada, Koicho. "The Pacifist Constitution in Post-war Japan—Economic Dividends or Political Burdens?" *Disarmament: A Periodic Review by the Nations* 19, no. 3 (1996): 46–62.

"Hard Target." *Far Eastern Economic Review* (September 24, 1998).

Heginbotham, Eric, and Richard Samuels. "Mercantile Realism and Japanese Foreign Policy." *International Security* 22, no. 4 (spring 1998): 171–204.

Hirano, Eri, and William Piez, eds. *Alliance for the 21st Century: The Final Report of the U.S.–Japan 21st Century Committee*. Washington, DC: The Center for Strategic and International Studies, August 1998.

Hosokawa, Morihiro. "Are U.S. Troops Needed in Japan? Reforming the Alliance." *Foreign Affairs* 77, no. 4 (July/August 1998): 2–5.

Hughes, Christopher. *Japan's Economic Power and Security: Japan and North Korea*. London: Routledge, 1999.

Inoguchi, Takashi. "Adjusting America's Two Alliances in East Asia: A Japanese View." Asia/Pacific Research Center, Stanford University, July 1999.

———. "The New Security Treaty Setup and Japan's Options." *Japan Echo* (winter 1995): 36–39.

International Institute for Strategic Studies. *The Military Balance 1999/2000*. London: International Institute for Strategic Studies, 2000.

Ishihara, Shintaro. *The Japan That Can Say No*. Trans. Frank Baldwin. New York: Simon and Schuster, 1991.

————. (Interview). "Japan, Wake Up!" *By the Way* 8, no. 4 (June/July 1998): 8–12.

Ishihara, Shintaro, and Akio Morita. *No to ieru Nihon* (The Japan that can say no). Tokyo: Kobunsha, 1989.

Ishihara, Shintaro, Shoichi Watanabe, and Kazuhisa Ogawa. *Soredemo no to ireu Nippon* (Japan which can still say no). Tokyo: Kobunsha, 1990.

Itoh, Mayumi. "Japanese Constitutional Revision." *Asian Survey* 41, no. 2 (March/April 2001): 310–327.

Japan Communist Party. *JCP's View on Relationship between Constitution's Article 9 and the Self Defense Forces*. Accessed on the Worldwide Web at the following address: http://www.jcp.or.jp/english/jps_weekly/e000930_03.html.

"Japan: Extending Tokyo's Reach." *Far Eastern Economic Review* (January 18, 2001).

"Japan's Defense Plan Creates Anxiety." *Beijing Review*, no. 2, January 11, 2001.

"Japan, U.S. Agree on SDI Participation." *Aviation Week and Space Technology*, July 27, 1987.

Johnson, Chalmers. "The Okinawan Rape Incident and the End of the Cold War." Working paper no. 16, Japan Policy Research Institute, February 1996.

————. "In Search of a 'Normal' Role." Institute on Global Conflict and Cooperation, University of California, July 1992.

Johnson, Chalmers, and E.B. Keehn. "The Pentagon's Ossified Strategy." *Foreign Affairs* 74, no. 4 (July/August 1995).

Joo, Seung-Ho. "Russia-North Korea Rapprochement and Its Implications for Korean Peace Regime." Paper presented at the International Studies Association Conference, Los Angeles, CA, March 14–18, 2000.

Kahn, Herman. *The Emerging Japanese Superstate*. Englewood Cliffs, NJ: Prentice Hall, 1970.

Kamiya, Matake. "Japan, Nuclear Weapons, and the U.S.–Japan Alliance." Paper presented at the conference on U.S.–Japan Security Relations, Washington, DC, May 2, 1996.

————. "The U.S.–Japan Alliance and Regional Security Cooperation: Toward a Double-Layered Security System." In *Restructuring the U.S.–Japan Alliance: Toward a More Equal Partnership*, ed. Ralph Cossa, 19–28. Washington, DC: Center for Strategic and International Studies, 1997.

Kaneko, Kumao. "Japan Needs No Nuclear Umbrella." *Bulletin of the Atomic Scientists* 52, no. 2 (March/April 1996): 46–51.

Katahara, Eiichi. "Japan's Plutonium Policy: Consequences for Nonproliferation." *Nonproliferation Review* 5, no. 1 (fall 1997): 53–61.

Katzenstein, Peter. *Cultural Norms and National Security*. Ithaca, NY: Cornell University Press, 1996.

Kim, Hyung Kook. "Japan, Korea, and Northeast Asia: A Korean View." In *Japan's Quest: The Search for International Role, Recognition, and Respect*, ed. Warren Hunsberger, 167–178. Armonk, NY: M.E. Sharpe, 1997.

"The Korean Peninsula: What If?" *Far East Economic Review* (June 29, 2000).

Koseki, Soichi. *The Birth of Japan's Postwar Constitution*. Ed. and trans. Ray Moore. Boulder, CO: Westview Press, 1997.

Kristensen, Hans. "Japan under the U.S. Nuclear Umbrella." Berkeley, CA: Nautilus Institute, July 21, 1999. Paper can be accessed on Worldwide Web at http://www.nautilus.org.

Kuchins, Andrew, and Alexei Zagorsky. "When Realism and Libralism Coincide:

Russian Views of U.S. Alliances in Asia." Asia/Pacific Research Center, Stanford University, July 1999.

Larimer, Tim, and Hiroko Tashiro. "National Colors." *Time South Pacific*, August 30, 1999.

Liu Huaqui. "No-First-Use and China's Security." Washington, DC: The Henry Stimson Center, 1998.

Luo, Tongsong. "Who Whips Up Anti-American Feeling?" *Beijing Review* 42, no. 23 (June 7, 1999).

Mack, Andrew. "Japan and the Bomb: A Cause for Concern." *Asia-Pacific Magazine* (June 1996), pp. 5–9.

McCormack, Gavin. "Nationalism and Identity in Post-Cold War Japan." *Pacifica Review: Peace, Security and Global Change* 12, no. 3 (October 2000): 249–254.

Mendel, Douglas. *The Japanese People and Foreign Policy: A Study of Public Opinion in Post-treaty Japan*. Berkeley: University of California Press, 1961.

Mendl, Wolf. *Japan's Asia Policy: Regional Security and Global Interests*. London: Routledge, 1995.

Menon, Rajan. "The Once and Future Superpower." *Bulletin of Atomic Scientists* 53, no. 1 (January/February 1997): 29–34.

Mochizuki, Mike. "The Future of the U.S.–Japan Alliance." *Sekai Shuho*, February 6, 1996.

———. "A New Bargain for a Stronger Alliance." In *Toward a True Alliance: Restructuring U.S.–Japan Relations*. Ed. Mike Mochizuki, 5–40. Washington, DC: Brookings Institution, 1997.

———. "Security and Economic Interdependence in Northeast Asia." Asia/Pacific Research Center, Stanford University, May 1998.

Mochizuki, Mike, and Michael O'Hanlon. "A Liberal Vision for the U.S.–Japan Alliance." *Survival* 40, no. 2 (summer 1998): 127–134.

———. "The Marines Should Come Home: Adapting the U.S.–Japan Alliance to a New Security Era." *Brookings Review* 14, no. 2 (spring 1996).

Monterey Institute of International Studies, Center for Nonproliferation Studies on the Worldwide Web at http://cns.miis.edu. Briefings on DPRK-Russia Joint Declaration that was released in July 2000.

Morimoto, Satoshi. "A Tighter Japan–U.S. Alliance Based on Greater Trust." In *Toward a True Alliance: Restructuring U.S.–Japan Security Relations*. Ed. Mike Mochizuki, 137–148. Washington, DC: Brookings Institution, 1997.

Morrison, Charles, ed. *Asia Pacific Security Outlook 1998*. Tokyo and New York: Japan Center for International Exchange, 1998.

Mulgan, Aurelia George. "Beyond Self-Defense? Evaluating Japan's Regional Security Role under the New Defense Cooperation Guidelines." *Pacifica Review: Peace Security and Global Change* 12, no. 3 (October 2000): 221–246.

———. "The U.S.–Japan Security Relationship." In *The New Security Agenda in the Asia-Pacific Region*. Ed. Roy Denny, 140–169. New York: St. Martin's Press, 1997.

Nakanishi, Hiroshi. "Redefining Comprehensive Security in Japan." In *Challenges for China-Japan–U.S. Cooperation*. Ed. Ryosei Kokubun, 44–69. Tokyo and New York: Japan Center for International Exchange, 1998.

Nakasone, Yasuhiro. "Japan's Firm Nonnuclear Resolve." *Japan Echo* 25, no. 5 (October 1998).

"News and Information Topics." *North Korea Quarterly* (spring/summer 1995): 11–23.

Nye, Joseph. "The Case for Deep Engagement." *Foreign Affairs* (July/August 1995): 90–102.

———. "China's Re-emergence and the Future of the Asia-Pacific." *Survival* 39, no. 4 (winter 1997–1998): 65–79.

Ogura, Toshimaru, and Oh, Ingyu. "Nuclear Clouds over the Korean Peninsula and Japan." *Monthly Review* 48, no. 11 (April 1997): 18–31.

Okamoto, Yukio. "Why We Still Need the Security Treaty." *Japan Echo* (winter 1995): 10–13.

Okimoto, Daniel. "The Japan-American Security Alliance: Prospects for the Twenty-first Century." Asia/Pacific Research Center, Stanford University, January 1998.

Okubo, Shiro. "Japan's Constitutional Pacifism and United Nations Peacekeeping." In *Japan's Quest: The Search for International Role, Recognition, and Respect*. Ed. Warren Hunsberger, 96–112. Armonk, NY: M.E. Sharpe, 1997.

Packard, George. *Protest in Tokyo: The Security Treaty Crisis of 1960*. Princeton, NJ: Princeton University Press, 1966.

Political Parties in Japan. Accessed on the Worldwide Web at the following address: http://www.kanzaki.com/jinfo/PoliticalParties.html#SDP.

"Problems of U.S. Bases in Okinawa Fuel Public Ire over Military Presence." In *Japan Economic Almanac 1997*, 30–31. Tokyo: Nihon Keizai Shimbun, 1997.

Pyle, Kenneth. *The Making of Modern Japan*. Lexington, MA: Heath and Company, 1996.

Quinones, C. Kenneth. "North Korea's 'New' Nuclear Site—Fact or Fiction." Berkeley, CA: Nautilus Institute, October 5, 1998.

Roper Center for Public Opinion Research. University of Connecticut, Japanese public opinion survey data. Accessed on the Worldwide Web at http://www.ropercenter.uconn.edu/jpoll/home.html.

Roy, Denny. "Hegemon on the Horizon? China's Threat to East Asian Security." *International Security* 19, no. 1 (summer 1994): 149–168.

Sato, Hideo. "Prospects for Global Leadership Sharing: The Economic Dimension." School of Public Affairs, Center for International and Security Studies, University of Maryland at College Park, Maryland/Tsukuba Papers on U.S.–Japan Relations, October 1996.

Segal, Gerald. "East Asia and the 'Containment' of China." *International Security* 20, no. 4 (spring 1996): 159–187.

Self, Benjamin. "Confidence-building Measures and Japanese Security." Washington, DC: The Henry Stimson Center, 2000.

Shambaugh, David. "China's Military Views the World: Ambivalent Security." *International Security* 24, no. 3 (winter 1999/2000): 52–79.

Shen, Dingli. "China's Negative Security Assurances." Washington, DC: The Henry Stimson Center, 1998.

Shirk, Susan. "Asia-Pacific Regional Security: Balance of Power or Concert of Powers?" In *Regional Orders: Building Security in a New World Order*. Eds. David Lake and Patrick Morgan. University Park: Pennsylvania State University Press, 1997.

Shuja, Sharif. "Japan's Asia Policy." *Contemporary Review* 274, no. 1600 (May 1999): 236–241.

Sigal, Leon. "Rogue Concepts." *Harvard International Review* 22, no. 2 (summer 2000): 62–66.

Simon, Sheldon. "Is There a U.S. Strategy for East Asia?" *Contemporary Southeast*

Asia: A Journal of International and Strategic Affairs 21, no. 3 (December 1999): 325–343.

Singleton, Royce et al. *Approaches to Social Research*. New York: Oxford University Press, 1988.

"Sino-Russia Joint Statement." *Beijing Review* 42, no. 51 (December 29, 1999).

Soeya, Yoshihide. "Japan's Dual Identity and the U.S.–Japan Alliance." Asia/Pacific Research Center, Stanford University, May 1998.

"Southeast Asia: China Steps in Where U.S. Fails." *Far Eastern Economic Review* (November 23, 2000).

"State Department Noon Briefing December 22, 1998" from *Daily Report*, Nautilus Institute, December 23, 1998.

Stockwin, J.A.A. *The Japan Socialist Party and Neutralism*. London: Melbourne University Press, 1968.

Takubo, Tadae. "The Okinawan Threat to the Security Treaty." *Japan Echo* (autumn 1996): 46–52.

Tamamoto, Masaru. "Japan's Search for Recognition and Status." In *Japan's Quest: The Search for International Role, Recognition, and Respect*. Ed. Warren Hunsberger, 3–14. Armonk, NY: M.E. Sharpe, 1997.

Tanaka, Akihiko. "Japan's Security Policy in the 1990s." In *Japan's International Agenda*. Ed. Yoichi Funabashi, 28–56. New York: New York University Press, 1994.

Tang, Tianri. "Japan's Stubborn 'History Syndrome' Requires Treatment." *Beijing Review*, no. 12 (March 22, 2001).

Teufel Dryer, June. "State of the Field Report: Research on the Chinese Military." *AccessAsia Review* 1, no. 1 (August 1997).

"TMD: Safety Net or Threat." *Far Eastern Economic Review* (February 4, 1999).

Tonelson, Alan. "Time for a New U.S.–Japan Security Relationship." *Comparative Strategy* 16, no. 1 (January–March 1997): 1–11.

Walt, Stephen. *The Origins of Alliance*. Ithaca, NY: Cornell University Press, 1987.

Wang, Hucheng. "Rising Military Budgets and International Security." *Beijing Review*, no. 14 (April 5, 2001).

Wang, Jianwei, and Xuinbo Wu. "Against Us or with Us? The Chinese Perspective of America's Alliances with Japan and Korea." Asia/Pacific Research Center, Stanford University, May 1998.

Wang, Jie. "Trampling on International Law Deserves Punishment." *Beijing Review* 42, no. 22 (May 31, 1999).

Wang, Jisi. "The Role of the United States as a Global and Pacific Power: A View from China." *Pacific Review* 10, no. 1 (1997): 1–18.

Wanner, Barbara. *United States, Japan Ink Accord on TMD Research*. Washington, DC: Japan Economic Institute, *JEI Report*, no. 33 (August 27, 1999).

"Wither US-Russian Relations?" *Beijing Review* 43, no. 9 (February 28, 2000).

Xiao, Li. "Japan's 'New Acts' Arouse Objections." *Beijing Review* 42, no 20 (May 17, 1999).

Xu, Zhixian, and Bojiang Yang. "New Acts of Historical Retrogression." *Beijing Review* 42, no. 24 (June 14, 1999).

Yamaguchi, Noboru. "Why the U.S. Marines Should Remain in Okinawa: A Military Perspective." In *Restructuring the U.S.–Japan Alliance: Toward a More Equal Partnership*. Ed. Ralph Cossa, 98–110. Washington, DC: Center for Strategic and International Studies, 1997.

Zhang, Tusheng. "Seven Issues in East Asian Security." *Beijing Review*, no. 9 (March 1, 2001).

Zhou, Bian. "The Trend in the Bush Administration's China Policy." *Beijing Review*, no. 8 (February 22, 2001).

Zhou, Xinhua. "Too Hasty to Become a Military-Political Power." *Beijing Review* 43, no. 21 (May 22, 2000).

Government and Public Organization Publications

Advisory Group on Defense Issues. *The Modality of the Security and Defense Capability of Japan: The Outlook for the 21st Century* (Higuchi Report). Tokyo, August 12, 1994.

Agreement under Article VI of the Treaty of Mutual Cooperation and Security between Japan and the United States of America, Regarding Facilities and Areas and the Status of United States Armed Forces in Japan, Washington, DC, January 19, 1960.

Akiba, Tadatoshi (Mayor of Hiroshima). "Letter of Protest," Hiroshima, February 4, 2000. Accessed on the Worldwide Web at http://www.pcf.city.hiroshima.jp/peacesite/English/Stage0/info/protest000204E.html.

"Appeal from Hiroshima and Nagasaki for a Total Ban and Elimination of Nuclear Weapons." Accessed on the Worldwide Web at http://www.ask.ne.jp/~hankaku/english/appeal.html.

Armitage, Richard. "A Comprehensive Approach to North Korea." Washington, DC: National Defense University, Strategic Forum, Institute for National Strategic Studies, March 1999.

Comprehensive Nuclear Test Ban Treaty Homepage. Accessed on the Worldwide Web at http://pws.ctbto.org.

Cox Report. Selected information made available to the public through a report issued on January 3, 1999, by the U.S. Congress's Select Committee on the People's Republic of China and its appropriation of U.S. nuclear weapons information. Accessed at http://www.conservativenews.org/SpecialReports/cox/index.html.

Cronin, Patrick. "The U.S.–Japan Alliance Redefined." Washington, DC: National Defense University, Strategic Forum, Institute for National Strategic Studies, May 1996.

Cronin, Patrick, and Ezra Vogel. "Unifying U.S. Policy on Japan." Washington, DC: National Defense University, Strategic Forum, Institute for National Strategic Studies, November 1995.

Defense Agency (Japanese). *Basic Policy for National Defense*, Tokyo, May 20, 1957. Accessed on the Worldwide Web at http://jda.go.jp/e/index_.htm.

———. *Defense of Japan 1997*. Tokyo: Japan Times, 1997.

———. *National Defense Program Outline in and after FY 1996*, Tokyo, November 28, 1995. Accessed on the Worldwide Web at http://www.jda.go.jp/index_.htm.

Department of Defense. *Annual Report on the Military Power of the People's Republic of China*. Report to the Congress. Washington, DC, June 2000.

———. *Annual Report to the President and Congress, 2000*. Washington, DC: Department of Defense, 2000.

———. *Report of the Quadrennial Defense Review*. Washington, DC: Department of Defense, May 1997.

————. *Report on the Allied Contributions to the Common Defense*. Washington, DC: Department of Defense, March 1999.

————. Washington Headquarters Services, Directorate for Information Operations and Reports. *Selected Manpower Statistics*. Active Duty Military Personnel Strengths by Regional Area and by Country. Washington, DC, Fiscal Year 1999.

————. *2000 Report to the Congress, Military Situation on the Korean Peninsula*. Washington DC: Department of Defense, September 12, 2000.

————. Office of International Security Affairs. *United States Security Strategy for the East Asia–Pacific Region* (East Asia and Pacific Region). Washington, DC: Department of Defense, February 1995.

————. Office of International Security Affairs. The United States Security Strategy for the East Asia-Pacific Region. Washington, DC: Department of Defense, November 1998.

Dolan, Ronald. "National Security." In *Japan: A Country Study*. Eds. Ronald Dolan and Robert Worden, 419–475. Washington, DC: U.S. Government Printing Office, 1992.

Framework for a New Economic Partnership between Japan and the United States, July 1993. Information on these bilateral talks can be accessed on the Japanese Ministry of Foreign Affairs' website at http://www.mofa.go.jp.

General Assembly, United Nations. *A Path to the Total Elimination of Nuclear Weapons*, New York, New York, November 2000. Submitted to the United Nations by the Japanese government.

The Government of Japan's Comments on the 1997 National Trade Estimates (NTE) Report, April 15, 1997. Accessed on the Japanese Ministry of Foreign Affairs website at http://www.mofa.go.jp.

Hiroshima City Homepage. Accessed on the Worldwide Web at http://www.city.hiroshima.jp/indexe.html.

Institute for National Strategic Studies. *1997 Strategic Assessment: Flashpoints and Force Structure*. Washington, DC National Defense University, 1997.

————. "The United States and Japan: Advancing toward a Mature Partnership." Special report. Washington, DC: National Defense University, October 11, 2000.

International Court of Justice. *Advisory Opinion: Legality of the Threat or Use of Nuclear Weapons*, July 8, 1996.

Japan Forum on International Relations. *The Policy Recommendations on the Perspective of Security Regimes in Asia–Pacific Region*. Tokyo: Japan Forum on International Relations, 1996.

Joint Announcement: U.S.–Japan Security Consultative Committee, Tokyo, December, 2, 1996. Accessed on the Japan Defense Agency's website at http://www.jda.go.jp/l/index_.ltm.

Management and Coordination Agency, Statistics Bureau. *Estimates on All Japan Population by Age Group and Sex*. Tokyo: Management and Coordination Agency, March 1998.

Ministry of Foreign Affairs. *Announcement by the Chief Cabinet Secretary on Japan's Immediate Response to North Korea's Missile Launch*, Tokyo, September 1, 1998. Accessed on the Worldwide Web at http:// mofa.go.jp/announce/announce/1998/9/901–2.html.

————. *Diplomatic Bluebook 1992*. Tokyo: Ministry of Foreign Affairs, 1993.

————. *Diplomatic Bluebook 1993*. Tokyo: Ministry of Foreign Affairs, 1994.

————. *Diplomatic Bluebook 1994*. Tokyo: Ministry of Foreign Affairs, 1994.

————. *Diplomatic Bluebook 1998*. Tokyo: Ministry of Foreign Affairs, 1998.

————. *Diplomatic Bluebook 2000*. Tokyo: Ministry of Foreign Affairs, 2000.

————. *Exchange of Notes Concerning a Program for Cooperative Research on Ballistic Missile Technologies Based on the Mutual Defense Assistance Agreement between Japan and the United States of America*, Tokyo, August 16, 1999.

————. "Is Japan Getting a Free Ride on Defense?" *Japanese Viewpoints*. Tokyo: Overseas Public Relations Office, Ministry of Foreign Affairs, September 1995. Accessed on the Worldwide Web at http://www.mofa.go.jp.

————. *Japan and the United Nations*, nd. Accessed on the Worldwide Web at http://www.mofa.go.jp.

————. *Japan-China Joint Declaration on Building a Partnership of Friendship and Cooperation for Peace and Development*, Tokyo, November 26, 1998.

————. *Japan-China Relations*, 1997.

————. *Japan-Russian Federation Joint Efforts for Disarmament and Environmental Protection: New Initiatives by the Government of Japan in the Areas of Assistance for Denuclearization, Disarmament and Non-proliferation*, Tokyo, May 1999. Accessed on the Worldwide Web at http://www.mofa.go.jp/region/europe/russia/fmv9905/joint.html.

————. *Japan's Assistance Programs for Russia*, Tokyo, May 1997. Accessed on the Worldwide Web at http://www.mofa.go.jp/region/europe/russia/assistance/index.html.

————. *Japan's Northern Territories*, Tokyo, 1999. Accessed on the Worldwide Web at http://infojapan.org/region/europe/russia/territory/index.html.

————. *Japan's Official Development Assistance, Annual Report 1999*. Accessed on the Worldwide Web at http://mofa.go.jp/policy/oda/summary/1999/index.html.

————. *Japan's Policy on the Russian Federation*, Tokyo, nd. Accessed on the Worldwide Web at http://www.mofa.go.jp/index.html.

————. *Japan's Policy toward the United Nations in the Post–Cold War World*. Nd. Accessed on the Worldwide Web at http://mofa.go.jp/policy/un/pamph96/japan.html.

————. *Joint Announcement, Japan–U.S. Security Consultative Committee*. September 1995. Accessed on the Worldwide Web at http://www.mofa.go.jp/region/n-america/security/index.html.

————. *ODA Summary, 1997*. Accessed on the Worldwide Web at http://www.mofa.go.jp.

————. *Press Conference by the Press Secretary*, Tokyo, October 2, 1998.

————. *In Quest of a New Role: The United Nations and Japan*, Tokyo, 2000. Accessed on the Worldwide Web at http://www.mofa.go.jp/policy/un/pamph/2000/index.html.

————. *Security*. Accessed on the Worldwide Web at http://www.mofa.go.jp/region/n-america/us/index.html.

————. *Statement by Mr. Keizo Obuchi Prime Minister of Japan at the Fifty-Third Session of the General Assembly of the United Nations*, New York, September 21, 1998.

————. *2000 Survey in the United States of Opinions toward Japan*. Tokyo: Overseas Public Relations Office, Ministry of Foreign Affairs, May 2000. Accessed on the Worldwide Web at http://www.mofa.go.jp/region/n-america/us/survey/survey2000.html.

————. *The United Nations and Japan 1995*. Tokyo: Ministry of Foreign Affairs, 1995.

Montaperto, Richard, and Hans Binnendijk. "PLA Views on Asia Pacific Security in the 21st Century." Washington, DC: National Defense University, Strategic Forum, Institute for National Strategic Studies, June 1997.

The National Institute for Defense Studies. *East Asian Strategic Review: 1997–1998*, Tokyo, January 1998.

————. *East Asian Strategic Review, 1998–1999* (summary), Tokyo, 1999.

————. *East Asia Strategic Review 2000* (summary), Tokyo, March 2000.

Nuclear Free Kobe (Resolution). Accessed on the Worldwide Web at http://www.prop1.org/prop1/jkobef.htm.

Nye, Joseph. "Strategy for East Asia and the U.S.–Japan Security Alliance." *Defense Issues* 10, no. 35 (1995).

Office of the Assistant Secretary of Defense for International Security Affairs, East Asia Pacific Region. *A Strategic Framework for the Asian Pacific Rim*. Washington, DC: Department of Defense, 1992.

Office of the Secretary of Defense. *Proliferation: Threat and Response*. Washington, DC: Department of Defense, January 2001.

Okinawa Homepage on Worldwide Web at http://www.pref.okinawa.jp.

People's Republic of China. Foreign Ministry. Information Office of State Council. Accessed at the Foreign Ministry of the People's Republic of China's website at http://www.fmprc.sou.cn/e/c/ec.htm.

China's National Defense in 1998, White Paper, Beijing, July 1998.

————. *China's National Defense in 2000*, White Paper, Beijing, 2000. Accessed on the Worldwide web at http://www.china.org.cn/english/2791.htm.

————. *Foreign Policy*. Accessed on the Worldwide Web at http://www.fmprc.gov.cn/e/c/ec.htm.

Perry, William. U.S. North Korea Policy Coordinator and Special Advisor to the President and the Secretary of State. *Review of the United States Policy toward North Korea: Findings and Recommendations*. Washington, DC, October 12, 1999.

Prime Minister's Office, Public Relations Office. *Opinion Surveys on Foreign Affairs*. Tokyo: Prime Minister's Office, January 1998.

————. *Opinion Surveys on Foreign Affairs*. Tokyo: Prime Minister's Office, 1999.

————. *Opinion Surveys on Foreign Affairs*. Tokyo: Prime Minister's Office, January 22, 2001.

The Report of the Tokyo Forum for Nuclear Non-proliferation and Disarmament. *Facing Nuclear Dangers: An Action Plan for the 21st Century*, Tokyo, July 25, 1999.

Saito, Toshio. "Japan's Security Policy." Washington, DC: National Defense University, Strategic Forum, Institute for National Strategic Studies, May 1999.

Secretary of State Madeleine K. Albright, Japanese Foreign Minister Kono, Japanese Defense Minister Torashima, and U.S. Secretary of Defense William Cohen. *Press Conference by the U.S.–Japan Security Consultative Committee*, New York, New York, September 11, 2000.

Security Treaty between the United States of America and Japan, San Francisco, September 8, 1951.

Seekins, Donald. "The Political System." In *Japan: A Country Study*. Eds. Ronald

Dolan and Robert Worden, 303–366. Washington, DC: U.S. Government Printing Office, 1992.

Special Action Committee on Okinawa (SACO). *The SACO Final Report*. Tokyo, December 2, 1996.

———. *The SACO Final Report on the Futenma Air Station*, Tokyo, December 2, 1996.

Speech by Prime Minister Ryutaro Hashimoto at Columbia University. *Japan–U.S. Relations: A Partnership for the 21st Century*, New York, New York, June 23, 1997.

Statement by Mr. Masahiko Koumura Minister for Foreign Affairs of Japan at the Fifty-fourth Session of the General Assembly of the United Nations, September 1999. Accessed on the Worldwide Web at http://www.mofa.go.jp/announce/fm/koumura/index.html.

Statement by Secretary of State for Foreign Affairs Masahiko Koumura to the United Nations Conference on Disarmament Issues in Sapporo, July 22, 1997. Accessed on the Worldwide Web at http://mofa.go.jp/press/c_s/disarmament.

Statement of Secretary of State-Designate Colin L. Powell, Prepared for the Confirmation Hearing of the U.S. Senate Committee on Foreign Relations, Scheduled for 10:30 a.m. January 17, 2001.

Subcommittee for Defense Cooperation. *Interim Report on the Review of the Guidelines for U.S.–Japan Defense Cooperation*. Honolulu, Hawaii, June 7, 1997.

Subcommittee on Unfair Trade Policies and Measures. *1998 Report on the WTO Consistency of Trade Policies by Major Trading Partners*. Tokyo: Ministry of International Trade and Industry, Industrial Structure Council, 1998.

Treaty of Mutual Cooperation and Security between Japan and the United States of America, Washington, DC, January 19, 1960.

United Nations. *Charter of the United Nations*, San Francisco, June 26, 1945. Accessed on the Worldwide Web at http://www/un.org/aboutun/charter/index.html.

United States General Accounting Office. *China Trade: WTO Membership and Most-Favored-Nation Status*. Washington, DC: U.S. General Accounting Office, June 17, 1998.

———. *Nuclear Nonproliferation: Difficulties in Accomplishing IAEA's Activities in North Korea*. Washington, DC: U.S. General Accounting Office, July 1998.

———. *Overseas Presence: Issues Involved in Reducing the Impact of the U.S. Military Presence in Okinawa*. Washington, DC: U.S. General Accounting Office, March 1998.

———. *United Nations: Financial Issues and U.S. Arrears*. Washington, DC: U.S. General Accounting Office, June 1998.

U.S. Arms Control and Disarmament Agency. *World Military Expenditures and Arms Transfers 1996*. Washington, DC: U.S. Arms Control and Disarmament Agency, 1997.

U.S. Bureau of the Census, Foreign Trade Division, Data Dissemination Branch, Washington, DC.

U.S. Department of State. *Background Notes: Japan, April 1998*. Washington, DC: U.S. Department of State, 1998.

———. *Background Notes: North Korea, June 1996*. Washington, DC: U.S. Department of State, 1996.

———. *Dispatch Magazine* 7, no. 39 (September 23, 1996).

————. Office of the Spokesman, Press Statement. *Report on the U.S. Visit to the Site at Kumchang-Ni, Democratic People's Republic of Korea*, Washington, DC: June 25, 1999.

————. Bureau of Verification and Compliance. *World Military Expenditures and Arms Transfers, 1998*. Washington, DC: U.S. Government Printing Office, April 2000.

U.S. International Trade Commission. *Vector Supercomputers from Japan*. Washington, DC: U.S. International Trade Commission, October 1997.

U.S.–Japan Common Agenda for Cooperation in Global Perspective, July 1993.

U.S.–Japan Joint Declaration on Security—Alliance for the 21st Century, Tokyo, April 17, 1996.

U.S.–Japan Security Consultative Committee. *Completion of the Review of the Guidelines for U.S.–Japan Defense Cooperation*. New York, September 23, 1997.

————. *Guidelines for Japan–U.S. Defense Cooperation*. November 27, 1978.

Verbatim Excerpts of Oral Statements to the International Court of Justice on the Legality of the Threat or Use of Nuclear Weapons, October 30–November 15, 1995.

The White House, Office of the Press Secretary. *Press Briefing*, Washington, DC, December 7, 1998.

Index

Anthony DiFilippo is professor of sociology at Lincoln University in Pennsylvania. He is the author of several other books, the most recent of which is *Cracks in the Alliance: Science, Technology, and the Evolution of U.S.–Japan Relations*. During the last ten years, he has published widely on the U.S.–Japan relationship; initially, he concentrated largely on science and technology and its connection to security, and in recent years he has focused on the Japan–U.S. bilateral military alliance.

DiFilippo's professional articles on the Japan–U.S. security relationship have recently appeared in the *Japan Quarterly*, the *Asian Survey* and *Pacifica Review: Peace, Security, and Global Change*. DiFilippo has also contributed a number of op-ed articles to major Japanese newspapers, including the *Asahi Shimbun*, the *Japan Times*, and the *Nihon Keizai Shimbun*.